MW00904834

Profiting from Hedge Funds

Profiting from Hedge Funds

Winning Strategies for the Little Guy

John Konnayil Vincent

WILEY

Cover Design: Michael Rutkowski
Cover Photography: ©iStockphoto.com/urbancow

Copyright © 2013 by John Wiley & Sons Singapore Pte. Ltd.

Published by John Wiley & Sons Singapore Pte. Ltd.
1 Fusionopolis Walk, #07-01, Solaris South Tower, Singapore 138628

All rights reserved.

No part of this publication may be reproduced, stored in a retrieval system, or transmitted
in any form or by any means, electronic, mechanical, photocopying, recording, scanning,
or otherwise, except as expressly permitted by law, without either the prior written
permission of the Publisher, or authorization through payment of the appropriate photocopy
fee to the Copyright Clearance Center. Requests for permission should be addressed
to the Publisher, John Wiley & Sons Singapore Pte. Ltd., 1 Fusionopolis Walk, #07-01,
Solaris South Tower, Singapore 138628, tel: 65–6643–8000, fax: 65–6643–8008,
e-mail: enquiry@wiley.com.

Limit of Liability/Disclaimer of Warranty: While the publisher and author have used their
best efforts in preparing this book, they make no representations or warranties with respect
to the accuracy or completeness of the contents of this book and specifically disclaim any
implied warranties of merchantability or fitness for a particular purpose. No warranty may
be created or extended by sales representatives or written sales materials. The advice and
strategies contained herein may not be suitable for your situation. You should consult with
a professional where appropriate. Neither the publisher nor the author shall be liable for
any damages arising herefrom.

Other Wiley Editorial Offices
John Wiley & Sons, 111 River Street, Hoboken, NJ 07030, USA
John Wiley & Sons, The Atrium, Southern Gate, Chichester, West Sussex, P019 8SQ,
    United Kingdom
John Wiley & Sons (Canada) Ltd., 5353 Dundas Street West, Suite 400, Toronto, Ontario,
    M9B 6HB, Canada
John Wiley & Sons Australia Ltd., 42 McDougall Street, Milton, Queensland 4064, Australia
Wiley-VCH, Boschstrasse 12, D-69469 Weinheim, Germany

ISBN 978-1-118-46520-2 (Cloth)
ISBN 978-1-118-46519-6 (ePDF)
ISBN 978-1-118-46517-2 (ePub)

Typeset in 11.5/14 pt. Bembo Std by MPS Limited, Chennai, India.
Printed in Singapore by C.O.S. Printers Pte. Ltd.

10 9 8 7 6 5 4 3 2

To my loving parents,
K. J. Vincent and Annies Vincent,
for their inspiration and guidance

Contents

Acknowledgments

Let me begin by acknowledging the Almighty for the blessings and wonderful provisions showered upon me throughout my life. My career progression to wealth management has been no exception, for it has been a wonderful ride.

Words fail to express the tremendous gratitude I owe Nick Wallwork at John Wiley, one of the most experienced English language finance/business publishers in the world. My articles at Seeking Alpha, a premier website for actionable stock market opinion, analysis, and discussion caught Nick's attention and he sowed the seeds for this book of strategies individual investors can implement to create alpha on their own. His insight and vision deserves credit for this maiden effort. On a related note, I salute Seeking Alpha for developing an ecosystem for investment researchers to network and develop ideas.

I have also drawn inspiration from several individuals who successfully migrated from other fields into investment management. Among them are Dr. Michael Burry, founder of Scion Capital, LLC hedge fund; Asif Suria, founder of Insider Trade Reports; Mazin Jadallah, founder of AlphaClone LLC; James Altucher, managing director of Formula Capital Hedge Fund; Mohnish Pabrai, founder of Pabrai Investment

Fund; Francis Chou, president of Chou Associates Management, Inc.; and several contributors at Seeking Alpha. Their intrepid sense of going all out in fulfilling their passion immensely helped my own transformation.

I extend my sincere thanks to the hedge fund managers profiled herein for explaining their operating styles through the media over the years. That was my primary source of information for the profiles in this book.

I recognize fully the efforts of Gemma Rosey, development editor; Jules Yap, editorial executive; Stefan Skeen, senior production editor; Barbara Hanson, copy editor; and the entire Wiley team for their unwavering support throughout the development of this book.

My partner in crime and beloved wife, Shara, has been the guiding and motivating force behind me, giving encouragement at times of difficulty and setbacks. Her critical suggestions, patient understanding, and realistic expectations helped me to comprehend the bigger picture. Her passion and enthusiasm to follow a new path, along with her pleasant disposition, fascinates me. She put in a tremendous effort to edit the initial drafts of the manuscript.

While we were writing this book, our two wonderful daughters Ann Gina Konnayil and Becka Jill Konnayil held up really well in a brand new environment, despite the fact that their parents were working with a very tight schedule. For that, they deserve our special mention and admiration.

I am blessed with a lot of well-wishers, friends, and family members. I thank all of them for being there.

Preface

Managing one's assets appropriately is indeed a monumental task. While select money managers with the elusive Midas touch easily outperform the market averages by wide margins over long periods of time, the majority of other money managers and individual investors unfortunately underperform the market averages. As these three groups—fruitful money managers, their struggling colleagues, and individual investors—represent the bulk of the market, it is evident the former gains at the expense of the latter two.

The track record of individual investors as a group has plenty of room for improvement. Equities and mutual funds are generic investment options available to all individuals, regardless of their net investable asset status. Net investable assets are the total value of an individual's investments, excluding his or her primary residence and retirement accounts. Individuals with investable wealth of less than $100,000 are at the lower end of this spectrum, while the superwealthy, with net investable assets exceeding $10,000,000, are at the other end. An uptick in the net investable assets of an individual means better investment prospects, as the chance to wrap one's fingers around such choice privileges as separately managed account (SMA) composites, hedge funds, private equity partnerships, venture capital, angel investment, and so on are available only to those higher up in the net investable assets ladder. The best among these exclusive opportunities manage to beat the market averages handsomely.

In order to improve the individual investor's situation, financial gurus such as Vanguard's John Bogle[1] professed the strategy of owning index funds so that an investor can mimic the performance of the market. Eliminating the risk of underperforming the market averages is the chief benefit of such an approach. However, this relative stability has a high hidden price, the cost of which becomes apparent only when one compares the difference in the amount of money that could have been made had the investments beaten the market by a few percentage points over a long period of time.

Those money managers that are ahead of the curve make it seem all too easy to post compounded annual returns net of all fees in the vicinity of a whopping 15 percent or higher. Clearly, consistent outperformance by wide margins is not an accident, and cannot be explained away by statistical probabilities. These highly successful managers have special investment allocation skills that allow them to take their returns from ordinary to extraordinary levels over long periods of time. The wealth difference created is huge, as is shown in the following table, which summarizes returns over 30 years for a $100,000 initial investment:

Duration (years)	Final Value @ 8%	Final Value @ 10%	Final Value @ 15%	Final Value @ 20%
5	$146,932.81	$161,051.00	$201,135.72	$248,832.00
10	$215,892.50	$259,374.25	$404,555.77	$619,173.64
15	$317,216.91	$417,724.82	$813,706.16	$1,540,702.16
20	$466,095.71	$672,749.99	$1,636,653.74	$3,833,759.99
25	$684,847.52	$1,083,470.59	$3,291,895.26	$9,539,621.66
30	$1,006,265.69	$1,744,940.23	$6,621,177.20	$23,737,631.38

- A $100,000 portfolio grows to slightly over one million dollars over a period of 30 years, if investment returns come in at the long-term compounded annual market growth rate of 8 percent.
- A $100,000 portfolio grows to around $1.75 million over 30 years, if investments grow at 10 percent, beating the market by a modest

2 percent. At that level of outperformance, the difference in dollar amount is over $0.75 million for the same time frame.

- A $100,000 portfolio grows to a massive $6.62 million over 30 years, if investments grow at 15 percent, beating the market by 7 percent. At that level of outperformance, the difference in dollar amount hovers close to an incredible $5.62 million, that is, over 6.2 times the returns compared to the market returns.

Having recognized the striking difference in returns even moderate levels of outperformance can generate, it is only logical that an individual investor would also want to pursue strategies aimed at beating the market indexes with a high level of confidence. The seemingly straightforward way for an individual investor to partake in the performance of superstar money managers is to invest directly with them. Unfortunately, this is easier said than done! The majority of the wizards don't accept a layperson's money and invest on their behalf even for a reasonable fee, for a variety of reasons. The Securities and Exchange Commission (SEC) regulations aimed at protecting investors from fraud are a major deterrent. The regulations include:

- **Securities Act of 1933**:[2] This law governs the offer and sale of securities in the United States. Funds offering to sell securities must first register and meet either the registration requirements or an exemption. Section 4(2) of the Securities Act exempts any transactions by an issuer not involving any public offering. To qualify under this exemption, there are rules under Regulation D (504, 505, and 506, a set of requirements that govern private offerings). Many of the investment management firms rely on Rule 506 to claim such exemption. Under that rule, offerings can be made to an unlimited number of accredited investors, and up to 35 other purchasers. Also, such offerings cannot employ general solicitation or advertising to market the securities. What does it take to be an accredited investor? One way to be an accredited investor is to have a net worth of at least $1 million, alone or with a spouse. The Dodd-Frank Wall Street Reform and Consumer Protection Act of 2010[3] further restricted this requirement by excluding a person's primary residence from the net worth calculation. Another way to qualify is to have income exceeding $200,000 in each of the two most recent years, or joint income with a spouse exceeding $300,000. Either of these requirements limits accessibility to the vast majority of individual investors. The regulatory curb on advertisements also makes it hard for investment management firms to reach individual investors.

- **Securities Exchange Act of 1934**:[4] This law governs the secondary trading of securities in the United States. The rules under Section 12(g) require that, if an investment management firm has over 500 holders of record (investors), and assets in excess of $10 million, it must be registered under the Securities Exchange Act. In their effort to avoid Securities Exchange Act registration, many investment managers try to have fewer than 500 holders of record. One way to achieve this is by having a very high minimum requirement. It is not unusual for highly successful hedge funds to have this threshold set at upward of $25 million which, needless to say, excludes a large number of individual investors.

- **Investment Company Act of 1940**:[5] This law regulates investment companies. It requires them to disclose material details about their financial health and also restricts certain activities, such as short selling, by mandating coverage requirements. Many funds rely on statutory exclusions under Section 3(c) that define an investment company to avoid being classified as an investment company. Section 3(c) (1) excludes issuers if the outstanding securities are owned by not more than 100 investors. Funds making use of this exclusion typically resort to very high minimum investment requirement to discourage most investors. Section 3(c) (7) excludes issuers if the outstanding securities are owned exclusively by qualified purchasers. Who are these qualified purchasers? To be a qualified purchaser, an individual investor has to own more than $5,000,000 in investments, which eliminates a high percentage of investors.

- **Investment Advisors Act of 1940**:[6] This regulates the activity of investment advisors. Many advisers use certain exemptions under the Dodd-Frank Act of 2010, which among other things, do not allow holding themselves out generally to the public as an investment advisor.

Moreover, many superlative money managers do not view managing individual investor accounts as their ticket to fame. Some of their typical preferred activities include the following:

- **Management of university endowment funds, charitable foundation trusts, and similar entities**: Some of the world's finest money managers are engaged in managing trusts and university endowments. One of the largest such trusts is the Bill & Melinda Gates Foundation Trust, with assets over $37 billion; and leading university endowments include the likes of Harvard ($32 billion) and Yale ($22 billion). Because they employ the cream of the top money managers, it is not much of a surprise that these endowments and trusts have fantastic track records.

- **Family offices**: *Family offices* are establishments set up by wealthy families to manage their money. These offices typically provide auxiliary services, such as tax, estate planning, and other legal matters. Several eminent money managers have long since exited the business of investing outsiders' money through a hedge fund to investing their own wealth through a family office structure. This trend has gained momentum recently, following the SEC adoption of a rule under Dodd-Frank Act defining family offices that are to be excluded from the Investment Advisors Act of 1940. The most high-profile conversion to date has been Soros Fund Management, the hedge fund that was run by billionaire George Soros. In July 2011, the fund decided to convert to a family office and return outside investors' money, thereby closing the doors on them.

- **Management of liquid assets of large corporations**: Managing the cash assets of large corporations is a complicated undertaking that sometimes gets assigned to professional investment management gurus. Managing insurance float is a variation on this theme and, under this category, are some of the most prominent experts, such as Warren Buffett and Ian Cumming. It is possible for individual investors to own shares of the publicly traded corporations these giants represent, such as Berkshire Hathaway, Leucadia National, and so on. However, owning such shares do not provide the individual with the same benefit as would exist if his or her money was part of the pool 'of investments that Buffett or Cumming manages. As things stand, it is impossible for individual investors to directly participate in the money management schemes of such managers.

- **Private equity funds, venture capital funds, and other miscellaneous pools**: There exists an array of unregistered investment vehicles that rely on exemptions to maintain their status quo under the SEC. They are structured as limited partnerships with investors committing to fund up to a certain amount of money. Private equity funds are pools of capital that invest in illiquid securities. When the fund manager identifies an opportunity, capital calls to investors allow them to obtain funds just in time and stay fully invested. Venture capital funds are pools that invest in start-up opportunities. They are also different in that they play an active role in the management of portfolio companies and exit as soon as a good return on investment is realized. Such entities largely bypass the vast majority of individual investors, as they rely on SEC exemptions to stay unregistered.

Hedge funds and mutual funds, on the other hand, seek individual investor capital but many of them are bounded because of their need to stay outside the radar of federal regulation. Most hedge funds set the entry bar high—their minimums start at upwards of a million dollars. Hedge funds cannot be marketed like a retail mutual fund. As for mutual funds, it is very rare to find one that beat the indexes consistently over long periods of time. There are exceptions but there are the following caveats as well:

- **Capital gains**: Mutual funds periodically distribute realized capital gains to their investors; such distributions are taxable. Besides, mutual funds can have unrealized capital gains that will eventually be distributed. In that case, a fund can fail to fascinate as an investment option, even if it has outperformed the indexes consistently over long periods of time. Sequoia Fund is an example of a highly successful mutual fund that has outperformed the S&P 500 by around 4 percent annually over 42 years. The fund, however, has a net unrealized appreciation of the fund's portfolio of over 40 percent of Net Asset Value (NAV), which makes it less desirable for prospective investors.

- **Fund closings**: Some of the best performing mutual funds are unwilling to take new investors on board. While this puts the fund beyond the reach of new investors, it is not completely out of circulation, as existing investors are generally allowed to add to their position. This is most prevalent among the best performing small cap funds, and is mostly due to the managers' belief that increasing the size of the fund could prove detrimental to the fund's performance. Examples of best performing mutual funds closed to new investors include the Royce Premier Fund, a small-cap–focused fund with an outstanding 20-year ~4 percent annual outperformance of the Russell 2000 index, and the Calamos Convertible Fund with a 27 year track record of outperformance. The Sequoia Fund also fits into this list.

- **High minimums**: Some mutual funds also resort to high minimums to keep at bay performance chasers who move in and out of funds frequently. Consequently, the fund becomes off-limits for genuine investors, too.

An alternative to investing directly with the best money managers is to invest in a fund of funds (FoFs). *FoFs* are investment companies that invest in other funds instead of investing in individual securities. On a comparative basis, FoFs have relatively lower investment minimums thus making them more readily accessible to individual investors. However, many factors such as those listed below make them less desirable than investing directly with the best money managers:

- **Fees and performance**: FoFs add another layer of decision making between the investor and the fund managers with whom they invest. On the one hand, the funds are diversified among other funds, but the extra management layer translates to additional fees (1 percent or more, plus a performance fee is typical) being tacked on. Further, as the returns will depend on the proficiency of the fund manager as well as on the asset allocation prowess of the FoF manager, FoFs mostly lag behind the returns achieved by the top managers.

- **Minimum requirements**: FoFs generally do not register under the Securities Act of 1933, so they rely on the private placements route to attract assets. This results in a much smaller market reach than that which could have been attained with a retail distribution network. Consequently, FoFs target high net-worth individuals which, in turn, cause them to keep large investment minimums (upward of $25,000).

- **Regulation:** Although FoFs may be registered under the Investment Company Act of 1940, the underlying funds in which they invest may not be. Investors are extremely dependent on the ability of the FoF managers to do proper due diligence in the selection of fund managers with whom they invest. The magnitude of this problem was highlighted by the[7] Madoff scandal when it was disclosed that many FoFs invested with the Ponzi scheme. Such vulnerability takes the joy out of investing!

Audience

A practical and gratifying alternative to investing directly with the awe-inspiring money managers is to monitor their moves, comprehend their investment rationale, and apply their proven strategies to one's own portfolio. Strategies to emulate the moves of remarkable money managers are the basis of this three-part book. Its purpose is to get individual investors to the next level by beating market averages with a high degree of confidence via incorporating cloning strategies in their own portfolios.

Overview

Part One begins with an explanation of the regulatory requirements that permit the public to scrutinize the investment activity of most money managers, albeit with a time delay. This section explains the simplest ways and means of cloning investment specialists individually, by inspecting their different investment styles, philosophies, and trades. An eclectic selection of 12 investment authorities is presented with particulars on:

- Characteristics that distinguish their portfolios from others.
- Analysis of their major moves over the years.

- Discussion of their largest positions (highest percentage allocations in the portfolio) and largest additions over the years.
- A peek into how selected stock picks, based on their bias (bullish, bearish, or neutral), would have performed.

The strategies put forth can be implemented into one's portfolios without further analysis of the securities themselves. The idea is to capitalize on the legwork already done by the best money managers or, put simply, let's not keep reinventing the wheel! Each chapter analyzes the strengths and weaknesses of the strategies to clone the moves of the best money managers one at a time, and also provides clues as to picking managers to follow.

Part Two discusses schemes that combine the moves of a selected set of money managers from Part I to construct cloned portfolios. These strategies apply rule-based criteria to the portfolios of the carefully chosen managers, so as to arrive at a list of potential securities in which to invest. The concept of model portfolios as a structured mechanical approach to follow the activities of the experts is introduced. A set of portfolio allocation models are presented with particulars on how assets can be spread among the different choices:

- Equal allocation model
- Weighted allocation model
- Ten-five-two allocation model

Nailing down these asset allocations is not complicated. The choices are based on the source manager's largest positions and the largest new additions. The money moves of a selected set of specialists from those introduced in Part I are used to present actual portfolios that can be constructed with this approach. Techniques to rebalance such portfolios quarterly, based on the changes made during the previous quarter, are explored. Back-tested progression spreadsheets that show how the portfolios would have performed over the years are analyzed. A description of alternatives to the long-only models is also covered:

- Incorporating bond and cash allocations.
- Hedging based on market sentiment.
- Net long versus neutral versus short.
- Cloning the asset allocation.
- Chapter summaries evaluating the strengths and weaknesses of the models.

Part Three presents rules-based filtering techniques based on money manager trading activity. The concept of building money manager investment bias spreadsheets to capture their preferences is introduced. A technique to create a prioritized manager bias spreadsheet by comparing the price range the manager traded with the price when the information became public is presented. The procedure is applied to the portfolios of the selected managers to create a prioritized manager bias spreadsheet. A strategy to invest based on these bias spreadsheets is introduced. A spreadsheet showing the back-tested performance of stock picks using this procedure against the selected manager portfolios is presented and analyzed.

This section also cites two other SEC regulatory requirements that allow the investing public to scrutinize certain other types of activity in security trading:

- SEC filings related to beneficial ownership of more than 5 percent in a public company, reported within 10 days of such activity.
- SEC filings related to insider trading that directors, officers, or 10 percent owners are required to file within two days of such activity.

Methods to filter and prioritize security selections using information from these regulatory filings are discussed. A strategy to invest based on this information is presented. The process is applied to the filings of the selected managers to present stock picks and their performance over the holding periods recommended by the strategy.

The best money managers are known to employ several stock selection strategies. Those techniques are introduced:

- Margin of safety
- Buying low and selling high
- Basic Q&A checklist
- Quantitative checklist
- Fair value estimates (FVE)

The importance of having different types of positions that are optimally sized is covered:

- Low probability versus high probability bets
- Positions that correlate inversely with the overall market

- Market neutral positions
- Keeping your powder dry
- Right sizing positions

The final chapter pulls everything together, with a discussion on the relative strengths and weaknesses of the different approaches proposed throughout the book.

Notes

1. John C. Bogle, *The Little Book of Common Sense Investing: The Only Way to Guarantee Your Fair Share of Stock Market Returns* (Hoboken, NJ: John Wiley & Sons, 2007).
2. Securities Act of 1933, May 27, 1933.
3. Dodd-Frank Wall Street Reform and Consumer Protection Act, January 05, 2010.
4. Securities Exchange Act of 1934, June 6, 1934.
5. Investment Company Act of 1940, August 22, 1940.
6. Investment Advisors Act of 1940, Aug. 22, 1940.
7. Bernard Madoff, former non-executive chairman of the NASDAQ stock market, and the confessed operator of a Ponzi scheme.

Part One

TRACKING 12 OF THE GREATEST MONEY MANAGERS

Chapter 1

Introduction

Investors are spoiled for choices when it comes to investment styles. There is no consensus on style even among the greatest money managers. Choosing of money managers to shadow requires careful consideration, as not all investment styles are conducive to cloning. Classifying money managers by their style is a practical initial step. This can be confusing, for many managers do not adhere solely to one style. Listed here are the most popular investment styles. Though they are often interchangeable, there are some differences among them:

- **Directional**: Directional managers forecast the turn of individual securities, as well as that of the overall market, based on analysis. Regardless of the type of analysis, the underlying theme is that the strategies they employ (long/short, managed futures, global macro, and dedicated shorts) rely on the outcome of the study to make a buy/sell decision. The long/short strategy, a favorite among money managers, is when directional bets are made both on the long and the short side. Global macro strategy banks on the analysis of the macroeconomic developments of the world to make investment decisions. Managed futures tactics depend on commodity trading advisors (CTAs) taking futures contracts and options positions based on fundamental or technical analysis.

- **Event driven**: Event-driven managers are on the prowl to profit from some expected event, the effect of which is yet to be factored into the market. Events they are drawn to include turnarounds in distressed securities, including securities undergoing bankruptcies, changes to the management structure and/or operation made possible by shareholder activism often spearheaded by the manager, and so on. In risk arbitrage, the play is on the risk that a closure or breakup of an announced merger or spinoff deal will not happen, thereby realizing the risk premium as profits, when the deal closes.
- **Market neutral**: This is a nondirectional absolute-return strategy used by money managers who seek to earn profits regardless of the route the market/sector they invest in takes: up, down, or sideways. A common way to achieve this is by using a variation of the long/short model. Here, the manager simultaneously builds a 50 percent long position in certain securities and a 50 percent short position in other securities in the same market/sector. If the manager's stock selection skill can return 10 percent annualized (both on the long and short side), then, independent of the direction in which the market/sector moved, the portfolio would return 10 percent. For example, assume a manager invested $100,000 using this model ($50,000 long and $50,000 short), and that the market/sector went down 40 percent during the period. The long portion of the portfolio will return −30 percent (−40 percent mirroring the market and +10 percent from the manager's superior stock selection skills). In dollars, the investment of $50,000 on the long side has shriveled to $35,000. The short portion of the portfolio on the other hand will return +50 percent (+40 percent countering the market and +10 percent from the manager's ability to achieve 10 percent annualized return). The $50,000 invested in the short side has swelled to $75,000. The total portfolio will then show a value of $110,000 or a 10 percent return. Other market-neutral strategies include *pairs trading* and *delta neutral trading.* In pairs trading, the manager is on the lookout for perfectly correlated securities to develop

a temporary period of divergence. When a match is found, the positions are offset (short the outperforming security and long the underperforming one) to take advantage of the price discrepancy. In delta trading, securities and their related options are combined to create a composite position whose delta is zero (*zero delta* means there is no correlation to the underlying security involved).

- **Quants**: Quant funds utilize computer-based models that depend on quantitative analysis to come up with buy/sell decisions on the securities they invest in. The level of automation varies between funds: Some funds analyze and execute trades automatically using such models while in certain others the final investment decision to buy or sell a security rests with the human analyst, although the computer model provides the choices. There are also combination funds in which some trades are executed automatically while others require human input. The best quant funds include Renaissance Technologies, D. E. Shaw & Company, and AQR Capital Management, and sport long-term return percentages well into the teens.

- **Risk optimized**: This is a multi-asset class investment strategy. It applies an asset-allocation-model that combines noncorrelated relatively risky assets and builds diversified portfolios that are less risky overall but still contain a high expected return characteristic. The idea is based on the Nobel-Prize–winning modern portfolio theory (MPT), which formalized the concept of diversification in investing and on the capital asset pricing model (CAPM), which introduced the idea of factoring in an asset's nondiversifiable systematic risk (market risk) and the expected return when adding an asset to a portfolio.

- **Others**: Managers that do not fit well into any of the preceding investment styles may be classified by the type of securities or the sectors they focus on: value versus growth, small cap versus midcap versus large cap, developed versus emerging markets, domestic versus international versus foreign, etc.

Directional style can be readily cloned. Regardless of the directional style used, the positions are based on some analysis that triggered the manager to place a directional bet on a security. To duplicate, include one or more of the manager's positions in one's own portfolio. Event-driven styles are also easily emulated, although individual investors will have trouble replicating some of the moves. While it is not complicated to imitate a position that an event driven manager establishes in a public company, many event-driven managers focus on distressed securities that are not traded, thereby cordoning off such positions from individual investors. Some strategies of market neutral style can be cloned effectively. The long/short variant strategy is relatively simple to replicate in aggregate. To achieve this, identify the positions and ratios involved, and allocate cash similarly in one's own portfolio. On the other hand, pairs trading and delta trading are tricky. In pairs trading, the window of opportunity is so tiny that only those who are ahead profit. Followers can wind up being too late. In delta neutral, the positions that combine to achieve a zero delta are complex and may not be apparent to an outsider. Quant funds are best left alone largely due to the sheer volume of trades executed during a quarter. Risk optimized style may be simulated as long as market-traded securities are used. To follow the strategy, the whole portfolio is cloned.

13Fs: A Window into Hedge Fund Activity

Being privy to the moves of money managers is critical for effective cloning. The regulatory requirement of SEC Form 13F is helpful to a point in this regard. It insists that institutional investment managers with investment discretion of $100 million or more in qualifying securities file this form. This rather broad rule applies no matter whether the investment management firm concerned is registered as an investment advisor per the Investment Advisors Act. As such, almost all money managers have to file Form 13F. Every quarter, the SEC publishes the list of qualifying securities; the latest list has around 16,000 entries comprising of the shares of stocks listed in NYSE, AMEX, and NASDAQ, and closed and open-ended investment companies.[1] For each stock listed, related instruments such as call-and-put options, warrants, and so on, are also included. Investment managers have to report details on the number of securities owned, the market value of the securities as of the end of the quarter for which the report is filed, etc. 13F filings, however, have several limitations:

- Timeliness is not a virtue of 13F. The information is due only within 45 days from the end of every quarter, making the buy/sell activity derivable from the reports inherently late by at least 45 days. To put it in perspective, if the buy/sell activity was executed on the first day of a particular quarter, this data might be four and a half months old! This essentially renders cloning useless, if the strategy of the money manager was time sensitive.
- The 13F does not provide a complete reflection of a manager's moves as only long holdings in the U.S. markets are reported in it. Many of the best money managers invest globally in all kinds of securities and the U.S. listed long selection is only part of their overall portfolio. The 13F contains information only on this subset. It does not shed light on the key elements of the manager's asset allocation strategy such as bonds, cash, and other alternative investments. These limitations severely undermine cloning money managers focused on alternate investment strategies, such as dedicated short, and income focused, as well as money managers who prefer investing outside the United States.
- Investment managers can request confidential treatment of 13F trades and delay reporting up to one year.[2] The majority of such requests are rejected, as the onus is on the investment management company to establish that absence of such immunity would impede their competitive position. Even so, the filing company still scores, as they can delay disclosing the position until the SEC rejection letter is received.

Currently, all 13F filings are in text format and are accessible to the public via the EDGAR (Electronic Data-Gathering, Analysis, and Retrieval) system. An SEC review (September 2010) of the Section 13F reporting requirements recommended plugging loopholes and rectifying limitations. Among them are the timely handling of confidential treatment requests and enforcing the requirement to supply background documentation.[3] The review also recommended looking into expanding the definition of 13F securities, among other things. They observed that not only did the current text format used in 13F

filings make it very difficult to analyze and manipulate the data submitted, but that there was also lack of uniformity in reporting. The
recommendation calls for a more structured format, such as Extensible
Markup Language (XML). Once the recommendations are implemented, the system will become much more user friendly. Until then,
those wanting to study the moves of money managers have to work
around such limitations.

Filtering 13Fs for Relevant Activity

The information in the 13F filings in text format carries all the details
of a fund manager's long positions. It is easier if the numbers are analyzed using a spreadsheet. Table 1.1 is one such spreadsheet, with the
details of Mohnish Pabrai's (a California hedge fund manager) U.S. long
holdings as of Q1 2012, derived from his corresponding 13F filing.

From this spreadsheet, the following valuable information about
Pabrai's portfolio can be gleaned:

- Mohnish Pabrai is running a very concentrated portfolio with just
  eight positions.
- The total value of the holdings is $324.75 million.

Table 1.1   Mohnish Pabrai's U.S. Holdings: Q1 2012

Entity	Market Value as of 03/31/2012	Shares as of 03/31/2012
Bank of America (BAC)	$71,794,000.00	7,502,000
CapitalSource Inc. (CSE)	$14,275,000.00	2,162,900
Citigroup Inc. (C)	$66,064,000.00	1,807,510
Goldman Sachs Group Inc. (GS)	$62,947,000.00	506,130
Horsehead Holding Corp. (ZINC)	$20,959,000.00	1,840,100
Pinnacle Airlines Corp. (PNCL) & Calls	$2,652,000.00	1,964,185
Potash Corp. (POT)	$36,232,000.00	793,000
Terex Corp. (TEX)	$49,825,000.00	2,214,460
Total	**$324,748,000.00**	

- Pabrai's largest three holdings are Bank of America (BAC), Citigroup (C), and Goldman Sachs (GS). Combined (~62 percent of the total portfolio), they make for a huge bet on financials. The percentage is obtained by adding the corresponding figures in the Market Value column and dividing by the total value of the holdings.

The spreadsheet, however, lacks the comparative information that provides insight into the manager's investment bias during the quarter:

- What are the largest buys in the quarter?
- What are the largest sells in the quarter?
- What positions were newly added in the quarter?
- What positions were eliminated in the quarter?
- How does the portfolio compare to that of the previous quarter?

This information can be visualized by incorporating information from 13F filings of previous quarters. Table 1.2 is a spreadsheet with details of Pabrai's U.S. long portfolio holdings from Q4 2011 and Q1 2012. It succeeds in answering the comparative questions raised earlier:

- Bank of America (BAC), Citigroup (C), and Goldman Sachs (GS) are the three largest buys during Q1 2012; compare the market values for 12/31/2011 with the corresponding market values for 3/31/2012. The biggest increases indicate the leading buys.
- Berkshire Hathaway (BRK.B), Wells Fargo (WFC), and DIRECTV (DTV) experienced the three largest stake reductions during Q1 2012; compare the market values for 12/31/2011 with the corresponding market values for 3/31/2012. The largest decreases denote the main stake reductions.
- No new positions were added in Q1 2012; absence of rows with entries for 3/31/2012 (market value and number of shares) with corresponding empty columns for 12/31/2011 indicates this.
- Berkshire Hathaway (BRK.B), Brookfield Residential Properties, Cresud (CRESY), DIRECTV (DTV), and Wells Fargo (WFC) are the positions eliminated in Q1 2012; the presence of rows with entries for 12/31/2011 (market value and number of shares) with corresponding empty columns for 3/31/2012 indicates this.

Table 1.2   Mohnish Pabrai's U.S. Holdings: Q1 2012 and Q4 2011

Entity	Market Value as of 03/31/2012	Shares as of 03/31/2012	Market Value as of 12/31/2011	Shares as of 12/31/2011
Bank of America (BAC)	$71,794,000.00	7,502,000	$11,876,000.00	2,135,986
Berkshire Hathaway (BRK.B)			$33,949,000.00	444,941
Brookfield Residential Properties Inc.			$1,766,000.00	226,155
CapitalSource Inc. (CSE)	$14,275,000.00	2,162,900	$14,661,000.00	2,188,141
Citigroup Inc. (C)	$66,064,000.00	1,807,510	$13,316,000.00	506,124
Cresud (CRESY)			$3,444,000.00	302,376
Goldman Sachs Group Inc. (GS)	$62,947,000.00	506,130	$19,423,000.00	214,786
Horsehead Holding Corp. (ZINC)	$20,959,000.00	1,840,100	$16,714,000.00	1,855,001
Pinnacle Airlines Corp. (PNCL) & Calls	$2,652,000.00	1,964,185	$1,628,000.00	1,985,902
Potash Corp. (POT)	$36,232,000.00	793,000	$32,859,000.00	796,000
Terex Corp. (TEX)	$49,825,000.00	2,214,460	$30,629,000.00	2,267,112
DIRECTV (DTV)			$17,033,000.00	398,341
Wells Fargo & Co. (WFC)			$38,226,000.00	1,387,001
Total	**$324,748,000.00**		**$235,524,000.00**	

- The portfolio size increased by ~38 percent during the quarter, and it has become even more concentrated than in the previous quarter.

Historical holdings information can be studied by adding more columns from the 13F filings from the previous quarters into the spreadsheet.

Raw 13F Filings from EDGAR

Table 1.3 is a snapshot of the Information Table section of a raw 13F filing downloaded from SEC's online EDGAR search system.[4] (Pabrai's filing for Q1 2012). To download and view 13Fs from the EDGAR search system, enter the name of the investment firm the manager represents (for Pabrai, use Dalal Street for filings from Q1 2012 onward, or Pabrai Mohnish for previous ones), select Exclude in the "and Ownership Forms 3, 4, and 5" field, leaving other fields blank, and use the Find Companies button. If the search criterion results in a unique match, a list of filings from the firm is returned. Otherwise, a selection must be made from a list of matching investment management firms. The end result is a list of filings from the selected investment management firm. Download and view the filing required by using the Documents button for the corresponding 13F-HR for the date concerned. The filings are done within 45 days of the end of quarter; for a Q1 2012 filing, search for a 13F-HR row with a date around May 15, 2012.

Pabrai has a very straightforward 13F filing. The raw filing has eight columns and the information from columns 1, 4, and 5 are used to populate the spreadsheets presented earlier. As indicated by the column 4 title, the column value must be multiplied by 1,000 to get the dollar figures in each of its cells. The remaining transformation is a straight one-to-one copy. To cross-check, compare the total value in column 4 with Form 13F Information Table Value Total field (further up in the filing report).

Many 13F filings have additional information in the other columns. Table 1.4 is a snapshot of a part of the Information Table from Warren Buffett's 13F filing for Q1 2012. The table is formatted similarly, although it is not an exact match. The name of the issuer is duplicated in several rows. Multiple rows for the same issuer can be present for several reasons. A common cause is when the manager owns options or warrants associated with the issuer. The rows will then indicate under column 5 the class of securities, in addition to the number of shares using abbreviations (SH, PRN, CALL, PUT). In Buffett's case, duplication occurs because the holdings of the

Table 1.3 Snapshot of Pabrai's Q1 2012 13F Filing

Column 1	Column 2	Column 3	Column 4	Column 5			Column 6	Column 7	Column 8		
	Title of Class	CUSIP Number	Value (x $1,000)	Shares or Principal Amount	SH/ PRN	PUT/ CALL	Investment Discretion	Other Managers	Voting Authority		
Name of Issuer									Sole	Shared	None
\<S\>	\<C\>	\<C\>	\<C\>	\<C\>	\<C\>	\<C\>	\<C\>	\<C\>	\<C\>		
BANK OF AMERICA CORPORATION	COM	060505104	71,794	7,502,000	SH		Sole	n/a	7,502,000		
CAPITAL SOURCE INC.	COM	14055X102	14,275	2,162,900	SH		Sole	n/a	2,162,900		
CITIGROUP INC.	COM	172967424	66,064	1,807,510	SH		Sole	n/a	1,807,510		
GOLDMAN SACHS GROUP INC.	COM	38141G104	62,947	506,130	SH		Sole	n/a	506,130		
HORSEHEAD HLDG CORP.	COM	440694305	20,959	1,840,100	SH		Sole	n/a	1,840,100		
PINNACLE AIRL CORP.	COM	723443107	2,652	1,964,185	SH		Sole	n/a	1,964,185		
POTASH CORP. SASK INC.	COM	73755L107	36,232	793,000	SH		Sole	n/a	793,000		
TEREX CORP NEW	COM	880779103	49,825	2,214,460	SH		Sole	n/a	2,214,460		

12

Table 1.4 Snapshot of Buffett's Q1 2012 13F Filing

Name of Issuer	Title of Class	CUSIP	Market Value (In Thousands)	Shares or Principal Amount	Investment Discretion	Other Managers	Voting Authority Sole	Voting Authority Shared	Voting Authority None
\<S\>	\<C\>	\<C\>	\<C\>	\<C\>	\<C\>	\<C\>	\<C\>	\<C\>	\<C\>
AMERICAN EXPRESS CO.	COM	025816109	112,951	1,952,142	Shared-Defined	4	1,952,142	—	—
AMERICAN EXPRESS CO.	COM	025816109	996,662	17,225,400	Shared-Defined	4,5	17,225,400	—	—
AMERICAN EXPRESS CO.	COM	025816109	48,593	839,832	Shared-Defined	4,7	839,832	—	—
AMERICAN EXPRESS CO.	COM	025816109	112,428	1,943,100	Shared-Defined	4,8,11	1,943,100	—	—
AMERICAN EXPRESS CO.	COM	025816109	462,570	7,994,634	Shared-Defined	4,10	7,994,634	—	—
AMERICAN EXPRESS CO.	COM	025816109	6,958,005	120,255,879	Shared-Defined	4,11	120,255,879	—	—
AMERICAN EXPRESS CO.	COM	025816109	80,987	1,399,713	Shared-Defined	4,13	1,399,713	—	—
BANK OF NEW YORK MELLON CORP.	COM	064058100	43,287	1,793,915	Shared-Defined	2,4,11	1,793,915	—	—
BANK OF NEW YORK MELLON CORP.	COM	064058100	92,021	3,813,551	Shared-Defined	4,8,11	3,813,551	—	—
CVS CAREMARK CORPORATION	COM	126650100	318,371	7,106,500	Shared-Defined	4,8,11	7,106,500	—	—
COCA COLA CO.	COM	191216100	29,604	400,000	Shared-Defined	4	400,000	—	—
COCA COLA CO.	COM	191216100	2,970,880	40,141,600	Shared-Defined	4,5	40,141,600	—	—
COCA COLA CO.	COM	191216100	67,497	912,000	Shared-Defined	4,6	912,000	—	—
COCA COLA CO.	COM	191216100	533,286	7,205,600	Shared-Defined	4,8,11	7,205,600	—	—
COCA COLA CO.	COM	191216100	676,392	9,139,200	Shared-Defined	4,10	9,139,200	—	—

subsidiaries are separated into different rows. Column 6 indicates with whom Investment Discretion rests, which is listed as Shared–Defined in Buffett's filing, that is, there are multiple managers involved. Column 7 indicates the other managers involved, through a comma-separated list of indexes. The indexes point to manager details listed in the table of Other Managers, included earlier in the filing. In general, with duplicate rows, column 5 abbreviation is a good key to base a consolidation. In this 13F, the abbreviations are missing as the holdings with the same issuer name are all the same class of securities and, when transforming into a spreadsheet, the rows can be summed up into a single row for each issuer.

Depending on the number of managers one is planning to track, transformation of the spreadsheet can be accomplished by either manually copying each item, or by using a simple computer program or script that can parse the relevant details from the 13F, and output a comma-separated list that can be processed by Excel. It is quite tedious for investors attempting to follow a number of managers to go through the process of downloading each 13F Filing, then transforming them into spreadsheets that can be analyzed. SEC offers a product called the Edgar Public Dissemination Service (PDS), which automatically delivers all public filings acquired and accepted by EDGAR, just as the filings are sent to the SEC from EDGAR.[5] It is a privately operated system by Keane Federal Systems, which is also responsible for setting the annual subscription rates. A subscription agreement with Keane, along with hardware and software setup compatible with their technical guidelines, is needed to receive the files. The system is especially useful to monitor filings that are submitted with very little delay, such as Form 13-D (the beneficial ownership report) and 4G (the insider trading report). There are also other firms[6] that specialize in making available a database that can be mined for specific information obtainable from the filings received through EDGAR.

To select a dozen of the best managers an eclectic approach was used, as it gives the best opportunity to study their styles and come up with cloning strategies that would suit particular styles. Reputation and long-term records were relied on as secondary considerations.

Notes

1. Official List of SEC's Section 13(f) Security Users, at www.sec.gov/divisions/investment/13flists.htm.
2. Details of SEC's Section 13(f) Confidential Treatment Requests, at www.sec.gov/divisions/investment/guidance/13fpt2.htm.
3. Review of the SEC's Section 13(f) Reporting Requirements at www.sec-oig.gov/Reports/AuditsInspections/2010/480.pdf.
4. SEC's EDGAR search system at www.sec.gov/edgar/searchedgar/companysearch.html.
5. Details of SEC's EDGAR Public Dissemination Service (PDS) at www.sec.gov/info/edgar/ednews/dissemin.htm.
6. Firms such as Dataroma and AlphaClone.

Chapter 2

Bill Ackman

In Sweden, the big shareholders propose board members. In the U.S., board members elect new board members.

—*Bill Ackman*

Bill Ackman is founder and CEO of the hedge fund management firm Pershing Square Capital Management, established in 2004. His initial venture was Gotham Partners (1992), cofounded with classmate David Berkowitz, after receiving an MBA from Harvard Business School. Drawing on his prior real-estate experience with his father's firm Ackman Brothers & Singer, Inc., early investments were primarily in the real estate sector. In spite of realizing good returns, the firm had a choppy end. Gotham bought a controlling stake in a golf-course operator, and added to the debt burden by acquiring other courses. To salvage the struggling golf business, the company planned a merger with First Union Real Estate Equity and Mortgage Investments, a cash-rich real-estate business. The union did not materialize, as a New York judge ruled in favor of certain minority shareholders who had filed a lawsuit against the merger. Reports[1] that Eliot Spitzer, the New York attorney general, would investigate whether Gotham Partners manipulated stock prices by publishing intentionally misleading research and/or illegal trading practices, did not bode well for the partnership either. As redemptions increased, Gotham shelved the fund in an effort to equitably distribute both the liquid and illiquid assets.

Ackman teamed with Leucadia National's (LUK) Ian Cumming to create Pershing Square, LP in 2003, which became Pershing Square Capital Management in 2004. He launched four different funds between January 2004 and July 2007, three of which enjoyed stunning returns by outperforming the market averages by double digits annually. The fund that underperformed was Pershing Square IV (PSIV), formed exclusively to invest in Target Corporation options. In early 2009, the fund dipped almost 90 percent, forcing Ackman to issue a public apology. Though eventually it recouped most of its losses, Ackman admitted that for four years no profit was made on investment in Target Corporation.

Philosophy and Style

Bill Ackman is an activist hedge fund manager. Activist investors hold considerably large (10 percent is typical) stakes in public companies and persuade management to effect changes that they (the activist investors) are confident would make the company more valuable. The activities range from negotiating directly with management in order to propose and implement operational changes to full-fledged proxy battles that allow gaining control of the company. The proposed changes can include operational adjustments, executive management changes, splitting of the company, spinning off businesses, and so on.

Ackman's modus operandi can be summed as searching for undervalued companies, analyzing why they are so, and determining whether it is worth becoming an activist investor. The idea is to help resolve the problems responsible for the underrating. Once an opportunity is identified, Ackman strikes. He swiftly builds a position upwards of 10 percent, and engages management to bring about changes. If his efforts pan out in time, the market will adjust to bridge the undervaluation gap returning an impressive yield on his original investment. At this point, Ackman usually moves on. His selection process normally excludes mega caps, as it is tough to build meaningful stakes in them.

Mispriced probabilistic investments are another of Ackman's strengths. These situations happen when the investor identifies that the market has under- or overestimated the probability of an event. Ackman generally places small, highly leveraged bets in this area; if proved right, the payoff is huge and if wrong, the damage is limited. The purchase of MBIA Credit Default Swaps (CDS) in the early 2000s is a prime example of one such killer investment. CDS contracts function as insurance policies against default of company debt. As the market did not anticipate a change in MBIA's AAA rating for some time, its CDS contracts were available cheaply. Ackman's astute research revealed MBIA was incorrectly rated AAA, and that the contracts were thus mispriced. Ackman followed through and successfully pulled off a major economic gamble in 2008. The CDS contract price moved up from a mere 13 to as high as 1200 basis points from 2002 to 2008. Ackman's activity on MBIA is immortalized in *Confidence Game*, by Christine Richard.[2]

Marquee Trades

Several of Ackman's investments did spectacularly well over the years and quite a few had reasonable returns. However, there were also some that had no movement or resulted in losses. As with any investment style, Ackman's is not without risks but, compared with his gains, the losses pale. The following are among the investment calls that greatly impacted his portfolio performance.

- **Wachovia transaction**: The Wachovia investment was among the largest realized gains in his portfolio in 2008.[3] Ackman picked up 178 million shares of Wachovia at an average purchase price of $3.15 in the week following Citigroup's announcement to buy Wachovia's banking subsidiaries on September 29, 2008. Per his investment thesis, Ackman's estimate of the value of Wachovia after the Citigroup transaction was between $8 and $11, while the stock was trading below $2. This call was spot-on, as Wells Fargo offered to buy Wachovia at about $7 per share the following week. Ackman had unflinchingly committed almost an eighth of his portfolio value to this one transaction whose returns had an overall portfolio impact of 6.5 percent. The position sizing in this transaction is a tutorial on how to ensure high conviction bets have a sizable portfolio impact. This transaction, along with several others that year, helped the fund outperform the S&P 500 index by a whopping 24 percent. The index returned −37 percent while his fund returned −13 percent.

- **General growth properties (GGP)**: Ackman invested in General Growth starting in Q4 2008 (when it was trading below a dollar) and built a 25 percent stake for $60 million. On liquidity concerns, GGP share price had decreased by over 90 percent. The investment theory was that the company was solvent, as assets outdid liabilities. Ackman believed bankruptcy might enable restoring equity value as the pressure to handle large near-term debt maturities could be extended in such a situation. His conviction proved true, and GGP emerged from bankruptcy in early 2010 at $15 per share, returning over 25 times on the investment. The position sizing is reflective of Ackman's assessment of the risk involved in the investment. While his investment was limited to less than 1.5 percent of the portfolio, the huge 25-times return made it absolutely worthwhile, as it contributed substantially to the funds returns for 2010.

- **Short-side bets on mortgage guarantors and bond insurers**: From 2007 to 2008, Ackman played the short side, using CDS contracts and short-selling stock of companies such as Fannie Mae (FNMA), MBIA (MBI), and Assured Guaranty (AGO). These positions had a positive double-digit percentage impact on the portfolio. Here again, perfect position sizing was demonstrated: The CDS contracts were cheap, allowing the purchase of a large position with a trivial portfolio portion, but the impact was significant, as many of them returned multiple times.

Portfolio Analysis

Pershing Square's U.S. long portfolio details as of Q1 2012 are listed in Table 2.1.

Table 2.1 Pershing Square's U.S. Long Portfolio Holdings: Q1 2012

Stock	Market Value	Shares	% of U.S. Long Portfolio
Alexander & Baldwin Inc. (ALEX)	$176,594,000.00	3,644,870	2.19%
Beam Inc. (BEAM)	$1,219,342,000.00	20,818,545	15.10%
Canadian Pacific Railway (CP)	$1,834,943,000.00	24,159,888	22.73%
Citigroup Inc. (C)	$954,854,000.00	26,124,594	11.83%
Family Dollar Stores (FDO)	$165,468,000.00	2,614,863	2.05%
Fortune Brands Home & Sec (FBHS)	$294,044,000.00	13,323,249	3.64%
General Growth Properties (GGP)	$1,227,250,000.00	72,233,712	15.20%
Howard Hughes Corp. (HHC)	$227,889,000.00	3,568,017	2.82%
Kraft Foods Inc. (KFT)	$589,390,000.00	15,506,172	7.30%
JCPenney (JCP)	$1,384,454,000.00	39,075,771	17.15%
Total	**$8,074,228,000.00**		

Ackman voluntarily discloses positions beyond that which U.S. regulatory requirements call for. The call option on the Hong Kong Dollar (HKD) made public through a presentation at the Delivering Alpha conference on September 14, 2011[4] is a position with very high risk/reward potential. Ackman is convinced beyond a doubt that the options are mispriced. The HKD has been pegged to the U.S. dollar for over 28 years, resulting in zero volatility. Since options are priced based on their volatility, the call options can be purchased inexpensively making way for a huge leverage—annual premiums are less than 1 percent of notional value. Although the market perception is against HKD de-pegging from the dollar, Ackman's research points to the contrary. If HKD de-pegs and appreciates against the USD, the call options will surge manifold in value. Here again, Bill Ackman is seen going for the huge leverage, although for all practical purposes, it is a low-probability binary outcome bet. He also perceives this position as a leveraged bet against a dollar collapse, for then, Hong Kong will be forced to re-peg and/or de-peg.

Another such enormous position revealed to the public is his investment in Burger King. On April 3, 2012, Justice Holdings, a special purpose acquisition Company (SPAC) listed in the London Stock Exchange and backed by Ackman, purchased a 29 percent stake in Burger King Holdings for $1.4 billion from 3G Capital. The transaction is rather strange, given its passive approach. The stake was purchased at a very large premium compared to what 3G Capital paid for the whole company in a leveraged buyout in 2010. This is a waiting game; the nature of the wait, however, hinges on Burger King's performance following IPO on the New York Stock Exchange. Justice Holdings is 30 percent owned by Pershing Square and the ownership in Burger King is around 11 percent.

Table 2.2 summarizes how cloning Ackman's top positions would have performed, assuming the positions were established immediately after they became public knowledge. The purchase date listed is the first trading day following such regulatory filing and the buy price is the one at open. To calculate returns, the market open price as of 04/02/2012 is used. Ackman still holds all the positions in the table.

General Growth Properties (GGP) is undoubtedly the celebrity stock, returning a stunning 1,131 percent over a period of 3.5 years of ownership. In theory, cloning would have worked wonders; it needs to be understood that though GGP position is enjoying diva status now, at the time the stake was established, the position was on the petite side (around 1 percent of the U.S. long portfolio). One had to either copy Ackman's entire portfolio or glean from further research that GGP was a high risk/reward type of bet. Citigroup Inc. (C) has played spoilsport,

Table 2.2 Effect of Cloning Ackman's Top Positions

Stock	Purchase Date	Buy Price	Sell Date	Sell Price or 04/02/2012 Price	Return %
General Growth Properties (GGP)	11/26/2008	$1.38	NA	$16.99	1131.16%
Citigroup Inc. (C)	8/17/2010	$39.15	NA	$36.55	−6.64%
J C Penney (JCP)	10/11/2010	$32.85	NA	$35.43	7.85%
Beam Inc. (BEAM)	10/11/2010	$39.00	NA	$58.57	50.18%
Canadian Pacific Railway (CP)	8/11/2011	$57.90	NA	$75.95	31.17%

returning −6.64 percent in the 1.7 years of ownership. The justification behind this buy was that Citigroup was trading at a significant discount to tangible book, and was also expected to start returning capital to shareholders in the form of a dividend and/or buyback. Unfortunately, that logic has yet to gain traction. JCPenney (JCP) is also yet to pick up steam, having returned just 7.85 percent in about one and a half years of ownership. As this is a pure activist investment with a longer-term outlook, the short-term underperformance is reasonable. Beam Inc. (BEAM) has been a steady performer returning over 50 percent in less than one and a half years of ownership. The original investment was on Fortune Brands, a company that split (09/2011) into Beam Inc. (BEAM) and Fortune Brands Home & Security (FBHS). Canadian Pacific (CP), another activist investment with a long-term outlook, has already returned over 30 percent in the six months of ownership. Ackman successfully ran a proxy fight against the company board and replaced the CEO.

The stake establishments in GGP, JCP, BEAM, and CP became public from Ackman's regulatory filing (SC 13D) indicating above 5 percent ownership. His Citigroup position was disclosed in a 13F filing. The holdings listed in the 13F filings and/or beneficial ownership filings are relatively easy to duplicate in an ad-hoc manner. The price ranges in the table clearly prove that the time delay with these filings did not negatively impact the returns achievable overall. However, some transactions—the Wachovia deal, the short-side bets during the credit crisis, and the Hong Kong Dollar (HKD) call options—are not easy to emulate. The Wachovia transaction does not appear in the 13F filings, due to the very short-term nature of the transaction. The round-trip happened in Q4 2008 and, hence, required nothing to be reported. The inability to clone transactions due to the lack of available public information is indeed a drawback. Nevertheless, the positions reported/disclosed are the majority of Ackman's investments at any given time making cloning a very viable option.

Notes

1. David Einhorn, *Fooling Some of the People All of the Time* (Hoboken, NJ: John Wiley & Sons, 2008).

2. Christine Richard, *Confidence Game* (Hoboken, NJ: John Wiley & Sons, 2010).

3. William Ackman, Annual Investor Dinner Presentation, Pershing Square Capital Management, L.P., January 22, 2009.

4. William Ackman, "Linked to Win," Pershing Square Capital Management, L.P., Delivery Alpha Conference, September 14, 2011.

Chapter 3

Bruce Berkowitz

Virtually no member of the Forbes 400 list of wealthiest Americans accumulated significant wealth by being widely diversified.

—Bruce Berkowitz

Bruce R. Berkowitz is founder and managing member of money management firm Fairholme Capital Management LLC, established in 1997. Its flagship product, the Fairholme Fund (FAIRX), was floated on December 29, 1999. More recently, two other smaller funds were launched: the Fairholme Focused Income Fund (FOCIX) on December 29, 2009 and the Fairholme Allocation Fund (FAAFX), which followed exactly one year later. FAIRX consistently outperformed the S&P 500 index by very wide margins from 2000 to 2009. This performance was brought into the limelight when Morningstar[1] honored Berkowitz with the Domestic-Stock Fund Manager of the Decade and the Domestic-Stock Fund Manager of the Year awards in 2010.

Berkowitz, the first in his family to attend college, graduated with a bachelor's degree in economics from University of Massachusetts, Amherst, in 1980. He started his career as a data analyst at Strategic Planning Institute in Cambridge, Massachusetts, and he was soon transferred to Manchester, England. In 1983, he joined Merrill Lynch,

London, and, by 1989, was the financial consultant and portfolio manager for Shearson Lehman Brothers in the United States. Concentrated
portfolios were his trademark, so much so that, in 1994, he held just two
stocks: Berkshire Hathaway and Fireman's Fund Insurance Company.
Berkowitz went solo in 1997 to found Fairholme, partly because the
supervisors at Lehman resented his concentrated portfolio style. After a
decade of superior returns with FAIRX, the FOCIX fund was launched
in 2009 to meet investor demand for a product focused on income oriented investments. A year later, the FAAFX fund was launched, again following investor demand for a smaller fund that could take advantage of
small-quantity ideas; as FAIRX is a very large fund, it is not possible to
meaningfully participate in smaller cap opportunities.

Philosophy and Style

Berkowitz is a contrarian deep-value investor impervious to the fads
and fashions of the stock market. His succinct tagline, "ignore the
crowd," accurately sums up his investment philosophy. He adheres to
the value investing notion of not associating volatility with risk: *Risk* is
a measure of the probability of permanent loss of capital while *volatility*
is short-term price movement that does not significantly affect long-
term returns. Berkowitz has acknowledged that his contrarian value
investing style frequently causes him to buy shares cheap, only to see
them get cheaper.[2] To him, these are golden chances to stock up more
for less, as such fluctuations are a result of volatility, rather than a reduction in the fair value of the company concerned.

Berkowitz also subscribes to a narrow school within the value-
investing world of running very concentrated portfolios. From a
peripheral standpoint, his portfolio can seem well diversified, as it is
spread over 30 or so different securities. Deeper scrutiny will reveal
that the majority of the money is invested in only a handful of them.
He also holds significant amount of cash at any given time.

Investing mostly in listed securities using a long-only investment
strategy had been his tried and tested approach for the longest time.
During the financial crisis, he migrated to investing in distressed assets
in need of both capital and restructuring. While such a step usually is

a precursor to transforming into a hedge fund, Berkowitz is not into dealing with hedge fund investors, terming them high maintenance.[3]

The Fairholme Fund experienced large redemptions in 2011 due to so-called performance chasing among investors who took to the fund following his selection as the fund manager of the decade, but disappeared when the fund underperformed in 2011. The cash allocation helped in riding out the storm and the outflows resulted in making his portfolio sharp; the total number of positions came down from the high 30s to the low 20s during that period. Having permanent capital, for instance closed-end funds and/or insurance float, would alleviate some of these issues. Though Berkowitz has voiced a preference for permanent capital, he is yet to commit to any particular option.[4]

Marquee Trades

Bruce Berkowitz's core expertise lies in analyzing financial companies. In the late 1980s and early 1990s, his investments in financial institutions provided manifold returns within a few years. A third of his liquid net worth at the time was invested in Wells Fargo (WFC), which returned around seven times in as many years. The investment theory was that the bank possessed tremendous earnings power whose potential largely went unrecognized, as the earnings were disguised by provisioning for loan losses. While the general consensus then was that WFC was covering up something, Berkowitz was convinced that was impossible. He saw no room for skeletons when nonperforming loans had a cash-yield of 6.2 percent, foreclosed assets had stabilized, the loan portfolio had shrunk 20 percent, and they were paying 17 times their GAAP earnings in taxes.

The fund identified problems with the real estate market and exited the financial sector by 2008. Some of the funds were reallocated into businesses vulnerable to turbulence in the credit markets. Auto and equipment rental companies such as Hertz (HTZ) and United Rentals (URI) fit this category, as they were dependent on short-term asset-backed financing. In spite of respectable free cash flow, the market valued such companies as though they were on the verge of bankruptcy, on liquidity concerns. Berkowitz's contrarian view begged to differ from the market. His assessment was these companies could deleverage easily by selling equipment and generating significant additional cash flow, which, in turn, would result in higher utilization and increased cash flow. Fairholme Fund also focused on defense and healthcare areas during the financial crisis. The fund established huge positions in Pfizer (PFE), Forest Labs (FRX), Humana (HUM), United Health (UNH), Wellcare (WCG), and Wellpoint (WLP) in the healthcare sector and Boeing (BA), General Dynamics (GD), Northrop Grumman (NOC), and Spirit Aerosystems (SPR) in the defense sector. Both sectors were trading in the six-times free-cash–flow range, which Berkowitz considered very cheap. To him, the fear of spending cuts in the defense sector and nationalization of healthcare were overrated. Per his calculation, homeland security would be a huge catalyst for the defense sector, and healthcare companies would thrive even if pushed toward nationalization. All told, the fund displayed three years of stellar performance from 2008 to 2010, returning over 60 percent cumulative compared to below 12 percent cumulative for the S&P 500 Index.

For certain types of investments, Berkowitz relies on consultants and a small number of other experts. His biggest project to date has been in distressed securities, which he debuted in 2009. Charlie Fernandez, a restructuring expert, was hired in 2007 to guide the fund in transforming to investing in this area. They invested in distressed securities, such as AmeriCredit and General Growth Properties (GGP), and insightfully purchased both senior debt and equity. This business acumen netted the fund billions of dollars in profits within a year.

Portfolio Analysis

Fairholme's U.S. long portfolio details as of Q1 2012 are listed in Table 3.1. The fund also has a cash allocation of around 10 percent and a large 11 percent allocation to AIA Group,[5] the spinoff of AIG's Asia Group listed in the Hong Kong exchange.

Financials and real estate is practically the whole portfolio! Berkshire Hathaway (BRK.A and BRK.B) and Leucadia National Corporation (LUK) have been a presence in the portfolio since its inception, although the sizing has varied over time. This is due to the unwavering

l   Fairholme's U.S. Long Portfolio Holdings: Q1 2012

	Market Value	Shares	% of US Long Portfolio
nternational Group (AIG)	$2,819,861,000.00	91,464,833	36.31%
l5 Strike	$261,240,000.00	24,575,760	3.36%
rica (BAC)	$984,165,000.00	102,838,555	12.67%
haway A (BRK.A)	$191,749,000.00	1,573	2.47%
haway B (BRK.B)	$78,474,000.00	967,019	1.01%
. (CIT)	$763,869,000.00	18,522,529	9.84%
orp. (LUK)	$474,524,000.00	18,180,980	6.11%
)	$453,303,000.00	46,255,370	5.84%
orp. (SHLD)	$1,113,893,000.00	16,813,480	14.34%
(JOE)	$474,185,000.00	25,715,428	6.11%
folio each)	$150,397,000.00	NA	1.94%
	$7,765,660,000.00		

blind trust associated with the proprietors of these holding companies—Warren Buffett and Ian Cumming. Sears Holdings Corporation (SHLD) and St. Joe Companies (JOE) are other long-term holdings in the portfolio, established in 2005 and 2007 respectively. The rationale behind them is that their liquidation values in a normal environment will be many times his average purchase prices. American International Group (AIG), Bank of America (BAC), CIT Group (CIT), and MBIA Inc. (MBIA) account for the massive portfolio shift into financials that began in early 2010. The four positions account for around 65 percent of the U.S. long portfolio value, making them a heavily concentrated investment that bets on an eventual turnaround in financials.

Table 3.2 summarizes how cloning Berkowitz's top positions would have performed, assuming the positions were established immediately after they became public knowledge. For positions that were since sold, the first trading day following the regulatory filing announcing the sale is taken as the sell date. For positions that are still held as of Q1 2012, 04/02/2012 is taken as the sell date. The prices at market open on the dates shown are taken as the buy and sell prices in the table.

Table 3.2   Effect of Cloning Berkowitz's Top Positions

Stock	Purchase Date	Buy Price	Sell Date	Sell Price or 04/02/2012 Price	Return %
Wells Fargo (WFC)	12/01/1992	$5.26	11/15/2006	$33.83	543.16%
Berkshire Hathaway (BRK.A)	04/01/1999	$74,600	NA	$121,950	63.47%
Leucadia National (LUK)	04/01/1999	$10.11	NA	$25.99	157.07%
Sears Holding (SHLD)	11/15/2005	$112.64	NA	$66.50	−40.96%
St. Joe Companies (JOE)	02/14/2008	$39.39	NA	$18.89	−52.04%
Pfizer Inc. (PFE)	08/15/2008	$19.87	05/17/2010	$16.20	−18.47%
Hertz Global Holdings (HTZ)	11/14/2008	$5.01	11/16/2010	$11.73	134.13%
Northrop Grumman (NOC)	11/14/2008	$42.86	02/16/2010	$59.38	38.54%
Humana (HUM)	02/14/2009	$41.54	05/17/2011	$78.15	88.13%
American International Group (AIG)	05/17/2010	$39.62	NA	$30.85	−22.14%
Bank of America (BAC)	05/17/2010	$16.39	NA	$9.54	−41.79%

Wells Fargo (WFC), a huge position in his portfolio, was made public through comments to the media in 1992.[6] The position was trimmed through the years, and eliminated completely in Q3 2006. Cloning WFC would have been immensely profitable, although it would have required the patience of many saints to sit tight while riding out the volatility. Berkshire Hathaway (BRK.A) and Leucadia (LUK) are core holdings established at inception, but whose sizes have varied over the years. The sizing adjustments are an indication for those attempting to clone these positions: Sizable increase in the position signals a buy and vice versa. Sears (SHLD) and St. Joe Companies (JOE) are long-term holdings with substantial negative returns. Bank of

America (BAC) and American International Group (AIG), the recently established financial positions in the table, are also in the negative turf. This is not a huge surprise for, as a value investor, Berkowitz is often an early bird; the volatility should not have an impact in the long-term, if the investment thesis on them unfolds as anticipated. When attempting to follow Berkowitz's trades, it is critical to realize that price fluctuations are part of the game. Pfizer Inc. (PFE) is a position that shows a small negative return using the cloning model, although Berkowitz himself probably realized a modest profit. This is a risk with most cloning strategies as it is impossible to follow the money managers in real time. But, then again, that risk is fairly minor, especially with value investors, as they tend to maintain positions for long periods of time. Per Table 3.2, Hertz (HTZ), Northrop Grumman (NOC), and Humana (HUM) show handsome returns. Berkowitz also realized similar positive returns on them. Overall, Berkowitz's portfolio is very conducive to cloning and the evidence from the table suggests such strategies are worth mulling over.

Notes

1. Nadine Youssef, "Morningstar Names Bruce Berkowitz, David Herro, and Bill Gross Fund Managers of the Decade," *PR Newswire*, January 12, 2010.

2. Fred Fraenkal, "An Interview with Bruce Berkowitz," Fairholme Funds Inc., February 8, 2012.

3. Scott Cendrowski, "Bruce Berkowitz: The Megamind of Miami," *Fortune*, December 10, 2010.

4. Margaret Cannella and Bruce Berkowitz, "Columbia Business School Value Investing Conference Panel," The Heilbrunn Center, February 10, 2012.

5. "Portfolio Manager's Report 2011," Fairholme Capital Management, LLC, December 31, 2011.

6. Bruce Berkowitz, "Interview with Outstanding Investor Digest," *Outstanding Investor Digest* VII, no. 9 and 10, November 25, 1992.

Chapter 4

Warren Buffett

Invest within your circle of competence. It's not how big the circle is that counts; it's how well you define the parameters.

—Warren Buffett

W arren Buffett is chairman and CEO of the holding company Berkshire Hathaway Inc. based in Omaha, Nebraska. He oversees a number of the conglomerate's subsidiaries. Renowned as the most successful investor of the twentieth century, Buffett is among the wealthiest individuals in the world.

Buffett, born in 1930, is the son of U.S. Congressman Howard Buffett. He was fascinated with making money from a very early age, buying his first stock at the age of 11. His investment philosophy was profoundly impacted by Benjamin Graham's classic, *The Intelligent Investor*. Buffett has declared that book, which he read while in college, as by far the best book on investing ever written. Buffett received his master's in economics from Columbia in 1951 under the tutelage of Benjamin Graham and David Dodd. His investment career also took off under Graham, when he worked as a securities analyst at Graham-Newman Corporation from 1954 to 1956. The Buffett partnership was started in 1957 and the rest, as the world will attest, is history.

The book value of Berkshire had a compounded annual gain of 19.8 percent between 1965 and 2011 for an overall gain in BV of 513,055 percent. This is against the compounded annual gain of 9.2 percent and overall gain of 6,397 percent of the S&P 500 index for the same period.[1] The 10.6 percent annual outperformance over a period of 47 years is truly one of epic proportions that outruns the rest of the investment community by a huge margin. To provide some perspective, on a $10,000 investment, that level of outperformance over that long a time, would have resulted in a terminal value of around $48.69 million compared to just around $626,000 with the S&P 500 index. Part of the BV progress came from the growth in the subsidiaries while the rest comes from investment returns. Buffett uses the float of Berkshire Hathaway's insurance operations as the primary fund for his investment operations.

Philosophy and Style

Warren Buffett officially rejected the efficient market theory as early as 1984, after profiling the investing performance records of nine persons (including himself) who significantly beat the market over long periods of time.[2] The common thread was that they were all taught by Benjamin Graham and David Dodd how to exploit gaps between price and value. The value investing philosophy focuses on the idea that risk becomes proportionally smaller as the purchase price of a business drops below intrinsic value.

Buffett considers his investment style as being 85 percent Benjamin Graham and 15 percent Philip Fisher. Benjamin Graham is regarded as the father of value investing, while Philip Fisher is a pioneer in growth investing. Graham's core investing philosophy revolves around business valuations often being wrong. Patient investors buy businesses when prices fall well below their intrinsic value and vice versa. Graham introduced the related concept, *margin of safety,* which stands for the difference between the purchase price and intrinsic value of an investment. Obviously, the higher that number, the more attractive the investment. While Buffett subscribed to these core ideas wholeheartedly, he recognized their shortcomings, too: The approach would overlook high quality businesses at higher valuations. Fisher's investment approach filled this void. It seeks out businesses able to increase earnings consistently over the long term. Once an opportunity is identified, the plan is to hold it for the very long term. Knowing that substantial effort is required to find such companies, Fisher advocated maintaining a concentrated portfolio of only a few stocks. To discover such gems, he preferred the *scuttlebutt* mode: searching information about a company through networking.

For Buffett, finding investments with a margin of safety is critical. Equally important is their ability to grow earnings consistently. Buffett runs a concentrated portfolio and expects to hold investments for the very long term, ideally forever. A double-barreled tactic to investing is also employed, viz, buying outright businesses with excellent economic characteristics that are run by outstanding managers and buying parts of businesses from the open market when it can be done at a pro-rata price well below what it would take to buy the entire business. Buffett also scouts for short-term arbitrage opportunities with excellent annualized returns.

Marquee Trades

Berkshire Hathaway bought several businesses outright, the majority of which have performed admirably over the years. See's Candies, purchased for ~$25 million in 1972, when earnings were in the $2 million range, is such an investment. Berkshire's 2011 annual report indicates See's had pretax earnings of $83 million; the total of such earnings since See's was acquired amounts to a massive $1.65 billion. The success and the reasoning of that investment are storied: See's has very low ongoing capex needs and has a virtual monopoly because customers overwhelmingly prefer their product compared to the competition. Businesses with these two characteristics are unaffected by inflation as they can raise prices without affecting volume.[3] Other outright purchases, from the 1980s on, include Nebraska Furniture Mart and Borsheim's Fine Jewelry (in the 1980s), Geico Corporation (1995), General Re Corp (1998), Burlington

Northern Santa Fe Corp (2009), and Lubrizol Corporation (2011). Geico was a minority holding in the portfolio beginning in the 1970s, and was bought fully in 1995. The performance of these and other such purchases over the years is reflected in the stunning book-value growth of Berkshire Hathaway Inc.

Buffett's long-term minority holdings in American Express (since 1964), Coca-Cola (since 1988), Gillette/Procter & Gamble (Gillette since 1989), and the *Washington Post* (since 1973) have all appreciated multiple times as of 2011. Combined they showed a total unrealized gain of ~$24 billion. While these investments showcase the power of patience when holding fundamentally sound businesses, there have also been investments that returned handsomely over shorter periods of time: Capital Cities (1979–96) returned over $2.2 billion when The Walt Disney Company acquired them, PetroChina (2003–08) added $3.6 billion (880 percent), and Freddie Mac brought in $2.5 billion (850 percent). To recap, perpetual holdings as well as shorter-term positions have contributed very significantly to Buffett's portfolio.

Although Buffett has struck gold repeatedly over the years in arbitrage opportunities, they have not attracted much publicity. Such prospects usually involve profiting from the difference in value between the market price and the announced buyout/liquidation price of a business. A variation on the same theme is to offer capital at advantageous terms to businesses with sound economic characteristics but nevertheless in dire need of capital. This window opens when the business is experiencing a rough patch, or the macro environment is such that even better companies have a hard time raising capital. Buffett's initial purchase of Gillette (1988) fell into this category: Gillette was losing market share in razors and barely managed to emerge unscathed from a hostile takeover attempt. By purchasing $600 million of preferred stock from the company, Buffett earned a seat on the board and an annualized dividend of 8.75 percent. With this transaction, he owned around 11 percent of the company as well. During the financial crisis, Buffett invested in several similar openings with capital injections of multiple billions each into Goldman Sachs, General Electric, Swiss RE, Dow Chemical, and Mars/Wrigley. In return, Berkshire Hathaway pocketed preferred shares or warrants that ensured an income stream while participating in the equity upside.

Portfolio Analysis

Table 4.1 lists Berkshire Hathaway's U.S. long portfolio details as of
Q1 2012, which consists of over $75 billion in U.S. equity invest-
ments. The company's 2011 annual report indicate ~$8 billion worth
of equity investments in businesses outside the U.S. The top allocations
there include Munich Re, POSCO, Sanofi SA, and Tesco plc. Berkshire
Hathaway's balance sheet denotes cash equivalents of ~$33.5 billion
and ~$44 billion in fixed and other investments.

The portfolio is heavily concentrated, with the top five holdings accounting for almost 74 percent of the overall U.S. long portfolio value. The selection revolves heavily around consumer staples and
financials. American Express, Coca-Cola, and Procter & Gamble are old-
timers, for they have weathered upward of 23 years with Buffett. Wells
Fargo & Co. has seen steady accumulation since its debut in Q1 2001,
and Moody's was initially purchased in 2000; they have both returned

Table 4.1   Berkshire Hathaway's U.S. Long Portfolio Holdings—Q1 2012

Stock	Market Value	Shares	% of US Long Portfolio
American Express (AXP)	$8,772,196,000.00	151,610,700	11.65%
Coca-Cola (KO)	$14,802,000,000.00	200,000,000	19.66%
ConocoPhillips (COP)	$2,211,963,000.00	29,100,937	2.94%
DirecTV (DTV)	$1,134,800,000.00	22,999,600	1.51%
International Business Machines (IBM)	$13,436,163,000.00	64,395,700	17.84%
Johnson & Johnson (JNJ)	$1,914,036,000.00	29,018,127	2.54%
Kraft (KFT)	$2,965,432,000.00	78,026,165	3.94%
Moody's (MCO)	$1,196,282,000.00	28,415,250	1.59%
Procter & Gamble (PG)	$4,923,411,000.00	73,254,136	6.54%
U.S. Bancorp (USB)	$2,187,165,000.00	69,039,326	2.90%
Wal-Mart Stores (WMT)	$2,858,538,000.00	46,708,142	3.80%
Wells Fargo & Co (WFC)	$13,462,596,000.00	394,334,928	17.88%
Misc. (<1% of US portfolio each)	$5,432,668,000.00	NA	7.21%
Grand Total	**$75,297,250,000.00**		

Table 4.2 Effect of Cloning Warren Buffett's Top Positions

Stock	Purchase Date	Buy Price	Sell Date	Sell Price or 04/02/2012 Price	Return %
Washington Post (WPO)	1974	$6.37★	NA	$375.17	5790%
The Coca-Cola Company (KO)	1988	$6.50★	NA	$73.83	1035%
Moody's Corporation (MCO)	02/15/2001	$14	NA	$42.14	201%
Wells Fargo & Co. (WFC)	05/16/2001	$22.62	NA	$33.83	49.56%
PetroChina (PTR)	05/16/2003	$23.10	11/15/2007	$195.90	748%
Wal-Mart Stores (WMT)	08/22/2005	$46.86	NA	$61.08	30.35%
ConocoPhillips (COP)	05/16/2006	$64	NA	$75.99	18.73%
Johnson & Johnson (JNJ)	11/15/2006	$66.56	NA	$66.04	−0.78%
U.S. Bancorp (USB)	02/15/2007	$36.60	NA	$31.55	−13.80%
POSCO (PKX)	03/02/2007	$96.50	NA	$84.42	−12.52%
Kraft Foods (KFT)	02/15/2008	$30.29	NA	$38.05	25.62%
DirecTV (DTV)	11/15/2011	$45.60	NA	$49.22	7.94%
International Business Machines (IBM)	11/15/2011	$187.49	NA	$208.96	11.45%

★The Buy Price for Washington Post (WPO) and The Coca-Cola Company (KO) were taken as Berkshire Hathaway's cost-basis (derived from the cost-basis listed in the Annual Report).

handsomely. Wal-Mart, Kraft Foods, Johnson & Johnson, ConocoPhillips, and U.S. Bancorp are more recent investments, picked up between 2005 and 2007. The former three positions have already proven their mettle, while the latter two have yet to. International Business Machines, almost 18 percent of the U.S. long portfolio stake established in Q3 2011, has already made significant strides.

Table 4.2 summarizes how cloning Buffett's top positions would have performed, assuming the positions were established immediately after they became public knowledge. For positions that were since sold, the trading day following the date the sales became public information is taken as the sell date. For positions that are held as of Q1 2012, April

2, 2012 is taken as the sell date. The prices at market open on the dates shown are taken as the buy and sell prices in the table.

The annualized returns of the *Washington Post* and the Coca-Cola Company at around 11.32 percent and 10.66 percent respectively are no laughing matter when their dividends, which would add a few more percentage points, are factored in. The star of the table however is PetroChina, which in spite of its relatively short five-year holding period returned at an annualized rate of 54 percent. The performance is truly satisfying when its high single digit dividends are also considered. Buffett had a 400 percent return on paper in BYD Company during the peak of the financial crisis after holding it for just one year. But, he returned it all in the following years, proving that he too is vulnerable! Replicating that investment would have resulted in a roller-coaster experience. Cloning the other more recent investments in the table would have resulted in modest annualized returns and in some cases minor losses. Buffett will probably hold the purchases for a lengthy period and hence patience is vital when following his trades. The positions overall show very respectable returns and dividends will add to this. Overall, Buffett's stock portfolio is a very good candidate for cloning.

Notes

1. Warren Buffett, "2011 Annual Letter to Shareholders" Berkshire Hathaway, Inc., February 25, 2012, www.berkshirehathaway.com/letters/letters.html.

2. Warren Buffett, "The Superinvestors of Graham-and-Doddsville," Columbia Business School Magazine, 1984.

3. Mary Buffett and David Clark, *Buffettology: The Previously Unexplained Techniques That Have Made Warren Buffett the World's Most famous Investor* (New York: Rawson Associates, 1997).

Chapter 5

Ian Cumming
and Joseph S. Steinberg

Don't overpay, no matter what the madding crowd is up to.[1]
—*Ian M. Cumming and Joseph S. Steinberg*

Ian Cumming and Joseph Steinberg run Leucadia National Corporation, a holding company with many subsidiaries, and large investments in other companies. Subsidiaries include Hard Rock Hotel and Casino in Biloxi, Mississippi, Idaho Timber, Conwed Plastics, and Crimson Wine Group. The large investments are in Jefferies Group, Inc., and Mueller Industries, Inc.

Cumming and Steinberg, classmates at Harvard Business School Class of 1970, formed Leucadia in 1980 with the takeover of Talcott National. Diversification attempts in the 1960s had left Talcott, a factoring business founded in 1854, in financial difficulties. Leucadia sold the factoring business and acquired American Investment Company, a small loan and life insurance business soon after. The insurance operations were expanded organically and via acquisitions throughout the 1980s. The pattern continued in 1991 with the acquisition of Colonial Penn for $150 million. The insurance operations of Leucadia's businesses are often compared to Warren Buffett's Berkshire Hathaway, as both companies engage in using the float in the insurance businesses to invest in a diversified range of businesses in other sectors.

The book value of Leucadia National grew at a compounded annual growth rate (CAGR) of 18.5 percent from 1979 to 2011, compared to the 8 percent growth of S&P 500 Index, including dividends.[2] That level of performance is exceptional, but becomes even more so when the benefits of annual dividends and the special dividend of $4.53 per share paid out in 1999 are considered. The 1999 payout is interesting as it offers a glimpse into their minds: Asset prices increased in the late 1990s to the point that Cumming and Steinberg were incapable of finding suitable businesses to invest in. In their 1997 letter to shareholders, they detailed the drastic step of liquidating and returning funds to investors as a plausible option. They did not follow through on this. Instead, a special dividend distribution of $812 million to shareholders was made, proving their preference for returning cash to waiting around looking for investments in a frothy market. The duo is scheduled to part ways as Ian Cumming has indicated he doesn't plan to pursue renewal of his contract after the current one expires in June 2015.

Philosophy and Style

Leucadia National's investing philosophy is concisely rendered by a comment from the 2007 Letter to Shareholders: "Investing for the long-term and fixing troubled companies' results in lumpy outcomes." The proprietors buy assets and businesses priced substantially below what they believe will be their intrinsic values, once the issue causing the undervaluation is resolved. The undervaluation could be due to the sector being out of favor, or because the business has significant operational problems. If it is the former, they wait for the market cycle to change and the concerned industry rebounds. For businesses in trouble, cash infusions are offered in exchange for equity and, in the process, earn a say in fixing the underlying problems. Either way, once the foreseen value is recognized by the market, they leave with a good return on their investment.

The fundamental theme of most of their twenty-first century investments is that they expect the underdeveloped world to raise its standard of living in the coming years. Thus, Leucadia has made several investments in the copper, iron ore, construction, and energy sectors, believing those areas will improve in value as consumption increases in other parts of the world.

Their inclination toward profitability rather than volume or market share sets their investment style apart from other value investors. Their 1993 Letter to Shareholders had the following listed as a guiding principle: "We search for niches, not dominance, on the theory that the world can tolerate many mice but few elephants." Thus, the greater share of their investments is in small and micro-caps. Joint ventures are another area of focus aimed at sharing expertise, risk, and returns.

Marquee Trades

The best investments in Leucadia's first two decades were insurance related. In 1986, they acquired Baldwin-United Corporation debt for about $107 million during its reorganization. The name was changed to Phl Corp, Inc. and Leucadia received 39 percent of common shares, certain miscellaneous assets, and board nominations. The miscellaneous assets netted cash distributions of $42 million by 1988. Following a tender offer, they increased ownership to 63 percent. The prize portion of the deal, however, was the conversion of surplus notes of Empire Insurance Company into 70 percent of the outstanding common shares, following their conversion from a mutual company to a stock company by January 1, 1988. It was a stroke of genius to recognize the hidden value of that instrument in the balance sheet, carried in the books at $25 million. Another irrefutably cool investment deal was the purchase of Colonial Penn Insurance Group for $127.9 million in cash (roughly one-third of GAAP net worth of $390.9 million) in 1991. The deal materialized as Florida Power & Light (FPL) wanted to sell Colonial Penn, a money-losing subsidiary. The payout came to pass in 1997—Leucadia waited until it became a money-spinning unit and sold it for $1.4 billion—a tenfold return in fewer than six years.

A twenty-first century blockbuster deal was a 2006 investment of $400 million in Fortescue Metals Group for 264 million shares of common and $100 million 13-year unsecured note that was to receive

4 percent of revenues from certain mines. In 2007, they boosted their stake by adding another 14 million shares for $44.2 million. With the capital infusion, FMG raised $2.1 billion in senior debt, developed its first mine, and commenced shipping iron ore from mid-2008. The efforts were rewarded in 2011 and 2012 when their stake (less 30.6 million shares) realized a total of $1.8 billion. In Compounded Annual Growth Rate (CAGR) terms, the four-and-a-half-times return over a period of five years is over 32 percent.

Leucadia enjoyed success in real estate transactions, too. The $21 million bankruptcy transaction in HomeFed Corporation was a classic wager. HomeFed owned several single-family developments in the San Diego area in 1996. Leucadia received around 40 percent of HomeFed, along with convertible notes that would increase their ownership to around 89 percent in three years. The entity was spun off to shareholders at around $1.79 per share in 1998. That stock traded as high as $70 in 2006 and currently trades in the 20s. Leucadia still controls over 31 percent of the outstanding stock of HomeFed.

Portfolio Analysis

Leucadia National's U.S. long portfolio details as of Q1 2012 are listed in Table 5.1.

Jefferies Group Inc. and Mueller Industries practically form the portfolio representing close to 98 percent of U.S. long stock holdings. Jefferies is a securities and investment banking firm; Mueller is a manufacturer of copper, brass, plastic, and aluminum products. Both

Table 5.1 Leucadia National's U.S. Long Portfolio Holdings: Q1 2012

Stock	Market Value	Shares	% of U.S. Long Portfolio
Cowen Group Inc. (COWN)	$2,693,000.00	993,758	0.17%
INTL Fcstone Inc. (INTL)	$34,141,000.00	1,618,044	2.13%
Jefferies Group Inc. (JEF)	$1,092,833,000.00	58,006,024	68.16%
Mueller Inds Inc. (MLI)	$473,719,000.00	10,422,859	29.54%
Total	$1,603,386,000.00		

these investments are expected to do well as economies around the world recover. At almost 70 percent of the portfolio, Jefferies Group is their largest single investment to date. The total investment is just over $980 million for 29 percent of the outstanding shares. Leucadia had a joint venture to trade high yield debt with Jefferies from 2000 onward, which provided excellent average returns in the 20 percent range for seven years. In their current mutual undertaking, the Jefferies High Yield Trading, LLC, they have invested around $350 million. The Mueller Industries stake, established in Q1 2011, represents close to 30 percent of the U.S. long stock holdings. Note: In March 2013, Leucadia National completed a merger with Jefferies Group.

Table 5.2 summarizes how cloning Leucadia's top positions would have performed, assuming the positions were established immediately after they became public knowledge. The purchase date listed is the first trading day following such regulatory filing and the prices at market open on the dates shown are taken as the buy and sell prices

Table 5.2 Effect of Cloning Leucadia's Top Positions

Stock	Purchase Date	Buy Price	Sell Date	Sell Price or 04/02/2012 Price	Return %
HomeFed Corporation (HOFD)	1998	$1.79	NA	$22.50	1,157%
Fortescue Metals Group (AMX:FMG)	04/02/2007	$2.01	NA	$5.91	194%
White Mountains Insurance (WTM)	04/02/2002	$339.50	11/15/2005	$633.50	86.60%
Eastman Chemical (EMN)	05/11/2006	$28.45	08/11/2007	$25.29	−11.11%
Americredit Corp.	01/01/2008	$7.64	10/01/2010	$24.46	220%
Jefferies Group Inc. (JEF)	05/15/2008	$17.54	NA	$18.91	7.81%
Mueller Industries Inc. (MLI)	05/17/2011	$36.32	NA	$45.36	24.89%

in the table. For positions since sold, the trading day following the date the sales became public information is taken as the sell date. For positions that are held as of Q1 2012, April 2, 2012 is taken as the sell date.

Purchasing HomeFed Corporation following Leucadia's lead in the wake of the spin-off in 1998 would have provided superior returns. The almost twelve-times return over a period of fourteen years adds up to an annualized yield of ~20 percent. Cloning the Fortescue, Americredit, and White Mountains investments would have generated similarly good results, but over a shorter period: Fortescue indicates annualized returns of over 24 percent over five years, Americredit ~90 percent over twenty-two months, and White Mountains ~20 percent over three-and-a-half years. Eastman Chemical disappointed with a small negative return over a period of fifteen months. Jefferies and Mueller show positive returns, but their investment thesis is yet to play out. Since Leucadia runs a very concentrated portfolio of around five positions, replicating them is not rocket science. Given their philosophy, their positions are very high-conviction bets, which provides some solace when emulating their shots. At any given time, they usually have investments in securities not publicly traded, and their subsidiaries are not publicly traded either making it impossible to clone those positions directly. A practical alternative is to monitor Leucadia's stock and consider a position when they trade below book value.

Notes

1. Ian Cumming and Joseph Steinberg, "2006 Annual Letter from the Chairman and President," Leucadia National Corporation, April 17, 2007, www.leucadia.com/c-p_letters/luk_c-p2006.pdf.
2. Ian Cumming and Joseph Steinberg, "2011 Annual Letter from the Chairman and President," Leucadia National Corporation, April 13, 2012, www.leucadia.com/c-p_letters/luk_c-p2011.pdf.

Chapter 6

David Einhorn

The goal of the portfolio construction is to try to create alpha on
both sides of the portfolio.

—David Einhorn

D avid Einhorn is founder and president of hedge fund Greenlight
Capital, established in 1996. Einhorn, a 1991 graduate of Cornell
University with a B.A. in government, entered the workforce
as an analyst at Donaldson, Lufkin & Jenrette. Two years later, he tested
the waters in the hedge fund industry with a position at SC Fundamental
Value Fund. Peter Collery, one of its proprietors, was a diligent researcher,
and greatly influenced Einhorn's investment research outlook. Peter
scrutinized SEC filings to vet businesses he was considering investing in:
He analyzed corporate behavioral issues, inconsistencies in the business
description compared to the results, aggressive accounting practices, and
so on. The experience dovetailed nicely when he launched his own
fund a few years later; after all, the devil is in the details.

Einhorn shot into prominence with his shorting of Lehman
Brothers' stock, and profiting immensely from its eventual bankruptcy. The stock was shorted initially in 2007, and the position
was announced during a speech at the Grant's Spring Investment
Conference in April 2008.[1] The presentation raised concerns about

Lehman's balance sheet not being materially different from Bear Stearns, a business the government bailed out in March 2008. It also questioned Lehman's accounting practices, observing many more billions in write-downs that should have been taken than they did. Although the popular press largely resented Einhorn's efforts at the time, he was vindicated when, a few months later, Lehman reported a $2.8 billion quarterly loss on their way to declaring bankruptcy in September 2008.[2]

Einhorn is well-known for his staunch stance against fraudulent businesses, and his active role in exposing such practices in the marketplace.[3] Warren Buffett once noted that shorting stocks of companies run by crooks is difficult, because they will fight dirty to save themselves. That captures the essence of the peril in short selling for money managers. Einhorn witnessed this behavior firsthand in the six-year-long battle with the management at Allied Capital. Einhorn kicked off this saga in 2002 by recommending the shorting of Allied stock on the grounds they defrauded Small Business Administration, among other things.[4] Allied countered, alleging Einhorn was engaged in market manipulation, and the SEC announced its intention to investigate Einhorn. In 2007, after Allied and Einhorn had traded several barbs to make the other appear culpable, the SEC ascertained that Allied violated securities laws through aggressive accounting practices. Einhorn's book, *Fooling Some of the People All of the Time,* details his version of this drama. Despite that experience, Einhorn is a determined advocate of detecting and rooting out fraud.[5]

Philosophy and Style

Greenlight Capital is a long-short value-oriented hedge fund focused on absolute returns. Since its inception in 1996, the prized Greenlight Capital, L.P. fund has returned ~20 percent annualized. The absolute return strategy has worked incredibly well over the years, save for one negative return year (2008). David Einhorn's value investing style examines the likely causes behind a business being mispriced, then scrutinizes it to determine whether mispricing actually exists. Einhorn invests only if the analytical edge is sizable and the mispricing is large. This deviates from the traditional value investing approach of first identifying a list of securities that are low-priced or expensive and analyzing whether the anomaly is justified. As a long-short fund, Einhorn looks for mispricing on either side: Undervaluation translates to going long and vice versa. The long-short style does not involve pairs trading: Each position, long or short, has to have favorable risk–reward characteristics.

Einhorn's approach also gauges the macro picture and the business cycle when considering an investment. However, he shies from placing bets based singly on the macro picture analysis or on the business cycle. The net exposure to the market is modified based on macro study, and the long-short ratio in specific sectors is adjusted according to the business cycle analysis. Unlike many hedge fund managers, he shuns leverage, does not use shorts as a hedge, and is not keen on timing the market.

On the average, Einhorn's portfolios sport upward of 30 positions, both on the long and the short side, though the short positions are sized at roughly half that of the long positions. A significant bias is placed on the long side, as markets tend to rise over time. He strongly supports concentrated bets with up to 20 percent of the capital in a single long position and 30 percent to 60 percent of the capital in the top-five long positions. The approach draws heavily from Joel Greenblatt's ideas on running a concentrated portfolio: Good ideas are hard to find, and so, when one is spotted, it is important to invest adequately for a good portfolio impact.[6]

Marquee Trades

In the initial years since its founding, the fund enjoyed exceptional success investing in special situations, such as demutualizations and spinoffs. In 1997, Greenlight established a position in Summit Holdings Southeast, a demutualized Florida workers' compensation specialist, which more than doubled in June 1998, when Liberty Mutual agreed to buy the company at $33 per share. The icing on the cake was that investment was a huge 15 percent of the fund's assets; that single position significantly impacted the fund's performance that year. The short positions also enjoyed success. Significant contributions were realized from shorting Boston Chicken, Samsonite, Sirrom Capital, and Century Business Services.

Einhorn has a reputation of being extremely cautious and disciplined when shorting businesses. Shorting something solely on valuation is not his style; the business has to have misunderstood fundamentals and deteriorating prospects. His preferred shorts are mostly suspected frauds. Century Business Services and Seitel were both businesses that Einhorn shorted successfully, based on his perception that their accounting was fraudulent. Century Business Services was shorted in 1998 when it was trading at around ~$25. The SEC was informed of the problem. A year later, the company restated their accounts and, by October 2000, the stock had dropped below a dollar. With Seitel, Einhorn uncovered the company was committing hari-kari, reporting earnings while burning cash. The accounting problem came to light in 2002, when the company went under and the CEO was sentenced to five years in prison. In the last decade, Einhorn's research has revealed fraud at businesses such as Chemdex, Orthodontic Centers of America, and Elan. Most of them were successfully shorted and resulted in immense profits over the years.

While short-side success has garnered attention for Greenlight, its long bets have also performed splendidly. The position in Agribrands (a spinoff from Ralston Purina), established in 1998, gave Greenlight reason to cheer when in two years the stock doubled following an acquisition offer from Cargill. Over 20 percent of Greenlight's total capital was allocated to that one investment thereby ensuring good portfolio returns. Lower conviction long-side bets that had a huge run, but limited portfolio impact, include the 2008 investment in Patriot Coal with an internal rate of return (IRR) of +2112%, and Jones Apparel Group, which quadrupled quickly in 2009. Lanxess, an investment Einhorn identified as the second most profitable position Greenlight had ever taken, was distinct as it involved two round trips from 2005 to 2010. The stock was first purchased in 2005 at prices in the teens and sold in 2007 at prices in the 40s. The same pattern of trades occurred again between 2008 and 2010.[7]

Portfolio Analysis

Table 6.1 lists Greenlight Capital's U.S. long portfolio details as of Q1 2012.

Apple Inc., established in Q2 2010 at $248.09, is by far the largest position in the partnership at over 15 percent of the U.S. long portfolio;

Table 6.1   Greenlight Capital's US Long Portfolio Holdings: Q1 2012

Stock	Market Values	Shares	% of U.S. Long Portfolio
Apple Inc. (AAPL)	$877,445,000.00	1,463,700	15.85%
Aspen Insurance Holdings (AHL)	$114,581,000.00	4,101,000	2.07%
Best Buy (BBY)	$182,676,000.00	7,714,375	3.30%
CA Inc (CA)	$69,878,000.00	2,535,772	1.26%
Carefusion Corp. (CFN)	$269,994,000.00	10,412,441	4.88%
CBS Corp. (CBS)	$153,568,000.00	4,528,681	2.77%
Computer Sciences Corp. (CSC)	$71,856,000.00	2,400,000	1.30%
Dell Inc. (DELL)	$198,610,000.00	11,964,405	3.59%
Delphi Automotive PLC (DLPH)	$252,633,000.00	8,194,661	4.56%
DST SYS INC (DST)	$85,018,000.00	1,567,734	1.54%
Einstein Noah Restaurant (BAGL)	$160,143,000.00	10,733,469	2.89%
Ensco PLC (ESV)	$203,377,000.00	3,842,365	3.67%
General Motors Company (GM)	$379,957,000.00	14,813,163	6.86%
HCA Holdings (HCA)	$103,290,000.00	4,175,000	1.87%
Huntington Ingalls Inds Inc. (HII)	$110,700,000.00	2,750,995	2.00%
Legg Mason Inc. (LM)	$94,962,000.00	3,400,000	1.72%
Liberty Media Capital (LMCA)	$86,387,000.00	980,000	1.56%
Market Vectors ETF (GDX)	$360,125,000.00	7,264,971	6.51%
Marvell Technology Group (MRVL)	$288,995,000.00	18,372,247	5.22%
Microsoft Corp. (MSFT)	$241,465,000.00	7,487,295	4.36%
NCR Corp. (NCR)	$182,093,000.00	8,387,490	3.29%
Seagate Technology (STX)	$391,803,000.00	14,538,126	7.08%
Sprint Nextel Corp. (S)	$194,555,000.00	68,265,000	3.51%
Xerox Corp. (XRX)	$124,373,000.00	15,392,717	2.25%
Misc (<1% of U.S. portfolio each)	$336,636,000.00	NA	6.08%
Total	**$5,535,120,000.00**		

Greenlight is sitting on huge profits there. Interestingly, the fund had a small position in Apple in Q4 2000 at an average purchase price of $14 per share, which it eliminated in the following quarter at around $18 per share. Einhorn has since classified that transaction among his worst sells of all times.[8] He believes Apple is erroneously valued as the market incorrectly perceives it to be already universally owned with

an unsustainably high market cap. Seagate Technology, a huge position established in Q2 2011, also boasts significant gains. The position
was established on the thesis that the market had mispriced Seagate on
undue concerns about macro weakness, technology substitution (flash
memory replacing hard-disks), and so on.

Table 6.2 summarizes how cloning Greenlight's top positions would
have performed, assuming the positions were established immediately
after they became public knowledge. For positions that were since sold,
the trading day following the date the sales became public information is taken as the sell date. For positions that are held as of Q1 2012,
04/02/2012 is taken as the sell date. The prices at market open on the
dates shown are taken as the buy and sell prices in the table.

Agribrands, a stake established in 1998, was made public only in
the first regulatory 13F-HR filing on 05/12/1999. Even so, following that trade would have snagged a 66 percent return over a period
of 18 months. Recognizing and mirroring the oversized allocation
(over one-fifth of the total capital) of that one investment would have
made the deal even sweeter. Einhorn has lauded M.D.C Holdings,
Inc., a long-term investment purchased on the day of Greenlight's
inception in 1996, and eliminated in Q2 2011, as among the biggest

Table 6.2   Effect of Cloning David Einhorn's Top Positions

Stock	Purchase Date	Buy Price	Sell Date	Sell Price or 04/02/2012 Price	Return %
Agribrands	05/13/1999	$32.88	12/2000	$54.50	65.75%
M.D.C Holdings (MDC)	05/14/1999	$10.37	08/16/2011	$18.43	77.72%
Market Vectors Gold Miners ETF (GDX)	02/13/2009	$36	NA	$49.49	37.47%
Apple Inc (AAPL)	08/16/2010	$247.58	NA	$601.83	143.1%
Seagate Technology (STX)	08/16/2011	$11.99	NA	$27.01	125.3%
General Motors (GM)	11/15/2011	$22.81	NA	$26.03	14.12%

contributors to the partnerships' returns of all time. Its holding information became public knowledge in 1999, and cloning that position would have provided rewards, although nowhere near as lucrative as those that Greenlight reaped. Greenlight trimmed its M.D.C. stake significantly in the interim periods at much higher prices, accounting for the discrepancy. The Market Vectors Gold Miners ETF position is part of Einhorn's large allocation to investments related to gold. Mimicking that position would have returned in the vicinity of 37 percent over three years. Apple Inc. and Seagate Technology are the stars, showing 143 percent and 125 percent returns in fewer than 20 and eight months, respectively. General Motors, on the other hand, showed modest returns over a five-month holding period. It is evident from the table that following Einhorn's major long moves would be a very profitable endeavor. Shadowing his long investments is easy and worthwhile, for he runs a concentrated portfolio and all positions are assured a favorable risk-reward characteristic, per his investigation. Since he is not given to the whims and fancies of the prevailing market, very short holding periods are a rarity. Thus, the vast majority of his long positions appear in the quarterly 13F filings, albeit with a time delay.

Following his short investments is a different ball game altogether. The table does not indicate any such investments as that information is beyond the scope of the 13F filings. The public becomes aware of them only if Einhorn volunteers these facts. All is not lost there, for Einhorn himself has revealed the specifics of such trades on several occasions.

Notes

1. David Einhorn, "Private Profits and Socialized Risk," Grant's Spring Investment Conference, April 8, 2008.
2. Louise Story, "Lehman Battles an Insurgent Investor," *New York Times*, June 4, 2008.
3. David Einhorn, "Q3 2008 Letter to Partners," Greenlight Capital, 10/01/2008.
4. David Einhorn, "Best Idea Speech," Tomorrow's Children Fund conference, May 15, 2002.
5. David Einhorn, *Fooling Some of the People All of the Time: A Long Short Story* (Hoboken, NJ: John Wiley & Sons, 2008).

6. Joel Greenblatt, *You Can Be a Stock Market Genius Even If You're Not Too Smart: Uncover the Secret Hiding Places of Stock Market Profits* (New York: Simon & Schuster, 1997).

7. David Einhorn, "Q4 2010 Letter to Partners," Greenlight Capital, January 18, 2011.

8. Consuelo Mack and David Einhorn, "WealthTrack Interview," November 19, 2010.

Chapter 7

Carl Icahn

CEOs are paid for doing a terrible job. If the system wasn't so
messed up, guys like me wouldn't make this kind of money.

—Carl Icahn

C arl Icahn is chairman of Icahn Enterprises, a diversified public
holding company engaged in businesses such as real estate,
metals, and consumer goods. He is also chairman of American
Railcar Industries and Federal-Mogul Corporation. Born in Brooklyn in
1936, Icahn's investment career started in 1961, as a registered representative of Dreyfus & Company, where he learned options and convertible
arbitrage. He founded the brokerage firm Icahn & Co. Inc. in 1968, and
purchased a seat on the New York Stock Exchange.

Icahn started acquiring large stakes in public companies in the late
1970s. The initial businesses he dabbled in included Tappan, whose shares
were trading at a large discount to book value.[1] The proxy fight that
ensued ended when the business was bought by Electrolux for a valuation that was more than double what Icahn paid. Icahn pioneered the
art of *greenmailing*: threatening the takeover of a business after purchasing
a large stake in it, which forces the business to buy the stake back at a
premium. It is akin to blackmailing, as Icahn is paid to walk away, but it
is perfectly legal. Prominent businesses that were successfully subjected to

this game plan include Marshall Field, American Can, Phillips Petroleum, Uniroyal, and BFGoodrich. Although he made his name as a dreaded corporate raider, Icahn did successfully increase shareholder value in several companies (Texaco, Nabisco Group Holdings, etc.), realizing profits for other shareholders as well.[2] Moreover, his forays included taking over or acquiring majority stakes and running companies such as TWA (1984 to 1991) and American Railcar (1994 onward).

Imposition of a 50 percent tax on greenmail profits, along with other changes, has rendered greenmailing obsolete.[3] Accordingly, Icahn made a tactical shift: The current strategy pressures management and boards to make operational changes to increase shareholder value. If the company fails to abide by his demands, he launches a proxy battle for board seats in an attempt to control the company. Depending on the situation, the demands can include stock buybacks, changes in management, spinning off businesses, and so on. Although greenmailing per se is no longer employed, a variation exists as a bargaining chip; Icahn offers to back off from the proxy battle if one or more of his demands are met.

Philosophy and Style

Carl Icahn's approach to investing has constantly evolved over the years and currently emphasizes activism. At the core of his activism theory is the belief that there is significant business mismanagement in corporate America. He has identified a number of corporate governance issues to target for activism: corporate boards failing to hold their business executives accountable, egregious executive pay scales, excessive board member compensation and perks, cumbersome provisions that are in the way of shareholders having a say in corporate board elections, and provisions that almost prevent the shareholders from uniting and causing changes in the way businesses are run. His main ideas on this theme are available through the website The Icahn Report™,[4] which functions to unite shareholders against mismanaged businesses and promote better frameworks.[5]

Icahn is convinced that the way in which promotions work in corporate America is responsible for incompetence at the top of many businesses. Political survivors ascend the corporate ladder easily. Those who steer clear of controversy and are not a threat to the executives higher up have better chances of being promoted. This results in many businesses having peacemakers, who are not CEO material. Corporate boards love having CEOs promoting camaraderie at the top because they meet the primary interest of the board members, viz, enriching themselves. Shareholders suffer as accountability simply does not exist. This also contributes to American businesses losing their edge globally. Because incompetent management and boards are key reasons for such businesses to be undervalued, Icahn relentlessly targets them to bring about changes.

Businesses with restructuring opportunities also beckon Icahn. It is not that these businesses lack competent executives at the helm; rather, it is their boards that thwart their efforts in carrying out large scale changes, such as splitting of businesses, supporting a merger, and so on.

Marquee Trades

In the late 1980s, Texaco was ordered to pay $10.53 billion dollars to Pennzoil, as compensation for acquiring Getty Oil, as Pennzoil already had a deal with Getty Oil. Such was the size of the payment that Texaco mulled Chapter 11 bankruptcy proceedings to protect its assets. Icahn smelled opportunity and, after building a 12 percent stake quickly, approached the CEO of Texaco and demanded they work out a quick settlement with Pennzoil. This well-oiled plan panned out well; Texaco agreed to settle the dispute for $3 billion. The rebound in its stock price allowed Icahn to walk away with a cool $600 million.

The Nabisco transaction that dragged on for six years from 1995 is a testimony to Icahn's tenacity. His main demand was to spin off the cookie business from the tobacco business; he had four failed bids during the period. At the end, when Nabisco stated its intention to sell itself or sell the stake in the cookie business, Icahn offered to buy the cookie unit for $5.2 billion. The bid was outbid and the unit taken away by Philip Morris at a substantial margin. Icahn laughed all the way to bank; his profit was over $600 million as his 10 percent stake in the company increased in value as a result of the premium bid.

Other deals in the last decade that provided handsome returns for Icahn included Kerr-McGee, MedImmune, and El Paso Corporation. Transactions such as Blockbuster and Yahoo did not have happy endings.

Portfolio Analysis

Ichan's U.S. long portfolio details as of Q1 2012 are listed in Table 7.1.

Icahn Enterprises LP, formerly American Real Estate Partners, is the holding company Icahn controls with over 92 percent of the outstanding shares. It has been in his portfolio since 2007. A huge stake in auto-parts supplier Federal-Mogul was first purchased in 2000. In October 2001, large asbestos-related claims forced it to seek

Table 7.1 Ichan's U.S. Long Portfolio Holdings: Q1 2012

Stock	Market Value	Shares	% of U.S. Long Portfolio
American Railcar Industries (ARII)	$278,568,000.00	11,848,898	2.85%
Amylin Pharmaceutical Inc. (AMLN)	$358,973,000.00	14,385,925	3.67%
CVR Energy Inc. (CVI)	$336,628,000.00	12,584,227	3.44%
Commercial Metals (CMC)	$154,958,000.00	10,455,991	1.59%
Federal Mogul Corp. (FDML)	$1,314,590,000.00	76,385,255	13.45%
Forest Labs Inc (FRX)	$914,487,000.00	26,361,686	9.36%
Hain Celestial Group Inc. (HAIN)	$312,390,000.00	7,130,563	3.20%
Icahn Enterprises LP (IEP)	$4,008,551,000.00	92,812,051	41.01%
Mentor Graphics Corp. (MENT)	$239,547,000.00	16,120,289	2.45%
Motorola Mobility Hldgs (MMI)	$1,020,240,000.00	26,000,000	10.44%
Navistar International Corp. (NAV)	$293,320,000.00	7,251,426	3.00%
Oshkosh Corp. (OSK)	$200,774,000.00	8,665,260	2.05%
Take-Two Interactive Software (TTWO)	$112,397,000.00	7,305,626	1.15%
Web MD Health Corp. (WBMD)	$171,400,000.00	6,700,525	1.75%
Misc (<1% of U.S. portfolio each)	$57,953,000.00		0.59%
Total	**$9,774,776,000.00**		

Chapter 11 bankruptcy protection. In December 2007, it emerged with Icahn owning 75.25 percent of the outstanding shares; Icahn acquired Federal-Mogul bonds that were swapped for equity. Motorola is an activist stake first purchased in Q1 2007 that paid off in 2012, with Google purchasing the Motorola Mobility spinoff. Motorola Solutions, the part left after the spinoff, was disposed of in Q1 2012. Forest Labs is a very recent activist stake first purchased in Q2 2011, and Icahn is seeking to replace the CEO. Most of the other positions in the table are also activist stakes, albeit smaller.

Table 7.2 summarizes how cloning Icahn's top positions would have performed, assuming the positions were established immediately after they became public knowledge. For positions that were since sold, the first trading day following the date the sales became public information is taken as the sell date. For positions that are held as of Q1 2012, 04/02/2012 is taken as the sell date. The prices at market open on the dates shown are taken as the buy and sell prices in the table.

Mylan, a position established in 2004, was exited in 2005 when his demand to abandon the deal to acquire King Pharmaceuticals was met. Per Icahn, his worst investment ever was Blockbuster: The debt load, along with the shift to digital, ultimately led Blockbuster to bankruptcy. Following that move would have been disastrous, resulting in a 93 percent loss. Cloning Imclone Systems and Biogen Idec on the other hand would have provided handsome returns. El Paso Corp, a

Table 7.2 Effect of Cloning Icahn's Top Positions

Stock	Purchase Date	Buy Price	Sell Date	Sell Price	Return %
Mylan Inc. (MYL)	08/20/2004	$17	11/15/2005	$20.05	17.94%
Blockbuster Inc.	Q4 2004	$9.54	Q1 2010	$0.67	−93%
Imclone Systems, Inc.	Q1 2004	$50.75	11/24/2008	$70	39.86%
Time Warner (TWX)	02/15/2006	$54.18	02/15/2007	$64.08	18.27%
El Paso Corp. (EP)	08/16/2011	$18.73	05/15/2012	$29.17	55.74%
Biogen Idec (BIIB)	02/15/2008	$62.47	08/16/2011	$91.36	46.25%

position disclosed in the 13G filing on 08/15/2011, is definitely the star returning over 55 percent in just nine months.

The risk in following Icahn's positions is that he is not consistently successful in forcing companies to meet his demands. Numerous federal and state laws make it hard for activism efforts to succeed.[6]

- Poison pill: Many states allow businesses to issue new stock to rebuff a hostile takeover attempt.
- Staggered board: A number of states allow businesses to spread out board elections over a period of time, thus blocking attempts to replace board members en masse.
- Right of domicile: In several states, management has the sole right to decide where a company is incorporated, making it impossible for activists to effect a change of domicile, even through a majority vote.

Businesses also put in bylaw provisions and other actions detrimental to activist efforts. Those include supermajority provisions that require large majority approval for major transactions, advance notice provisions that make it expensive to comply, and so on. Also, in many businesses, the CEO and chairman of the board is the same individual, resulting in a conflict of interest: The CEO represents management, while the chairman represents shareholders. Despite such problems, the table reveals several stakes that provide great returns and, hence, following him in a selective fashion may be quite worthwhile.

Notes

1. Ken Auletta, "The Raid: How Carl Icahn Came up Short," *The New Yorker*, 03/20/2006, www.newyorker.com/archive/2006/03/20/060320fa_fact4.
2. Diane Brady, "Icahn: The Once and Future Dealmaker," *Businessweek*, June 11, 2000, www.businessweek.com/archives/2000/b3685250.arc.htm.
3. Electronic Code of Federal Regulations, "Title 26: Internal Revenue, Part 156—Excise Tax on Greenmail," www.ecfr.gov/cgi-bin/retrieveECFR?gp=1& SID=d39fb3e01a2b9f1cc82aeae3020ee210&ty=HTML&h=L&n=26y17.0.1. 1.13&r = PART.
4. Carl Icahn, "The Icahn Report™," www.icahnreport.com.

5. Icahn, Carl. "The Icahn Plan: Join the United Shareholders of America." *Icahn Report*, October 7, 2008, www.icahnreport.com/report/2008/10/join-the-united.html

6. Icahn, Carl. "100 Million Reasons Why We Need Governance Changes Now: Join USA." *Icahn Report*, October 27, 2008, www.icahnreport.com/report/2008/10/100-million-rea.html

Chapter 8

Seth Klarman

The prevailing view has been that the market will earn a high rate of return if the holding period is long enough, but entry point is what really matters.

—Seth Klarman

S eth Klarman is founder and president of Baupost Group, LLC, a hedge fund he founded in 1982.[1] Baupost is among the largest hedge funds in the world, with almost $30 billion in assets under management (AUM).

Klarman was born in New York City but grew up in Baltimore; he had an obsession with numbers from childhood. From baseball statistics he graduated to stock tables and, by age ten, had already made his first stock purchase in Johnson & Johnson. While at Cornell, he was introduced to value investing via a summer internship at Mutual Shares, an investment firm founded in 1949 by Max Heine. Mutual Shares operates on the value-investing principles espoused by Benjamin Graham and, in 2010, was ranked as the best performing mutual fund over the last fifty years.[2] Klarman has since admitted that what he learned there was far superior to what an academic setting could offer. Immediately upon graduation, he had another eighteen-month stint at Mutual Shares.

Professor William Poorvu recognized Klarman's immense potential during a course on real estate at Harvard Business School. Soon thereafter, Poorvu and his friends enlisted Klarman's help in investing their money. Thus, Baupost was formed from initial capital of $27 million. The fund earned annualized returns of ~19% since inception compared to ~8% for the S&P 500 index for the same stretch of time. At over $16 billion dollars, the fund is riding high in net gains after all fees since inception.

Philosophy and Style

Klarman's investing philosophy is best covered in his 1991 book *Margin of Safety: Risk-Averse Value Investing Strategies for the Thoughtful Investor.* The fundamental idea is that a security is worth purchasing only if it is trading at a discount to its underlying value. If securities are picked up at a substantial discount, losses could be avoided or at least mitigated, should the scenario that caused the low end of the valuation range play out. In a nutshell, the discount makes for a cushion, or a margin of safety. Security valuation is a complex process, returning a range of values under different scenarios. Rather than compromising on a security with little or no margin of safety, Klarman prefers to hold onto good old cash.

Sensitivity analysis is used to determine the width of the margin of safety under different scenarios. Baupost Group acquired debt of several firms, including Washington Mutual and Ford Motor Credit Company, during the financial crisis of 2008, based on the sensitivity analysis that determined the value of the bonds in an economic depression to be above what they were trading at the time of purchase.

Klarman's viewpoint on market efficiency and risk differ starkly from the academic definition. He believes inefficiently priced securities are aplenty at any given time, but that investors need an edge to find them: truly long-term capital; a flexible approach that enables you to move opportunistically across a broad array of markets, securities, and asset classes; deep industry knowledge; strong sourcing relationships; and a solid grounding in value investing principles.[3] He focuses on risk before return. To him, risk does not imply volatility but rather the probability of losing and by how much.

He uses an absolute return bottom–up style of investing. Scrutinizing the economic and macro outlooks is also done: Worry top down but invest bottom up. This approach is preferred over its reverse, as economic and macro forecasting are difficult endeavors.

The fund shuns leverage, avoids short selling, and holds a significant amount of cash. These strategies avoid risk to a great extent, but fail to contain tail risk. *Tail risk* is the risk of unlikely, but possible, catastrophic events: the specific tail risks the firm tries to insure against are stock market corrections, surges in inflation, and currency devaluation.[4] Strategies include buying put options on market indexes to compensate for market correction, gold investments to counter currency devaluation, and credit default swaps that climb if the chances of default of the underlying instrument increase.

Marquee Trades

Baupost Group has trumped in insuring against disaster for quite some time. Buying way–out–of–the–money puts against frothy market indices, like the Nikkei, worked for them during the 1980s. The continuous climb of the U.S. markets in the 1990s made Klarman wary and so he kept his U.S. allocation very low. Out-of-the-money puts on the U.S. market indexes were placed to cover the tail risk of a U.S. market crash. The risk avoidance tactics against a persistently bubbly market made Baupost underperform the S&P 500 index significantly in the 1990s. However, his unwavering patience bore fruit in the last decade as the strategies propelled the fund to the top of the U.S. hedge-fund industry following strong returns compared to S&P 500 index.

A variation on the insuring theme is his tactic of hedging against U.S. dollar devaluation. Gold is undoubtedly the shiny favorite, and he has had significant exposure to this precious metal through owning gold stocks since 2006. His bets on gold rising in value against the U.S. dollar have certainly gilded his returns since then.

Seeking gains from mispriced distressed bonds is also a focus area for Klarman. When Nations Rent, a building equipment rental business, filed for bankruptcy in 2001, Baupost invested $100 million in the debt. During its reorganization in 2002, Klarman plunked down another $50 million in exchange for stock. By the time the company emerged from bankruptcy, Baupost controlled about two-thirds of the business. This move repaid him when, in 2006, Sunbelt Rentals acquired the company for $1 billion, and Klarman walked away with mid-20 percent annualized returns.

During the financial crisis, Klarman was extremely busy, investing as much as $100 million in a single day, mostly in distressed debt. Bonds of CIT Group and Washington Mutual paid off immensely as he succeeded in picking them up at a large discount to par and selling them closer to par during 2010 and 2011. Occasionally, he unearthed values in U.S. equity, with some trading at two-thirds of net working capital, a level identified by Graham as a compelling valuation. News Corporation, a long-term holding of Baupost initially purchased in 2005, traded as low as $5 in 2008. Baupost more than tripled his position during that time—his fundamental analysis on News Corp. determined that the breakup value based on the depressed environment at the time was $20 and in a more normal environment ranged between $20 and $30. The gamble worked as the stock recovered quickly.

Portfolio Analysis

Table 8.1 lists Baupost Group's U.S. long portfolio details as of Q1 2012.

Viasat, the largest holding in his 13F portfolio, was purchased in 2008, but most of the position was acquired during the market lows of 2009, allowing Baupost large gains on the position. The stakes in BP PLC, Hewlett Packard Company, and Microsoft were established in 2011, when they were trading at multiyear lows. The other major concentrations in the portfolio are in gold miners and pharmaceuticals.

Table 8.2 summarizes how cloning Klarman's top positions would have performed, assuming the positions were established immediately after they became public knowledge. For positions that were since sold, the trading day following the date the sales became public information

Table 8.1 Baupost Group's U.S. Long Portfolio Holdings: Q1 2012

Stock	Market Value	Shares	% of U.S. Long Portfolio
Alliance One International (AOI)	$33,126,000.00	8,786,700	1.12%
Allied Nevada Gold (ANV)	$130,535,000.00	4,012,750	4.41%
Aveo Pharmaceuticals Inc. (AVEO)	$63,101,000.00	5,084,652	2.13%
BP PLC (BP)	$419,441,000.00	9,390,900	14.18%
Enzon Pharmaceuticals Inc. (ENZN)	$61,566,000.00	9,000,878	2.08%
Hewlett Packard Co. (HPQ)	$411,068,000.00	17,250,000	13.90%
Idenix Pharmaceuticals Inc. (IDIX)	$80,758,000.00	8,249,000	2.73%
Microsoft Corp. (MSFT)	$225,785,000.00	7,000,000	7.64%
News Corp. (NWSA)	$296,471,000.00	15,041,665	10.03%
News Corp. Class B (NWS)	$212,847,000.00	10,658,335	7.20%
Novagold Resources Inc. (NG)	$71,800,000.00	10,000,000	2.43%
Syneron Medical Ltd. (ELOS)	$42,880,000.00	4,000,000	1.45%
Theravance Inc. (THRX)	$283,799,000.00	14,553,800	9.60%
Theravance Inc. Notes	$52,211,000.00	51,000,000	1.77%
Viasat Inc. (VSAT)	$506,205,000.00	10,499,992	17.12%
Misc (<1% of U.S. long portfolio each)	$65,361,000.00	NA	2.21%
Total	**$2,956,954,000.00**		

Table 8.2 Effect of Cloning Klarman's Top Positions

Stock	Purchase Date	Buy Price	Sell Date	Sell Price or 04/02/2012 Price	Return %
National Health Inv (NHI)	08/14/2002	$14.05	05/15/2003	$16.75	19.22%
Radvision Ltd. (RVSN)	08/14/2002	$4.15	02/14/2006	$19.91	380%
News Corp. (NW)	08/15/2005	$18.11	NA	$19.89	9.82%
Domtar Corp. (UFS)	05/12/2007	$114.96	02/14/2011	$90.05	−21.67%
Viasat Inc. (VSAT)	08/14/2008	$27.34	NA	$47.80	74.84%

is taken as the sell date. For positions that are held as of Q1 2012, April 2, 2012 is taken as the sell date. The prices at market open on the dates shown are taken as the buy and sell prices in the table.

The stocks in the table did reasonably well using the cloning strategy, with Radvision showing a whopping 380 percent return over 3.5 years. The bulk of the News Corp position, first established in Q2 2005, was purchased in 2008 at the mid-single-digit price range. Klarman has done very well with that wager, although the cloning model shows only a modest return. Domtar Corporation disappointed, down around 22 percent over a period of almost four years.

Klarman's 13F U.S. long portfolio is on the average only a small portion (~10 percent) of his assets under management. His market hedges, investments in liquidations, bankruptcies, other distressed instruments, and foreign investments are difficult to follow; for competitive reasons, he plays his cards close to the vest. He rarely gives interviews or divulges any of his positions to the public voluntarily. Still, given his philosophy of purchasing securities only if there is a margin of safety, cloning based on the 13F and other regulatory filings is a reasonable strategy.

Notes

1. "The 20 Biggest Global Hedge Funds," The Hedge Funds Blog Man, 2012.
2. John Waggoner, "Fundline: Best Fund for Past 50 Years Turned $100 into $49,000," *USA Today*, 1/5/2010, www.usatoday.com/money/perfi/funds/2010–01–04-mutual-funds-best_N.htm.
3. Seth Klarman, "Letter to Shareholders," Baupost Group, 06/15/2010.
4. Seth Klarman and Jason Zweig, "Opportunities for Patient Investors," Interview at the CFA Institute 2010 annual conference on 05/16/2010, *Financial Analysts Journal*, September/October 2010.

Chapter 9

John Paulson

The beauty of shorting a bond is that the maximum you can lose is the spread over the benchmark; yet if the bond defaults, you can potentially make more.[1]

—John Paulson

John Paulson is founder and president of Paulson & Company, a hedge fund based in New York City. Paulson grew up in Queens, in New York City, and enrolled at New York University in 1973. He became passionate about striking it rich after a visit with his wealthy uncle in Ecuador. In his first really profitable venture, he made $25,000 in commissions by facilitating the export of garments from Quito to department stores in the United States. After receiving a finance degree in 1978, Paulson earned an MBA from Harvard Business School in 1980 as a Baker Scholar. Following the most lucrative career option, he took to consulting. Upon realizing the kind of cash that he was seeking was beyond the reach of even partners in consulting, he moved to Wall Street.

Paulson got a head start in risk arbitrage in the mid-1970s while at New York University, via a seminar by Robert Rubin, who was then a partner at Goldman Sachs. After a stint at private equity firm

Odyssey Partners LP, he gained experience in merger arbitrage while climbing the corporate ladder at Bear Stearns. He founded Paulson & Company in 1994 with a focus on merger arbitrage and gained a reputation of investing with very low correlation to the market. The fund, which was ~$2 million at inception, surpassed $500 million by 2003. The focus of the firm shifted dramatically after 2004, when Paulson began wagering against the real estate market. The exploits in that sector are vividly narrated in the book *The Greatest Trade Ever: The Behind-the-Scenes Story of How John Paulson Defied Wall Street and Made Financial History.*[2] The fund earned around $15 billion in 2007 and followed it up with another $5 billion in 2008, catapulting his firm to near the top of the hedge fund world both in terms of total returns since inception and by the size of the firm. In 2011, the fund's performance had a reversal, with flagship Advantage fund losing well over a third of its value.

Philosophy and Style

John Paulson's investment philosophy revolves around the goal of capital preservation. In its first decade, the fund consistently held diversified merger arbitrage positions, which produced respectable returns with low volatility and low correlation to the equity markets. Deals that break are a huge concern, as that would result in loss of capital; the firm's research aims to eliminate relatively risky deals. They also weight the portfolio to high-conviction bets and sometimes resort to shorting the weaker deals. Spinoffs, recapitalizations, and restructurings are generally not messed with, as they have more market correlation. Though the fund takes hundreds of positions every year, it is not unusual for an individual position with low risk to be allocated up to 12 percent of the portfolio.

As the assets grew, Paulson extended his focus into other areas, offering new products such as event funds, credit funds, recovery funds, and gold funds. Purists do not consider style drift as a virtue, for it is extremely hard to be an expert who can create significant outperformance from multiple areas. Despite this, with impeccable timing, Paulson pulled off a string of blow-out performances from 2007 to 2010. The winning positions included credit-default swaps on subprime mortgage bonds, shorts of businesses with significant subprime exposure, distressed debt of businesses in bankruptcy, and holding gold as a hedge against a falling dollar.

Paulson does not use much leverage in his flagship funds, although he did launch leveraged versions of some of his funds. He does not really consider size as a major deterrent to performance, citing his achievement while managing billions during the four years prior to 2010. That stance lost some credibility when the funds lost billions in 2011. The style drift, along with the size of the fund, did cause significant net market exposure, which he plans to curtail with hedging strategies.

Marquee Trades

By early 2005, Paulson was convinced that subprime mortgages were headed for trouble. As his analysis pointed out the great risk-reward potential of credit default swaps (CDS) in such an eventuality, CDS contracts were used as early as April 2005. Shorting triple-B subprime securities was another technique used to profit from the same event. As the securities were trading at just 1 percent over LIBOR, the downside risk was 1 percent, while the upside was 100 percent. The positions took flight in early 2007 but, with amazing foresight, Paulson held on to the majority of them which, in the following months, more than compensated him with massive returns.

During the credit crisis, Paulson was on the prowl for bargains in distressed debt. The smartest move from among such bets was an investment in Delphi Automotive debt, which was converted into equity at around 67 cents a share. The move proved to be a big hit when the firm emerged from bankruptcy in late 2011 and had an IPO at a share price of $22.

His fund started building a large exposure to gold in early 2009 with the expectation that inflation will surge and the U.S. dollar will tumble. Although the calamity never came to pass, gold still doubled, thereby accounting for a significant portion of his returns for 2010.[3]

Portfolio Analysis

Table 9.1 lists Paulson's U.S. long portfolio details as of Q1 2012.

Since early 2009, Paulson has had enormous exposure to gold, via shares of gold miners (AngloGold Ashanti Limited, Gold Fields Inc., and Nova Gold) and the SPDR Gold Trust ETF. The positions have

Table 9.1 John Paulson's U.S. Long Portfolio Holdings—Q1 2012

Stock	Market Value	Shares	% of US Long Portfolio
AMC Networks (AMCX)	$256,623,000.00	5,750,000	1.85%
American Capital Ltd. (ACAS)	$157,790,000.00	18,199,543	1.14%
Anadarko Petroleum Corp. (APC)	$468,657,000.00	5,982,345	3.38%
AngloGold Ashanti Ltd. (AU)	$1,224,358,000.00	34,290,702	8.83%
Bank of America Warrants 2019	$147,085,000.00	31,631,200	1.06%
Baxter Intl Inc. (BAX)	$322,812,000.00	5,400,000	2.33%
Capital One Financial (COF)	$457,068,000.00	8,200,000	3.30%
Caesars Entmt Corp. (CZR)	$182,376,000.00	12,372,835	1.32%
CNO Finl 2016 7% DBCV	$312,462,000.00	99,976,000	2.25%
CNO Finl Group Inc. (CNO)	$181,129,000.00	23,498,496	1.31%
Delphi Automotive (DLPH)	$1,438,898,000.00	45,534,758	10.38%
El Paso Corp. (EP)	$236,400,000.00	8,000,000	1.71%
Gold Fields Ltd. (GFI)	$262,121,000.00	18,857,600	1.89%
Goodrich Corp. (GR)	$179,084,000.00	1,427,649	1.29%
Hartford Finl Svcs Grp (HIG)	$789,882,000.00	37,470,676	5.70%
JPMorgan Chase 2018 Wrnts	$247,042,000.00	18,463,500	1.78%
Life Technologies (LIFE)	$243,016,000.00	4,977,792	1.75%
Medco Health (MHS)	$281,200,000.00	4,000,000	2.03%
MGM Resorts Intl. (MGM)	$512,782,000.00	37,649,200	3.70%
Motorola Mobility (MMI)	$431,640,000.00	11,000,000	3.11%
Mylan Inc. (MYL)	$574,605,000.00	24,503,400	4.14%
Novagold (NG)	$229,292,000.00	31,937,018	1.65%
Scripps Networks (SNI)	$146,070,000.00	3,000,000	1.05%
SPDR Gold Trust (GLD)	$2,806,452,000.00	17,310,952	20.24%
XL Group PLC (XL)	$244,915,000.00	11,291,600	1.77%
Misc (<1% of the U.S. portfolio each)	$1,531,264,000.00	NA	11.04%
Total	$13,865,023,000.00		

since been adjusted to favor the mining companies instead of physical gold, as gold miner stocks became mispriced, compared to the price of gold. Although the gold positions were hammered in 2012, he is very bullish on them and presented AngloGold Ashanti as one of his best ideas at the Ira Sohn Investment Conference. Paulson is sitting on huge gains on Delphi Automotive, the distressed debt position that got converted into equity. Even though he has trimmed his stake significantly, the position still accounts for over 10 percent of the U.S. long portfolio. Paulson has become an activist at Hartford Financial Services (HIG), a position that was first purchased in 2009; in 2012, he has been very vocal with calls to breakup the company to realize value for shareholders.[4] Yet to pay off is Mylan Inc, a ~4 percent position first purchased in Q1 2010. Caesar's Entertainment, a position established in Q1 2012, was another of his best ideas at the 2012 Ira Sohn Investment Conference.

Table 9.2 summarizes how cloning Paulson's top positions would have performed, assuming the positions were established immediately after they became public knowledge. For positions that were since sold, the trading day following the date the sales became public information is taken as the sell date. For positions that are held as of Q1 2012,

Table 9.2 Effect of Cloning John Paulson's Top Positions

Stock	Purchase Date	Buy Price	Sell Date	Sell Price or 04/02/2012 Price	Return %
Cardinal Health (CAH)	02/13/2003	$54.87	02/15/2007	$72.54	32.20%
Biogen Idec Inc. (BIIB)	08/15/2003	$33.10	05/17/2005	$38.44	16.13%
Sprint-Nextel (S)	05/17/2005	$20.91	05/16/2007	$20.10	4.03%
Boston Scientific (BSX)	08/15/2006	$16.36	08/16/2011	$6.42	−60.76%
Citigroup (C)	11/16/2009	$42.20	02/15/2012	$32.33	−23.39%
AngloGold Ashanti Ltd (AU)	05/18/2009	$36.06	NA	$36.74	1.89%
SPDR Gold Trust (GLD)	05/18/2009	$91.53	NA	$161.99	76.89%

04/02/2012 is taken as the sell date. The prices at market open on the dates shown are taken as the buy and sell prices in the table.

The returns achieved by cloning Paulson's positions are decidedly mixed. Following the stake establishment of SPDR Gold Trust in Q1 2009 would have returned over 75 percent in less than three years. The same success was not reflected in AngloGold Ashanti as it remained flat during the three years, in spite of the substantial uptick in the price of gold. The large stake establishments of Cardinal Health and Biogen Idec in 2003 would have resulted in modest annualized returns. Cloning the purchase of Boston Scientific in Q2 2006 would have been disastrous—by Q2 2011 when he completely sold-off the position, the price per share had fallen by over 60 percent. Paulson was less burnt as he trimmed the holdings in the interim quarters when the price was higher. He walked away from his large position in Citigroup with hundreds of millions in profits but surprisingly the cloning model shows negative returns: the time delay before the moves became public, the short-term holding period, and the volatility of Citigroup shares all adversely affected cloning.[5] In general, cloning money managers who specialize in risk arbitrage opportunities is not that effective. Timing is so critical that any delay can be fatal.

Many of Paulson's moves that raked in billions of dollars in profits were by using securities outside the scope of the 13F regulatory filings. The public became aware about the purchase of CDS contracts and the shorting of mortgage insurers only when he voluntarily disclosed the information in early 2007. Shadowing his moves into similar securities immediately after such disclosure would have resulted in handsome returns during the credit crisis.

Notes

1. Christine Williamson, "Excellent Timing: Face to Face with John Paulson," pionline.com, July 9, 2007.
2. Gregory Zuckerman, *The Greatest Trade Ever: The Behind-the-Scenes Story of How John Paulson Defied Wall Street and Made Financial History* (New York: Crown Business, 2010).

3. Sam Jones, "John Paulson's Real 2010 Success: Gold," *FT Alphaville*, 01/25/2011, http://ftalphaville.ft.com/2011/01/25/468871/john-paulsons-real-2010-success-gold/.

4. SEC Form SC 13D/A, "Hartford: Spin-Off of P&C Business Would Increase Shareholder Value By 60%," Paulson & Co. Inc., March 9, 2012, www.sec.gov/Archives/edgar/data/874766/000119312512106076/d315758dsc13da.htm.

5. "John Paulson Makes $1bn Betting on Citigroup Recovery," *The Telegraph*, January 24, 2011.

Chapter 10

Wilbur Ross

We spend a lot of time trying to figure out which industries will go bad a year from now and then within that universe, we try to figure out which companies are salvageable.[1]

—*Wilbur Ross*

Wilbur Ross, Jr. is CEO and Chairman of WL Ross & Co. LLC, a subsidiary of Invesco. Invesco is a diversified investment management firm with WL Ross & Co. focused on turning around financially distressed companies. Ross got his BA from Yale and an MBA with distinction from Harvard Business School. After a stellar 24-year career at Rothschild Inc., where he led the worldwide bankruptcy advisory practice, Ross founded WL Ross & Co. in 2000. During his last three years at Rothschild, he ran a private equity fund that inspired him to venture out on his own, raising $450 million to invest in distressed businesses. WL Ross & Co. came under the fold of Invesco in 2006. The products offered by them include funds in the absolute return and private equity sectors.

Ross is an anomaly among his peers; while most of them courted conservative investing in their golden years, Ross's appetite for risk took to the skies after starting his own gig at the age of 62. From 2001 to 2004, Ross raked in hundreds of millions of dollars by investing in dying businesses and giving them a second chance at life. The segments included steel milling, mining, metals, coal, and textiles. The amazing part is that these turnarounds happened when the U.S. economy was reeling from the back-to-back punches of the tech-bubble popping and the 9/11 terrorist attacks.

Philosophy and Style

Wilbur Ross, known as "the king of bankruptcy," defines his work as "Go into buildings that aren't completely burned down and put the fire out."[2] Inevitably, the plan involves a painful restructuring process for the employees and executives of the businesses concerned: layoffs, firings, wage freezes, benefit reductions, plant closures, and so on, along with hard negotiations with any unions involved are all part of the deal. The media overwhelmingly disdains turning around distressed securities through such actions and describes the activity with choice terms such as "dirty work," "vulture capitalists," and "bottom feeders." But not Ross, who sees his work as a phoenix that rises from the ashes—creating jobs and profits from dying businesses is very beneficial to society.[3]

Ross's philosophy encompasses pushing for improved efficiency and positive changes at all levels including government policies. He applauds efforts in returning U.S. manufacturing jobs through protectionist policies, such as trade restrictions and import tariffs. In the global stage, he looks to promoting fair trade practices and has said that the United States is in danger of exporting its standard of living and importing unemployment.[4] He sees China as engaged in stealth exportation of U.S. jobs. Until 2008, his investments were in businesses with a strong U.S. manufacturing base, enabling him to benefit from his efforts in the area. Since the crisis, he has shifted the focus to distressed securities in the financial sector.

Marquee Trades

For Wilbur Ross, patience pays. He initiates positions only after the targets lighten up by purging debilitating liabilities such as health-care and pension obligations, usually in the bankruptcy phase. He consolidated the assets of numerous bankrupt steel companies in the early 2000s and engineered a turnaround. At that time, the U.S. steel industry was on life support, beset by a series of bankruptcies over the prior five years, due to their high costs and inability to compete. His process swung into high gear with the purchase of Acme Steel and LTV Steel's integrated steel assets in early 2002. A number of other purchases, including Bethlehem Steel Corporation, U.S. Steel's Gary plate mill, and Weirton Steel, from 2003 to 2004, were modeled after the LTV purchase. International Steel Group (ISG) was organized using these consolidated assets with the unions accepting new work rules, and reduced benefits and compensation. A set of positive external events lined up making the turnaround of ISG seem almost instantaneous: the United States imposed a 30 percent tariff on foreign steel, international demand for steel picked up, and demand from U.S. automakers improved. Because Ross had foreseen the probability of some of these events coming to pass, he was able to call his shots with absolute conviction. In December 2003, ISG held a successful initial public offering (IPO), and the company was sold to Mittal Steel in 2005 for $4.5 billion. All told, WL Ross & Co. spent ~$2 billion consolidating assets, and was able to more than double their investment in three years with this resounding deal.

Over the last decade, Ross adopted comparable strategies to bump up businesses in three other sectors with similar problems: textiles, auto parts, and coal. International Textile Group (ITG), International Automotive Components Group (IAC), and International Coal Group (ICG) were based on this approach. ITG, a U.S. manufacturer of fabrics, was woven in 2004 through the consolidation of the assets of Burlington Industries, Cone Mills Corporation, Safety Components International (automotive fabrics), and BST Safety Textiles of Germany. IAC, a similar endeavor, is the amalgamation of certain assets of Lear Corporation and Collins & Aikman. The purchase of the nonunion properties of Horizon Natural Resources through a bankruptcy auction in May 2004 established ICG. Anker Coal Group came into the fold in 2005 and in 2011 the business was sold to Arch Coal, Inc.

Portfolio Analysis

Table 10.1 lists Wilbur Ross' U.S. long portfolio details as of Q1 2012.

The 13F indicates a very concentrated portfolio with just seven holdings accounting for 99 percent of the total portfolio value, of

Table 10.1   Wilbur Ross' U.S. Long Portfolio Holdings: Q1 2012

Stock	Market Value	Shares	% of U.S. Long Portfolio
Air Lease Corp. (AL)	$102,298,000.00	4,250,000	6.36%
Assured Guaranty Ltd. (AGO)	$327,680,000.00	19,835,370	20.38%
BankUnited Inc. (BKU)	$343,028,000.00	13,721,131	21.34%
Cascade Bancorp (CACB)	$65,143,000.00	11,468,750	4.05%
Exco Resources (XCO)	$195,612,000.00	29,504,077	12.17%
Sun Bancorp (SNBC)	$75,116,000.00	21,279,241	4.67%
(The) Governor and Company of the Bank of Ireland (LON:BKIR)	$484,979,000.00	2,933,635,858	30.17%
Misc (<1% of U.S. long portfolio)	$13,624,000.00	NA	0.85%
Total	**$1,607,480,000.00**		

which the top three positions account for over 70 percent of value. The top spot is the investment in Bank of Ireland, made public in Q3 2011. The deal involved WL Ross & Co and Fairfax Financial of Toronto each taking a 9.9 percent stake as part of a capital raise of 3.8 billion euros.[5] BankUnited position was established in May 2009 in a deal with Federal Deposit Insurance Corporation (FDIC); following the bank's failure, WL Ross & Co along with three other private equity groups paid $900 million for the bank. Following the financial crisis, Ross made numerous related investments. A $250 million cash infusion into Assured Guaranty Limited in February 2008 in exchange for common stock is the biggest among them. In the last four years, the size of that position has increased by ~50%. The stake in Exco Resources was established in Q4 2010. The investment theories on many of his current holdings are yet to play out completely, for quite a few of them are trading well below his cost basis.

Table 10.2 summarizes how cloning Ross' top positions would have performed, assuming the positions were established immediately after they became public knowledge. The purchase date listed is the first trading day following such regulatory filing and the prices at market open

Table 10.2   Effect of Cloning Wilbur Ross's Top Positions

Stock	Purchase Date	Buy Price	Sell Date	Sell Price or 04/02/2012 Price	Return %
International Coal Group	12/2005	$11	05/03/2011	$14.43	31.18%
Montpelier Re Holdings (MRH)	05/25/2006	$16.40	02/26/2010	$17.81	8.60%
Assured Guaranty Limited (AGO)	02/29/2008	$25.77	NA	$16.47	−36.09%
BankUnited (BKU)	01/28/2011	$29.50	NA	$25	−15.25%
Air Lease Corp. (AL)	04/19/2011	$27.25	NA	$24.01	−11.89%
(The) Governor and Company of the Bank of Ireland (LON:BKIR)	07/28/2011	€0.10	NA	€0.12	20%

on the dates shown are taken as the buy and sell prices in the table. For positions since sold, the trading day following the date the sales became public information is taken as the sell date. For positions that are held as of Q1 2012, April 2, 2012 is taken as the sell date.

Cloning Ross's top positions would have yielded mixed results, as indicated in Table 10.2. International Coal Group debuted in December 2005 at $11 per share and duplicating that position would have resulted in a very modest annualized return over the course of more than five years. In fact, holding onto this stock would have been downright grueling as the stock dipped to almost $1 per share during the crash of 2008 before bouncing back. Mimicking Montpelier Re Holdings at the time the stake establishment became public information (May 25, 2006) would have led to mildly positive returns over the course of the cloning period.[6] Ross himself fared only slightly better on both these transactions. The position in Bank of Ireland shows a good 20 percent short-term return, which is the same return Ross obtained on it, as the stake became public information immediately after he established the position. The other three positions in the table show negative returns but Ross is unfazed; not only is he holding them tight, he is also increasing the stakes at lower price points. Ross has a 195 percent unrealized return on his investment in BankUnited, as his stake was bought from FDIC prior to the IPO at ~$10 per share.[7] The Air Lease Corp. investment is also prior to the IPO making his cost basis much lower compared to the IPO price of $27.25. On the other hand, there is a sizable unrealized loss on the Assured Guaranty Limited position.

Many of Wilbur Ross's positions were established when the businesses involved were in bankruptcy. It is not possible to simulate such positions, as the negotiated details of the deals are generally private information. Ross successfully turned around several businesses and offered shares through initial public offerings (IPO). Cloning positions after the IPO is an option, but the returns are nowhere in the vicinity of those of Ross, as his cost basis would inevitably be much lower. Overall, ad hoc cloning is not very suited to following Ross's moves. A strategy which filters his moves based on position size and whether the cost-basis achievable by cloning is comparable to Ross's own cost basis should provide good returns, although the number of such positions will be very limited.

Notes

1. Nicholas Stein, "Man of Steel," *Fortune*, 05/26/2003, http://money.cnn .com/magazines/fortune/fortune_archive/2003/05/26/343116/index.htm.

2. Jack Simon and Wilbur Ross, "Wilbur Ross: I Put Out the Fire of Failed Businesses," BBC Today Radio Programme, 06/25/2012, http://news.bbc .co.uk/today/hi/today/newsid_9731000/9731547.stm.

3. Renee Montagne, Steve Inskeep, and Wilbur Ross, "Wilbur Ross: Finding His Calling," National Public Radio's *Morning Edition*, 09/15/2008, www .npr.org/templates/story/story.php?storyId = 94569826.

4. Daniel Gross, "The Bottom-Feeder King," *New York*. 05/21/2005, http:// nymag.com/nymetro/news/bizfinance/columns/moneyandmind/10279.

5. Lisa O'Carroll, "Wilbur Ross and Fairfax Rescue Bank of Ireland," the *Guardian* Ireland Business Blog, 07/28/2011, www.guardian.co.uk/business/ ireland-business-blog-with-lisa-ocarroll/2011/jul/28/banking-globalrecession.

6. Steve Gelsi, "Montpelier Re Holdings Gets $100M from Wilbur Ross," MarketWatch—Market Pulse, 05/25/2006, http://articles.marketwatch

.com/2006–05–25/news/30927718_1_montpelier-re-holdings-shares-reinsurance-firm.

7. Justin Doom, "BankUnited IPO Raises $783 Million as Blackstone, Carlyle Reduce Holdings," Bloomberg News, 01/29/2011, www.bloomberg.com/news/2011–01–27/bankunited-ipo-raises-783-million-as-buyout-firms-reduce-stake-in-lender.html.

Chapter 11

George Soros

There has to be both some form of credit or leverage and some kind of misconception or misinterpretation involved for a boom-bust process to develop.

—George Soros

George Soros is founder and chairman of Soros Fund Management LLC, a hedge fund management firm founded in 1969. Born in Budapest in 1930, he and his family, using false identities, survived the Nazi occupation that started in 1944. Soros describes the experience as "exhilarating," for they not only endured but helped many others.[1] Soros immigrated to England in 1947, and graduated from the London School of Economics in 1952. His career started in earnest after a move to New York City in 1956, as an arbitrage trader at F. M. Mayer. Steadily climbing the corporate ladder, he became manager of the Double Eagle hedge fund in 1967, while working for First Eagle Funds. Soon after, he started his own hedge fund management firm, Soros Fund Management.

Soros Fund Management's flagship product, Quantum Fund, returned over 30 percent per year in its first two decades. By the late 1980s Soros ranked near the top of the world's wealthiest list and gave up day-to-day management of the firm. The aggressive strategies of the fund continued through the 1990s, until his partner Stanley Druckenmiller quit as portfolio manager in 2000. In 2001, the hedge fund was renamed Quantum Endowment Fund and converted to a less aggressive investment vehicle. In 2011, the fund converted to a family office structure to avoid registration with the SEC as a private investment adviser per the new rules under the Dodd-Frank act.

Philosophy and Style

George Soros believes in the significance of reflexivity in markets and his philosophy on the same was published in his 1987 book, *The Alchemy of Finance: Reading the Mind of the Market.*[2] *Reflexivity* revolves around how expectation/pricing affects fundamentals and how those modified fundamentals in turn affect expectation/pricing resulting in a self-reinforcing pattern that moves markets toward disequilibrium. With this hypothesis, boom-and-bust cycles that appear periodically in the markets are easily explained: For example, in the housing bubble, an increase in overall home prices in the market made banks open to lending more for the same house. This, in turn, made housing accessible to a broader clientele, further increasing home prices. The trend is recognized and reinforced, as home prices became artificially inflated to unsustainable levels (disequilibrium) at which point the trend reversed, and banks' willingness to lend plunged, causing a sharp deceleration in overall home prices.

Soros's investment philosophy is primarily based on holding highly leveraged short and long positions that enable profiting from market trends identified from his reflexivity principles. He is convinced about the herd mentality of market participants and seeks to exploit such trends; he moves with the herd for the most part, but exits ahead of them based on his instinct. The reliance on instinct makes such trades hard to comprehend and copy.

Marquee Trades

Soros's early trades amassed profits that took advantage of the boom-bust cycles associated with certain types of equity leveraging. The conglomerate boom-bust cycle that originated in the late 1960s is a case in point. Around that time, it dawned on many defense-oriented businesses enjoying respectable growth rates and strong valuation that such growth rates were not sustainable. By acquiring low-quality businesses in diverse areas, they turned themselves into conglomerates. As the firms purchased businesses with their highly valued stock, on a per-share basis, their growth rates appeared to be accelerating—for example, if Company X with a Price-to-Earnings (PE) ratio of 20 acquires Company Y with a PE of 10 using Company X's stock, the per-share-earnings of the combined business increases, thereby causing an illusion of accelerating growth. The misconception led to stock price appreciation in the short term. Ultimately, the shares crashed when it became evident that the growth rates were not sustainable. Soros profited both on the uptrend and in the crash that followed. Soros also benefited from the boom-bust cycle in REITs. A legislation permitting tax-free distribution if 95 percent of the income is distributed resulted in the mushrooming of mortgage trusts. Their share prices swiftly doubled, allowing more shares to be issued at inflated prices. A few years later, many of these trusts collapsed when the sentiment reversed. Soros anticipated the trend and profited from the up cycle. He returned later to play the short side, and realized more than 100 percent profits in some of them, as he continued shorting more shares as the prices fell.

Soros's hall-of-fame trade is the shorting of the British pound in 1992. His fund manager Stanley Druckenmiller's macro analysis concluded that the Bank of England didn't have enough reserves to prop up the currency and that it couldn't afford to raise rates.[3] Soros's genius involved recognizing the potential of the trade and prodding Druckenmiller to go all in. The $10 billion bet paid off in a few months when the pound sterling was devalued following Great Britain's withdrawal from the European Exchange Rate Mechanism (ERM) on September 16, 1992 (Black Wednesday). The short position netted the fund over $1 billion and the trade earned Soros the nick-name "The Man Who Broke the Bank of England."

In 2007, upon sensing the imminent financial crisis, Soros returned to active trading after a hiatus of almost 20 years. His trades since his comeback are related to taking advantage of the unraveling of what he terms the "super bubble," a situation that developed over the last 25 years.[4] Three major trends feed this fire: ever increasing credit expansion, globalization of financial markets, and removal of financial regulations. He envisages the bursting of the super bubble as the end of U.S. dominance, and the mighty dollar loses its reserve currency status. Although the premise has not come to pass, his trades have still been very successful, with the fund showing handsome returns over the last four years.

Portfolio Analysis

Table 11.1 lists Soros Fund Management's U.S. long portfolio details as of Q1 2012.

At any given time, Soros holds hundreds of positions spread all over the map. Over 70 percent of the holdings reported in the 13F filings are positions less than 1 percent each. A handful of sizable long positions indicates a clear bias on certain individual securities. PowerShares ETF Trust QQQ PUTS and S&P 500 SPDR PUTS are large short positions that collectively account for ~12% of the overall portfolio. Shorting the U.S. market indexes confirms Soros has positions in place to profit, should his super-bubble scenario prove spot on over the long term. Adecoagro SA, a large farming operation from South America, which had an IPO in early 2011, was established prior to its IPO. Agricultural boom is the next bubble identified and Adecoagro is a play on that uptrend. Other potential boom–bust scenarios on his radar include raw materials, energy, and asset bubbles in certain emerging markets. Westport Innovations is focused on providing technologies using natural gas in petroleum-based fuel engines. Here, too, Soros is positioned to profit from the boom–bust potential of natural gas adoption trend in the United States and the rest of the world.

Table 11.1 George Soros' U.S. Long Portfolio Holdings: Q1 2012

Stock	Market Value	Shares	% of U.S. Long Portfolio
Acacia Research Corp. (ACTG)	$105,666,000.00	2,531,518	1.55%
Adecoagro S A (AGRO)	$272,402,000.00	25,384,049	3.98%
CVR Energy Inc. (CVI)	$100,195,000.00	3,745,600	1.47%
Chevron Corp. (CVX)	$73,137,000.00	682,000	1.07%
Comverse Tech. (CMVT)	$111,065,000.00	16,166,666	1.62%
Dish Network (DISH)	$68,052,000.00	2,066,597	1.00%
Interoil Corp. (IOC)	$80,758,000.00	1,570,858	1.18%
Motorola Solutions Inc. (MSI)	$139,011,000.00	2,734,816	2.03%
PowerShares QQQ PUTS	$294,856,000.00	4,365,000	4.31%
S&P 500 SPDR (SPY) PUTS	$509,336,000.00	3,619,500	7.45%
Suntrust Banks (STI)	$77,054,000.00	3,188,000	1.13%
Westport Innovations (WPRT)	$120,820,000.00	2,952,606	1.77%
Misc (<1% positions, notes, etc.)	$4,884,441,000.00	NA	71.44%
Total	**$1,952,352,000.00**		

Table 11.2 summarizes how cloning Soros's top positions would have performed, assuming the positions were established immediately after they became public knowledge. The purchase date listed is the first trading day following such regulatory filing and the prices at market open on the dates shown are taken as the buy and sell prices in the table. For positions since sold, the trading day following the date the sales became public information is taken as the sell date. For positions that are held as of Q1 2012, April 2, 2012 is taken as the sell date.

Cloning the Oracle position after its appearance in the Q1 1999 13F filing would have resulted in a home run, as the stock appreciated over 300 percent during an 18-month holding period. Following Qualcom would also have brought favorable results, for the stock more than doubled in the 15-month holding period. JetBlue Airways Corporation disappointed, as the stock lost more than 50 percent of its value during the seven-year holding period; the pinch was probably not felt by Soros as he undoubtedly realized handsome profits on this position by trimming at higher prices along the way. Mimicking the

Table 11.2   Effect of Cloning Soros's Top Positions

Stock	Purchase Date	Buy Price	Sell Date	Sell Price or 04/02/2012 Price	Return %
Oracle Corporation (ORCL)	05/18/1999	$6.12	02/15/2001	$25.56	318%
Qualcom Inc. (QCOM)	08/17/1999	$19.75	02/15/2001	$42.34	114%
JetBlue Airways Corp (JBLU)	08/15/2002	$11.97	05/18/2009	$5.16	−56.90%
Petroleo Brasileiro (PBR)	08/15/2006	$23.19	11/15/2011	$26.79	15.52%
Adecoagro S A (AGRO)	05/17/2011	$10.40	NA	$10.80	3.85%
Westport Innovations (WPRT)	05/18/2010	$17.24	NA	$40.87	137%

Petroleo Brasileiro position would have resulted in modest returns over a five-year holding period; here again, Soros must have made decent money as he actively adjusted his positions throughout the holding period. Westport Innovations and Adecoagro are recent acquisitions that are still held.

Although the table imparts the impression that cloning Soros's portfolio is a viable option, his trading philosophy makes it extremely hard to do so. Most of the positions in the table had huge allocations at one point or another, although most of them started out as much smaller stakes. As there are hundreds of similarly sized positions, it is hard to identify the positions to clone. Soros trades very frequently and adjusts his positions regularly, thus making mimicking a tall order. He uses short positions as a hedging strategy, and as a way to play the crash in a boom-bust cycle. These short positions are generally hard to track, as they do not figure in the 13F reports. Soros sometimes buys put options instead of shorting securities directly and, while these are reported in the 13F filings, the information is incomplete, making cloning impractical. For example, Table 11.1 shows that Soros acquired large short positions on the S&P 500 Index and the NASDAQ-100 Index through put options on S&P 500 SPDR and PowerShares QQQ ETFs. However, the 13F information does not list the strike prices and expiration dates.

Soros's strategy is very consistent, as many of his positions attempt to profit from boom-bust trends. Therefore, a strategy endeavoring to identify the trends Soros is playing in and applying the same in one's own portfolio is the best approach to follow Soros.

Notes

1. George Soros, *The New Paradigm for Financial Markets: The Credit Crisis of 2008 and What It Means* (New York: PublicAffairs, 2008).

2. George Soros, *The Alchemy of Finance: Reading the Mind of the Market* (New York: John Wiley & Sons, 1987).

3. Katherine Burton, "Druckenmiller Calls It Quits After 30 Years as Job Gets Tougher," Bloomberg, 08/19/2010, www.bloomberg.com/news/2010-08-18/druckenmiller-calls-it-quits-after-30-years-as-hedge-fund-job-gets-tougher.html.

4. DealBook. "George Soros Sees a 'Superbubble,'" *New York Times*, 04/11/2008, http://dealbook.nytimes.com/2008/04/11/george-soros-the-face-of-a-prophet.

Chapter 12

David Swensen

Only with confidence created by a strong decision-making process can investors sell mania-induced excess and buy despair-driven value.

—David Swensen

D avid Swensen is chief investment officer at Yale University's endowment fund, which is among the largest university endowments in the United States, with assets over $19 billion as of 2011.[1] Upon completing his PhD in economics from Yale in 1980, Swensen spent a few years in Wall Street: at Salomon Brothers as an associate in corporate finance developing new financial technologies and at Lehman Brothers as a vice president specializing in swap activities. In 1985, he returned to Yale to run its $1 billion endowment fund at the insistence of James Tobin and William Brainard, his PhD dissertation advisors. Under Swensen's stewardship, the endowment went on to return over 19 times, and its performance beat institutional fund indices by wide margins. The results take on an extraordinary hue when the spending from the endowment is also factored in: From $45 million in 1985, it reached $987 million in 2011.[2] Over the last decade, spending has grown at an annual rate of 11 percent and as of 2011 accounts for 37 percent of the university's revenues. It was just 10 percent of the university's revenues when Swensen took control.

The 2009 fiscal year was very rare in that the endowment dropped almost 25 percent. For the same period, global equity markets dropped around 30 percent. The large negative return drew disapproval from critics who were quick to pronounce the model broken, and condemned it for underestimating the risk of holding equity like instruments.[3] Still, the poor performance of that lone year did not dent Swensen's long-term record.

Swensen's outperformance with the Yale Endowment encouraged other college and university endowments to follow in his footsteps. Swensen's book, *Pioneering Portfolio Management: An Unconventional Approach to Institutional Investment* (2000), introduced his strategies and coined the term "the Yale model." However, the Yale model failed to assist institutional investors, because they sorely lacked superior investing skills.[4] Swensen also came across as ineffective in his simple index-funds based allocation strategy for individual investors presented in his book, *Unconventional Success: A Fundamental Approach to Personal Investment* (2005).[5] Following his equity oriented index fund recommendations would have resulted in large negative returns during the financial crisis. In essence, his efforts at teaching portfolio management to institutional investors and individual investors definitely fall short. But his record at Yale is impeccable.

Philosophy and Style

Yale Endowment's portfolio management philosophy is centered on David Swensen's two core ideas: equity bias with a long time horizon and diversification.[6] Equity bias with a long time horizon is based on the notion that, in the long term, a diversified portfolio of equities outperforms debt-based asset classes such as short-term treasury bills and longer-term bonds. In fact, over the last two centuries, equities handsomely outperformed bonds. From 1925 through 2006, equity returns varied between 3,000 (diversified stocks) and 16,000 (small cap stocks) times while debt-investment returns varied between 19 (short-term treasury bills) and 72 (bonds) times. The need for diversification arises from the necessity to limit exposure to volatility. Without this, the ability to stay solvent and fully invested through a market crash is hard to achieve. The Yale Endowment follows these ideas to a T, with an overwhelming majority of the portfolio allocated in diversified equity like investments and a very small (<5 percent) bond/cash allocation.

While other portfolio managers rely on market timing and other trend-following methods, Swensen is not keen on them; to him, they are zero-sum games. His resources are spent primarily on bottom-up security selection in equity like assets. The assets are diversified over efficiently priced marketable securities (domestic stocks and foreign stocks) and inefficiently priced alternatives (absolute return, private equity, and real assets). The allocation is heavily tilted in favor of alternatives, and those assets accounted for over 80 percent of the portfolio as of 2011, way up from ~60 percent in 2000 and nil in 1985. Swensen channels security selection efforts into market areas that are less efficient, for therein lies true rewards; the difference between the top and bottom quartile performance of funds in the venture capital area is over 40 percent, while the gap is in the low-single digits in the marketable security areas. The alternatives are less liquid but are not a concern, given the endowment's long time horizon (forever).

Marquee Trades

In 1989, Yale's Investments Office formed an absolute return asset class and in the process became the first institutional investor to create an independent asset class for diversifying equity strategies.[7] Over the next 23 years, the strategy paid huge dividends while reducing overall risk. The excellent returns were mainly attributable to manager skill, equity like orientation, and investments in less market efficient areas that featured outstanding risk-reward characteristics.

Yale initiated investing in private equity (PE) in the form of leveraged buyouts as early as 1973 and the venture capital field by 1976. Undoubtedly, PE is the best performing asset class for Yale, returning an unprecedented 30.3 percent annualized since inception. Very successful venture capital investments include companies such as Oracle, Amgen,

Cisco Systems, Netscape Communications, and Dell Computer. Lucrative investments were also made in companies, such as Yahoo, Amazon.com, and Juniper Networks during the late 1990s. As the Internet bubble developed, the endowment reversed course and played the short side—huge bets against Internet stocks in 1999 and 2000 brought in substantial gains. The about-turn doesn't qualify as market timing for the overall portfolio allocation was not impacted with these wagers.

The asset class real assets (RA) not only delivered a steady ~10 percent annualized returns, but also provided the portfolio with good diversification, predictable cash flow, and a hedge against inflation. The RA asset class includes illiquid and inefficient investment options, such as real estate, oil and gas, and timberland. By collaborating with specialized managers with deep market knowledge, Yale is able to play these fields to its advantage. Focus on less efficiently priced areas, such as natural forests instead of plantation forests, have also helped the endowment achieve good returns with very low correlation to other asset classes.

During the financial crisis, a large short position in subprime mortgage-backed securities helped cushion setbacks in other parts of the portfolio. The endowment also profited from positions in the distressed securities area, such as bank loans purchased at well below par during the wake of the financial crisis. Such positions, based largely on macros analysis, helped protect assets while keeping the allocation percentages intact.

Portfolio Analysis

Yale's U.S. long portfolio details as of Q1 2012 are listed in Table 12.1.

Yale Endowments 13F long portfolio is very light representing only ~0.6 percent of the total assets. The bulk of the domestic equity allocation (6.7 percent as of 2011 fiscal year) is with other fund managers, as in a fund-of-funds model. Yale, having recognized the efficiency of the domestic equity area, prefers active management by engaging talented fund managers with strong bottom-up research capabilities to capture the competitive advantage. On the other hand, the petite

Table 12.1   Yale Endowment's U.S. Long Portfolio Holdings: Q1 2012

Stock	Market Value	Shares	% of U.S. Long Portfolio
iShares MSCI EAFE Index (EFA)	$2,910,000.00	53,000	2.27%
iShares FTSE/China Index Fd (FXI)	$4,575,000.00	124,786	3.56%
Linkedin Corp (LNKD)	$2,966,000.00	29,085	2.31%
SPDR Trust Series I (SPY)	$2,111,000.00	15,000	1.64%
Vanguard MSCI Emerging Mkts (VWO)	$112,457,000.00	2,587,000	87.59%
Misc (<1% of the U.S. long portfolio)	$3,367,000.00	NA	2.62%
Total	**$128,386,000.00**		

13F portfolio is a medley of Exchange Traded Index Funds (ETF) and underfollowed smaller capitalization stocks.

Table 12.2 summarizes how cloning Yale's top positions would have performed, assuming the positions were established immediately after they became public knowledge. The purchase date listed is the first trading day following such regulatory filing and the prices at market open on the dates shown are taken as the buy and sell prices in the table. For positions since sold, the trading day following the date the sales became public information is taken as the sell date. For positions that are held as of Q1 2012, 04/02/2012 is taken as the sell date.

The returns are indeed an assortment. Acadia Realty Trust, established in Q2 2000, would have returned a compounded 182 percent over nine years. Juniper Networks, a top holding from the same period would have stung, for it went down 85 percent in the following year. Juniper Networks, which began as a venture capital investment for Yale, provided the endowment with a big bang on its initial public offering (IPO) in June 1999. Following Yale's lead and purchasing the shares at IPO would have been a much better option. Cloning Douglas Emmett, Inc. would have resulted in an over 50 percent loss in fewer than three years. The remaining positions, mainly ETFs on world indices, would not have fared any better.

Overall, Yale's 13F portfolio is not an ideal contender for cloning. The biggest drawback is that the 13F portfolio is less than 1 percent of the total endowment assets and is not representative of Yale's overall bias. Even within the domestic equity portion of the overall portfolio,

Table 12.2   Effect of Cloning Yale Endowment's Top Positions

Stock	Purchase Date	Buy Price	Sell Date	Sell Price or 04/02/2012 Price	Return %
Acadia Realty Trust (AKR)	08/15/2000	$5.88	11/14/2009	$16.56	182%
Juniper Networks (JNPR)	08/15/2000	$169.25	11/15/2001	$24.75	−85.38%
iShares Trust MSCI Emerging (EEM)	08/16/2004	$17	02/15/2005	$23.47	38.06%
Douglas Emmett, Inc. (DEI)	02/15/2007	$27.81	11/16/2009	$13.17	−52.64%
iShares Trust MSCI EAFE (EFA)	11/15/2007	$81.55	NA	$54.66	−32.97%
Vanguard MSCI Emerging Markets (VWO)	02/15/2012	$44.10	NA	$43.37	−1.66%

the assets represent less than 10 percent. As such, the impact of these positions on Yale's endowment is very low. Historical holdings activity from the 13Fs indicates that the majority of the portfolio is used to make bets based on macro analysis; the positions are intended to insulate other parts of the endowment and are generally of shorter-term duration making the timing of the moves critical. Hence, the time delay associated with the 13F filings is a detrimental factor when attempting to follow Swensen. A much better option is to implement his ideas on portfolio management and asset allocation into one's own portfolios.

Notes

1. "2011 NACUBO-Commonfund Study of Endowments Results," National Association of College and University Business Officers (NACUBO), January 17, 2012, www.nacubo.org/Documents/research/2011_NCSE_Public_Tables_Endowment_Market_Values_Final_January_17_2012.pdf.
2. "The Yale Endowment Update 2011," Yale University Investments Office, June 30, 2011, www.yale.edu/investments.

3. "Report Blasts Harvard, Endowment Model," Bloomberg, May 20, 2010, www.pionline.com/article/20100520/DAILYREG/100529991.

4. Rick Ferri, "The Curse of the Yale Model," *Forbes*, April 16, 2012, www.forbes.com/sites/rickferri/2012/04/16/the-curse-of-the-yale-model.

5. Aaron Pressman, "Revisiting the Debate over Yale's Investing Guru, David Swensen," *BusinessWeek*, June 17, 2009, www.businessweek.com/investing/insights/blog/archives/2009/06/revisiting_the.html.

6. David Swensen, ECON-252–08: "Financial Markets (2008)," Lecture 9—Guest Lecture by David Swensen, Open Yale courses, February 13, 2008, http://oyc.yale.edu/transcript/976/econ-252–08.

7. "The Yale Endowment Update 2000," Yale University Investments Office, June 30, 2000, www.yale.edu/investments.

Chapter 13

Prem Watsa

A clear understanding of the fundamental value of our holdings allows us to go against the crowd. It is lonely at times, but it works.[2]

—Prem Watsa

Prem Watsa is the founder, chairman, and CEO of Fairfax Financial Holdings Limited, a Toronto, Ontario based insurance and investment management company. The insurance business is organized under a decentralized model through subsidiaries, such as Odyssey Re, Crum & Forster, Zenith Insurance Company, and Northbridge Financial. The investment management company is centralized, and operates as Hamblin Watsa Investment Council Limited (HWIC). Watsa, a chemical engineering graduate from the Indian Institute of Technology (IIT Madras), obtained his MBA from the Richard Ivey School of Business, London, Ontario. He was introduced to the Benjamin Graham style of value investing at his first posting as an analyst at Confederation Life in 1974.[1]

The insurance business greatly appealed to Watsa after his colleague at GW Investments, Francis Chou, highlighted how Warren Buffett invests with insurance float. Fairfax Financial Holdings was established in 1985, after Watsa took over the reins at Markel Financial, a troubled trucking insurance business, by providing a cash infusion of $5 million. Since its inception, Fairfax had a stunning compounded annual growth rate (CAGR) of 23.5 percent through 2011. The returns, along with the similarities to Buffett's business model, have earned him the nicknames "Canadian Warren Buffett" and "Buffett of the North."[3]

Fairfax had a rough patch in the early 2000s. On liquidity concerns, the business was afflicted with credit downgrades and, at one point, the stock was trading at half its book value ($75). The company was also subjected to what Watsa terms as a "bear raid" by a group of hedge funds; an $8 billion lawsuit is moving forward.[4] The U.S. Securities and Exchange Commission (SEC) compounded problems by subjecting Watsa and the auditors of the business to a reinsurance accounting probe. Fairfax not only rebounded from these setbacks but also thrived: During the financial crunch, Fairfax was one of the few businesses that prospered. Book value grew by 53 percent in 2007, 21 percent in 2008, and 33 percent in 2009.

Philosophy and Style

Prem Watsa's investment philosophy is a contrarian long-term value-oriented style focused on establishing positions at the maximum pessimism point. A salient trait that propels him against the flow is a thorough understanding of the fundamental value of positions. This single-minded value approach gives him the strength to stay steadfast even when the market tumbles. Another vital element that lets him stay ahead of the curve is flexibility, a valued lesson imparted by his mentor, John Templeton. Shorting was rejected initially, but was called upon in the late 1980s to profit from irrational market behavior. Likewise, hedging was employed as a strategy in the late 1990s as a protection against heightened tail risk; being prescient is trendy only if positions are established to profit from foreseen events.

Watsa looks for parabolic curves in asset pricing, as he considers such patterns bubbly and without a happy ending. Hedges, if cheaply available, are established to profit from them. Over the years, Watsa noticed such patterns in Internet stocks, commodities, housing, gold, and so on, and profited by establishing hedges in some of them. A major tail risk he is currently insuring against is the possibility of deflation in the United States; Watsa sees the current environment in the United States as being similar to the conditions that prevailed in the 1930s and also finds parallels to Japan from the early 1990s: 0 percent interest rates and 10 percent deficits year after year.

In the insurance businesses, Watsa focuses firmly on the bottom line. According to him, focusing on growth in the insurance business is dangerous, for it is easy to grow by cutting price, and under reserving can go undetected for years. Unlike most other companies, there is no growth target at all; performance is measured based on underwriting profit and reserves. This approach allows the insurance subsidiaries to shrink in a soft cycle and expand aggressively at other times while meeting capital constraints. There are no layoffs during soft cycles.

When making acquisition decisions, Watsa is especially partial to founder-run businesses. Acquired businesses are assured of a friendly and permanent home. This philosophy is evident with current equity allocations as well: Fairfax holds large positions in founder-run businesses such as BlackBerry (previously Research In Motion) and Dell Inc. He believes the biggest determinant of a company's valuation is its management's track record. His valuation theses for potential investments rely heavily on studying management track records.

Fairfax does not see an edge in consensus when it comes to investing money. It allocates capital to each of its asset managers and gives them the liberty to forge ahead with their own investment decisions. Watsa considers consensus among managers as implying a minimal margin of safety; when a company is analyzed heavily by the investment community, it leaves no room for misconceptions to cause a margin of safety.

Marquee Trades

Prem Watsa's initial letter to shareholders in 1985 detailed an ambitious long-term return objective of 20 percent on common shareholders' equity. The initial strategy involved re-underwriting and repricing the entire insurance business. Doing so initially resulted in large losses and a huge reduction of the entire business. By Q3 1985, the strategy showed promise; Watsa went against the grain and shrunk the business even further by holding out for better premiums. The story unfurled successfully the following year, as it reported a net income of $6.5 million. What made it all the more spectacular was that the highest profit level Markel had ever achieved in its prior 12-year history was less than a million.

Equity investments in the starting years were concentrated in the natural resource, industrial, and banking sectors. The company realized handsome gains from the portfolio, with significant contributions from Royal Bank, Princeton Mining, and Algoma Steel. In 1990, it posted a realized gain of $2.4 million in Nikkei Puts as the Japanese stock market declined by ~ 40 percent. Though the balance sheet had significant unrealized losses then, Watsa held onto them and converted most of them into realized gains in the bull market that followed. Case in point was a stake in Magna held at a cost basis of $6.8 million: In 1990, the position had dwindled down to an unrealized loss of $3.2 million but, within a year, it altered into a realized gain of $5.4 million.

The big winners of the late 1990s and early 2000s were positions outside North America. A $200 million investment in the Korean market (1998–99) fetched Fairfax more than $120 million in profits. Likewise, Latin American stocks generated profits of ~$250 million in 2000. Over the years, Fairfax realized significant gains from hedging strategies: shorting Internet stocks via put contracts, purchasing put bonds as a way to profit from a fall in interest rates, S&P 500 Index puts to profit from a U.S. market crash, and short positions on individual securities. The trade that towered over others came in 2008, when Fairfax gathered a cumulative gain close to $2 billion from credit default swaps that had an original acquisition cost in the neighborhood of $270 million.

All things considered, Fairfax is a great model portfolio that details how diversification across asset classes along with a healthy dose of hedging can help harvest gains constantly. Gains are reaped by liquidating the outperforming positions, even though other parts of the portfolio may be showing unrealized losses. When those underperforming positions turn robust in their turn, usually with a shift in market sentiment, they are liquidated to show more realized profits. Independent of which asset class is outperforming at any given time, the portfolio manages to realize gains thereby ensuring good absolute returns.

Portfolio Analysis

Prem Watsa's U.S. long portfolio details as of Q1 2012 are listed in Table 13.1.

Fairfax's U.S. long portfolio stands at slightly over $2 billion, which is about 50 percent of the overall common stock portfolio and just about 10 percent of the total investment portfolio. 100 percent of the equity positions are hedged to counter the risk of a market crash in the coming years; still, over the long term, they are very bullish on equities. Currently, the portfolio has large unrealized losses in BlackBerry (BBRY) and Dell Inc. (DELL) as these positions have plunged significantly since his purchase.

Table 13.1   Prem Watsa's U.S. Long Portfolio Holdings: Q1 2012

Stock	Market Value	Shares	% of U.S. Long Portfolio
Abitibibowater Inc. (ABH)	$250,332,000.00	17,505,751	11.45%
Dell Inc. (DELL)	$148,922,000.00	8,976,589	6.81%
Frontier Communications Corp. (FRO)	$77,459,000.00	18,620,000	3.54%
Johnson & Johnson (JNJ)	$392,343,000.00	5,947,300	17.95%
Level 3 Commn Inc. Note 7% 3/1	$97,875,000.00	75,000,000	4.48%
Level 3 Commn Inc. (LVLT)	$332,588,000.00	12,931,094	15.21%
BlackBerry (BBRY)	$394,116,000.00	26,848,500	18.03%
Sandridge Energy (SD)	$34,080,000.00	4,347,000	1.56%
US Bancorp (USB)	$140,789,000.00	4,448,310	6.44%
USG Corp. (USG)	$116,857,000.00	6,794,000	5.35%
Wells Fargo & Co. (WFC)	$100,852,000.00	2,956,660	4.61%
Misc (<1% of U.S. long portfolio)	$99,753,000.00	NA	4.56%
Total	$2,185,966,000.00		

Table 13.2 summarizes how cloning Watsa's top positions would have performed, assuming the positions were established immediately after they became public knowledge. The purchase date listed is the first trading day following such regulatory filing and the prices at market open on the dates shown are taken as the buy and sell prices in the table. For positions since sold, the trading day following the date the sales became public information is taken as the sell date. For positions that are held as of Q1 2012, April 2, 2012 is taken as the sell date.

Fairfax's holdings prior to Q2 2007 are not available through the EDGAR system. The results of cloning based on the last five years are presented in Table 13.2. It shows very mixed results, although International Coal Group was a huge winner that more than doubled over the course of slightly fewer than four years. Of the four holdings that are still being held—Pfizer, Johnson & Johnson, Dell Inc., and BlackBerry—three show unrealized losses. Duplicating BlackBerry would have been a real disaster for it lost 75 percent of its value in fewer than two years, although it is yet to completely play out. News Corp and WellPoint show losses as Watsa's disposal became public in a 13F filing during the market lows of 2009; Fairfax probably realized better prices on them.

Table 13.2   Effect of Cloning Prem Watsa's Top Positions

Stock	Purchase Date	Buy Price	Sell Date	Sell Price or 04/02/2012 Price	Return %
International Coal Group	Q2 2007	~$5.98	05/03/2011	$14.60	144%
Pfizer Inc. (PFE)	08/10/2007	$24	NA	$22.54	−6.08%
Johnson & Johnson (JNJ)	08/10/2007	$60.70	NA	$66.04	8.80%
Dell Inc. (DELL)	08/10/2007	$26.13	NA	$16.52	−36.78%
News Corp. (NWS.A)	05/15/2008	$14.32	02/17/2009	$6.01	−58.03%
WellPoint Inc. (WLP)	05/15/2008	$50.78	02/17/2009	$42.40	−16.50%
BlackBerry (BBRY)	11/15/2010	$59.38	NA	$14.67	−75.29%

Overall, cloning Watsa's portfolio is a good option, in spite of the fact that the results from the limited data set are mixed so far. He is very patient and holds positions for extended periods, giving time for his theses to play out. His long-term value-oriented style is also very conducive to cloning.

Notes

1. Prem Watsa, "Ben Graham Value Investing Conference," Richard Ivey School of Business, Ontario, 02/16/2011, www.bengrahaminvesting.ca/Resources/ Video_Presentations/Guest_Speakers/2011/Watsa_2011.htm.

2. John Reese, "Prem Watsa's Stock Picking Aces the Guru Test," the *Globe and Mail*, 06/11/2012, www.theglobeandmail.com/globe-investor/investment-ideas/prem-watsas-stock-picking-aces-the-guru-test/article4249305.

3. Prem Watsa, "End of Year Letter to Shareholders," Fairfax Financial Holdings Limited, 2011.

4. Debbie Baratz, "Fairfax's Watsa Moves Forward with $8 Billion Lawsuit," ValueWalk, 07/03/2012, www.valuewalk.com/2012/07/fairfaxs-watsa-moves-forward-with-8-billion-lawsuit.

Part Two

MECHANICAL APPROACHES TO FOLLOWING THE MASTERS

Chapter 14

Introduction

The evaluation of an eclectic selection of the best fund managers in the first part of this book introduced a varied number of investment styles and philosophies. The study substantiated that, no matter the game plan, the best practitioners are extremely successful over the long haul. This section gets into the nuts and bolts of the next logical step: how to construct mechanically cloned portfolios that are highly likely to outperform the market. Individual investors, even those who have absolutely no interest in analyzing businesses or actively making buy/sell/hold decisions, stand to benefit immensely from this approach, for they too can play the field with a fair chance of success.

Research has categorically established that cloning based on disclosed positions of active fund managers is a very viable strategy for individual investors:

- Massachusetts Institute of Technology Department of Economics in 2000 concluded that copycat funds have the potential to generate returns comparable to the primitive funds they are designed to mimic. This research was based on a broad sample of diversified U.S. equity mutual fund data from 1992 to 1999.[1]

- Erasmus University in 2010 analyzed the performance of impersonator funds and their performance characteristics twice, before and after the 2004 SEC regulation that increased the mandatory reporting frequency of mutual fund holdings from semiannually to quarterly.[2] Their conclusion was that portfolio disclosure was costly to actively managed funds; mimicking portfolios in spite of the lag was a boon to competitors. The fact that the copycat funds not only enjoyed elevated performance but also actually managed to outperform their target funds in both timeframes was a real kicker. Also, recent performance of the source portfolios was indicative of imitating being more successful.

- The combined efforts of three individuals from Harvard Business School, the London School of Economics, and the Universitat Pompeu Fabra in 2010 confirmed that the best ideas of the active fund managers outperformed the market.[3] They recognized overdiversification as the cause of poor overall performance of fund managers, not a lack of stock-picking skills. In essence, the odds are high for a portfolio based on the best ideas of a selected set of active fund managers to outperform the market indexes.

- The research project of Mazin Jadallah (founder and CEO of AlphaClone) yielded impressive results with mechanical cloning strategies: The project studied the effects of lag on mechanically cloned portfolios and established that a significant portion of them outperformed the S&P 500 index.[4] Since 2000, two-thirds outperformed the market and nearly half outdid the same by over 4 percent. The research stamped its approval on mechanically cloned portfolios outperforming the market indexes. AlphaClone was thus set up to pursue such strategies.

A word of caution is not amiss here: Cloning some of the top positions of the managers on an ad-hoc basis does not guarantee superior returns. The results of cloning presented in Part One for each of the masters are a testimony to that. The glaring limitations that exist with the ad-hoc method of cloning are:

- Manager selection is an often overlooked critical factor when constructing a mechanically cloned portfolio. As the examples in the earlier section showed, being blindsided by the might of a great manager whose style is not conducive to cloning does not make for good returns.

- The ad-hoc approach has no calculation guidelines to determine how much to allocate for each selection. An asset allocation strategy is an absolute requirement when attempting to clone.
- The manager's current sentiment is not captured when replicating top positions. As most managers build positions in phases, by the time a position is identified as an ideal cloning candidate based on size, the average purchase prices the manager achieved might be very different from the purchase price of the cloned position. Understanding the manager's sentiment is an important consideration when cloning positions mechanically.

These limitations need to be addressed to construct model portfolios with great return potential.

Manager Selection

Academic research provides pointers on choosing and cloning money managers successfully:

- The American University and the University of Nevada tracked Warren Buffett's Berkshire Hathaway from 1976 to 2006.[5] They analyzed the behavior of a portfolio that mimicked the investments following their public disclosure at the beginning of the subsequent month. To say the findings were amazing is putting it mildly. Over that time period, when Berkshire Hathaway outperformed the S&P 500 index by an outstanding 11.4 percent, the cloned portfolio lagged its original only slightly, and managed to outperform the S&P 500 index by a striking 10.75 percent.
- Mebane Faber and Eric Richardson presented case studies of cloning Berkshire Hathaway, Greenlight Capital, and Blue Ridge Capital, using a very simple mechanical strategy in their book *The Ivy Portfolio.*[6] The studies focused on the period from 2000 to 2008, when the S&P 500 had a dismal annualized return of negative 3.5 percent. The emulated portfolios, on the other hand, not only outdid the S&P 500 by significant margins, but also exhibited

handsome annualized positive returns: 6.48 percent for Berkshire Hathaway, 12.58 percent for Greenlight Capital, and 3.5 percent for Blue Ridge Capital. Although the case studies probably picked the best performing portfolios from a larger set of money managers, it does indicate the strong potential for outpacing with certain fund manager portfolios. It is also significant that all three of these case studies involved value-oriented managers.

- A University of Toledo research paper (March 2012) probed the existence of hedge fund herding.[7] The widely held notion is that hedge funds destabilize markets by excessive trading and by engaging in herding. The primary conclusion of the paper contradicted such beliefs: Hedge funds were less likely to herd, momentum trade, and so on, compared to non-hedge–fund institutions. Their finding, when the aggregate institutional demand for a security increases the returns on them from then on decreases, highlights the fact that unlike most other professions, seeking consensus for an investment pick is not a good thing. Investors looking to clone need to be cognizant of this relevant fact—no matter how tempting it is to take comfort in the numbers, that security could be a recipe for underperformance. The study also found disparity in the data from hedge funds and non-hedge–fund institutions: increase in hedge fund demand forecasted good returns while increase in non-hedge–fund demand forecasted poor returns. This outcome endorses the need for being very careful with manager selection.

- A University of Maryland Department of Finance case study (2003) showcased replication in a very bullish manner by establishing money as smart in chasing winning managers and mimicking the trades of such fund managers as a smart strategy.[8] A key part of the research probed the persistent nature of the performance of successful managers. Surprisingly, this was tied to both consumer and manager behavior—consumers by chasing previous year's winning funds and the managers, in their turn, by investing those inflows into momentum stocks causing them to spike in value. The findings led many to question whether manager talent was the reason for the winning stock picks. This brought to light the risk of cloning managers with good recent performance: The strategy can be very successful over the short term, but whether the outperformance will endure is a game of chance.

- An Arizona State University research paper (2011) explored why hedge funds avoided disclosure as far as possible by using 13F confidential treatment requests.[9] The study confirmed that managers sought confidentiality treatment to protect their research, which inevitably helps to create market-beating returns. Also, it is a tactic by which managers avoid front running by other investors. *Front running* involves anticipating a fund's trades then trading against it. The fact that the undisclosed positions earn good returns over the confidentiality treatment period is very relevant for those into cloning.

- Commercial databases track the performance of the hedge fund universe and provide information mined from their 13F filings. The overall performance of the hedge fund industry is shown in a favorable light in these databases. Studies have stressed that this reputable act has to do more with reporting biases than the hedge fund managers as a whole being more skillful stock pickers compared to other investors. A study by the finance departments of Quinnipiac University, University of Kentucky, and University of Alabama examined the effects of selection bias and also the effect of funds that stopped reporting (delisted and/or dead funds).[10] The outcome was that the funds that chose to report to commercial databases outperform those that do not. This is especially true with delisted funds, whose performance is worse than the funds that continue reporting. Another paper on the same theme by Burton G. Malkiel of Princeton University and Atanu Saha of Analysis Group focused on the effects of backfill bias and survivorship bias on reported overall hedge fund returns.[11] *Backfill bias* is the tendency of managers to report previous returns only if they are favorable, while *survivorship bias* is based on the fact that the underperforming hedge funds eventually die out without finding a place in the database. The study concluded that both backfill bias and survivorship bias result in reported results being significantly better than what would have been otherwise, and that there is substantial risk of selecting a dismally performing fund. Strategies that attempt to follow the performance of the hedge fund world are to be used only with caution. For cloning to succeed, it is imperative to be selective when it comes to picking managers.

From the manager profiles in Part One, it is easy to find the better managers to shadow:

- Core value managers are the cream of the crop when it comes to mechanical cloning. Their stock picks are backed by solid bottom-up research, and they are inclined toward holding tight to their positions for extended periods of time.

- Managers with a sizable stake in the U.S. markets rank higher in the preferred list. The 13F holdings disclosed every quarter contain only the U.S. listed positions and ADRs. Shadowing managers who invest primarily outside the United States will result in a portfolio with little bearing on the manager's overall portfolio.

- Managers who employ long positions as hedges are not user friendly when it comes to cloning. With a mechanical cloning strategy against such manager portfolios, it is impossible to distinguish a hedged long position from a position established based on pure bottom-up valuation research.

- Managers focused on distressed securities are best avoided. By their very nature, their investment philosophy mandates most of their positions to be in companies that are either in bankruptcy or on their way to being so. It is quite normal for them to be messing with debt positions or securities that are no longer traded. Obviously, positions that are not mentioned in 13F filings are not easily cloned. Even those that are reported carry a lot of risk. Furthermore, these positions are usually held in combination with senior debt holdings—the debt holdings do not make it to the 13F, leaving mimicking such positions beyond the reach of individual investors.

- Managers who invest mostly in nonpublicly traded securities should be excluded. The 13F reports will contain no information on such holdings, rendering cloning impractical.

- Managers focused on turnaround opportunities and other event-driven prospects are complicated candidates. Their positions are relatively riskier with no guarantee for success. Moreover, timing is critical and the chances are great that followers will finish off with a higher cost basis when entering, and lower realized values when exiting, compared to the manager.

- Managers focused on market neutral trading strategies are best left alone. The strategies to achieve market neutrality involve a combination of long and short positions. The short positions are not reported in 13F filings, making it impossible to mimic the complete trade using that information. Timing is a key to pairs trading, so 13F information on even the long portion of the positions will be out of date because of the 45-day minimum delay before positions become public through 13F filings.

- Quant fund managers are best given a miss. For the most part, the information reported by Quant funds through 13F filings is outdated, overwhelming, and irrelevant. The computer models usually result in scores of trading and several open positions at any given point. The 13F filings will be chock full of positions that are not of any real value; for, by then, these positions will already be liquidated and replaced with others.

- Risk optimized managers are best avoided. Managers who focus on risk optimized strategies are not bounded by U.S. long positions, making only a portion of their holdings appear in the 13F filings. Risk optimized strategies are effective only when the entire portfolio is lifted, complete to the percentage allocation to each position. Cloning the whole portfolio is a futile task, as the public is aware of only a portion of the overall portfolio.

- Managers without a long-term track record but with good recent performance need time to mature. Evidence points to recently successful managers being able to maintain their victory run only for some period. That triumph is attributed more towards customer and manager behavior rather than investing skills. In short, cloning such managers likely results in only a chance for short-term success.

Picking managers to clone is more art than science. For the less creatively inclined, research chips in with helpful clues that allow easy elimination of managers whose philosophies and style do not lend to replicating. From the 12 managers profiled in Part One, the following three were selected as they have characteristics conducive to cloning:

- **Bill Ackman**: Majority of Ackman's positions are, at any given time, accessible to the public via his 13Fs. Moreover, his activist investment style tends to favor disclosing positions.
- **Warren Buffett**: Some of Buffett's big positions are forever. A majority of his other positions are long term in nature. His

portfolio is concentrated with the investments guaranteed to have a margin of safety. All sought-after values!

- **David Einhorn**: Although Einhorn runs a long/short portfolio with only the long positions featuring in 13F filings, per his research, each long holding is ensured to possess favorable risk-reward characteristics. Here also, it is a concentrated portfolio with lengthy holding periods. His overall philosophy and style makes duplicating a feasible strategy.

The picks are heavily tilted in favor of value-oriented managers who use bottom-up stock selection.

Bruce Berkowitz is a true value investor who tends to maintain positions for extended periods of time, a highly esteemed feature when it comes to cloning. However, his portfolio was not considered, as he has several specialized mutual funds with the combined picks showing up in the 13Fs. Ian Cumming and Joseph Steinberg's portfolio did not make the cut, as a majority of their investments are not publicly traded and hence not reported in their 13F filings. Carl Icahn's portfolio lost out, as he specializes in the rather risky area of turnarounds; his cost basis on many of his positions is unachievable for followers. The minute his stake becomes public, the market would have adjusted to reflect the new circumstances. Seth Klarman operates in the bottom-up value field, which is exactly what the doctor ordered. However, his portfolio was not selected, as his secretive nature avoids disclosing positions as far as possible, and because his U.S. long portfolio allocation is very small. A mimicked portfolio based on his 13Fs would capture the performance of only a small portion of his overall portfolio. John Paulson's portfolio was excluded, as his expertise is in risk arbitrage. The recent big returns in his portfolio are from positions outside the scope of 13Fs. Wilbur Ross did not qualify, as his positions are primarily established during bankruptcies and hence do not make it to the 13Fs. George Soros's trend trading based on boom-bust cycles is heavily dependent on timing. Such strategies are difficult to shadow, given the 45-day minimum reporting delay for the 13Fs. David Swensen's portfolio was not included as his 13F holdings, which are only a very small part of his overall portfolio, is not representative of Swensen's bias. Although Prem Watsa's long-term value-oriented style is very conducive to cloning, his portfolio was not chosen, as he relies on extensive hedging strategies, which are generally not included in the 13F filings.

The next three chapters will look into the selected manager's 13F holdings history to construct, maintain, and analyze mechanically cloned portfolios.

Asset Allocation and Sentiment Capture

After manager selection, the essential building blocks to constructing a mechanically cloned portfolio with good return potential are asset allocation plans and sentiment capture choices.

- *Asset allocation* plans deal with mechanically splitting portfolio assets among the securities picked by a manager. Zeroing in on a particular plan is more about assessing the strengths and weaknesses of each choice and deciding on the best option for a particular situation.
- *Sentiment capture* involves mechanically selecting a determined number of positions from a manager's portfolio that reflect, as accurately as possible, his thought process. Here, too, there exists a few different options and again it is a question of deciding what works best for a specific situation.

Below are the three most common allocation choices that cover the gamut:

- **Equal allocation**: Here, each component of the portfolio receives equal attention—the same amount is invested in each. If five securities are involved and the capital is $50,000, then they receive $10,000 each. Though implementation is easiest for this approach, its flaw is that it fails to seize the manager's relative conviction (high conviction picks in the source portfolio will have higher percentage allocation and vice-versa but the model will not reflect this) among the picks.
- **Weighted allocation**: Positions with deeper conviction are given higher percentage allocation and vice-versa. The conviction level is gauged by the size of the position relative to the manager's overall 13F portfolio size.

- **10–5–2 allocation**: Based on their size in the source portfolio, the mechanically cloned portfolio picks are given a fixed weightage. The method targets to reflect the allocation style of certain managers: a very small number of highest conviction positions (over 10 percent), an average number of large high conviction positions (over 5 percent), and the rest in smaller positions (less than 2 percent).

Two of the most popular sentiment capture choices follow.

- **Top holdings (largest positions)**: The focus here is on the manager's largest positions. Technically, this strategy succeeds in capturing the manager's highest convictions but stops short of reflecting the manager's current bias. Some managers remain loyal to their core holdings even during overvaluation on the premise they will come out ahead in the long haul; worthwhile companies capable of continuing their healthy growth rates make this overvaluation temporary. The core positions are usually the largest holdings in a portfolio, so this cloning model can at times pick overvalued stocks.
- **Best ideas (largest new positions)**: The manager's largest new positions are shadowed here. On the upside, it successfully captures the manager's current sentiment, but these positions have to be constantly updated; they will have to be traded in and out based on every subsequent 13F. Money managers generally exercise patience and abstain from diving into a position all at once; the new additions are usually only a percentage of their eventual stakes. These models capture this style well. However, some value-oriented managers are notorious for nibbling at new positions, only to dispose of them a few quarters later. In such cases, the model captures only the noise. It should also be remembered that this model sidesteps the manager's large long positions that form the core of the portfolio.

A third sentiment capture model selects the most popular positions from among a set of managers that are followed. The model goes against the rule: Seeking consensus is not desirable when pursuing good returns. Since the strength is in numbers, numerous managers will need to be followed to be able to construct a meaningful portfolio

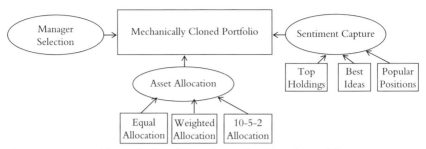

Figure 14.1   Building Blocks of a Mechanically Cloned Portfolio

featuring the most popular picks. As it is unlikely this model will prove successful over the long term, it will not be discussed further.

The flowchart in Figure 14.1 represents the building blocks used to construct a mechanically cloned portfolio.

The model portfolios would need to be updated every quarter, as soon as the 13Fs become public. To rebalance the models, periodic buying and selling of some parts of the positions is involved. These aspects will be discussed in later chapters.

Risk Avoidance

The models used to construct mechanically cloned portfolios can be applied to the 13Fs of a single manager or a group of managers. While leaning on the strategies of only one manager can simplify matters, it carries single-manager risk: most managers periodically experience rough patches, and the single-manager risk is encountering that scenario just when attempting to clone his/her holdings. The risk is minimal over the long term when following value-oriented managers with good track records.

Cloning the positions of a group of managers avoids single-manager risk. A small selection of managers is best for two reasons:

1. The universe of value oriented managers with outstanding long-term track records is small.
2. As the number of managers tracked goes up, the complexity of the models used increases.

Table 14.1   Glenn Greenberg's U.S. Long Portfolio Holdings: Q1 2012

Stock	Market Value	Shares	% of US Long Portfolio
Adobe Systems Inc. (ADBE)	$49,463,000.00	1,441,656	3.63%
Aon Corp. (AON)	$62,795,000.00	1,279,957	4.61%
Comcast Corp. (CMCSA)	$126,210,000.00	4,276,864	9.27%
Fiserv Inc. (FISV)	$142,263,000.00	2,050,188	10.45%
Google Inc. (GOOG)	$207,423,000.00	323,472	15.23%
Higher One Hldgs Inc. (ONE)	$97,763,000.00	6,539,352	7.18%
Laboratory Corp. Amer Hldgs (LH)	$81,658,000.00	892,050	6.00%
Motorola Solutions Inc. (MSI)	$96,671,000.00	1,901,857	7.10%
Oracle Corp. (ORCL)	$55,450,000.00	1,901,571	4.07%
Primerica Inc. (PRI)	$42,922,000.00	1,702,581	3.15%
Valeant Pharmaceuticals Intl. (VRX)	$236,942,000.00	4,413,146	17.40%
Visa Inc. (V)	$31,990,000.00	271,098	2.35%
VistaPrint Limited (VPRT)	$130,029,000.00	3,364,275	9.55%
Total	**$1,361,579,000.00**		

Constructing model portfolios using the 13Fs of the three managers selected individually and as a group will be discussed in the ensuing chapters.

Investors need to be mindful that the portfolios cloned from 13F filings are not cushioned against market corrections; the positions reported are all longs on U.S. market traded securities. In fact, the model portfolios should not be viewed as a replacement for the overall portfolio. It is not one size fits all. Instead, these should work well for long-only portions of the overall asset allocation. Certain mechanical strategies complement the long-only models allowing for distributing the entire portfolio mechanically. The final chapter of Part Two considers such options.

Constructing Model Portfolios Mechanically: A Primer

From a 13F filing, six different portfolios are possible from the combination of three asset allocation models (equal, weighted, and 10–5–2) and two sentiment capture choices (top holdings, best ideas). The 13Fs of

Glenn Greenberg's Brave Warrior Capital, a value-oriented hedge fund, is used to illustrate how the portfolios are constructed. Table 14.1 is his 13F portfolio as of Q1 2012 with the largest five positions highlighted.

The following sections illustrate the six model portfolios from Greenberg's 13Fs. The number of positions to use is not imposed by the models. Five is chosen for the demonstrations for the sake of convenience.

Equal Allocation Largest Positions

Table 14.2 demonstrates the sample portfolio when a capital of $50,000 is distributed equally among the five largest positions in Greenberg's portfolio as of Q1 2012.

The largest five positions in Greenberg's 13F (Table 14.1) account for more than 60 percent of his entire portfolio. Google leads this list at ~15 percent and Comcast Corp brings up the rear at ~ 9 percent. The model (Table 14.2) captures the largest positions reasonably well with 20 percent of the cash allocated for each selection. However, the other ~40 percent of Greenberg's portfolio is ignored. Increasing the number of selections used (from five) will alleviate that problem, but since the smaller positions are allocated the same percentage as the larger positions, it will end up diverging more from the asset allocation of the original portfolio.

A common concern with mechanically cloned portfolios is the amount of trading involved each quarter to keep the portfolio updated per the model. This model holds up very well in that regard: Value

Table 14.2   Sample Portfolio: Equal Allocation Largest Positions

Entity	Share Prices (03/31/2012)	Model Allocation	Share Count	% of Portfolio
Comcast Corp. (CMCSA)	29.51	$10,000.00	339	20.00%
Fiserv Inc. (FISV)	69.39	$10,000.00	144	20.00%
Google Inc. (GOOG)	641.24	$10,000.00	16	20.00%
Valeant Pharmaceuticals Intl. (VRX)	53.69	$10,000.00	186	20.00%
VistaPrint NV (VPRT)	38.65	$10,000.00	259	20.00%
Total		**$50,000.00**		

managers are generally not into frequent trading, so their largest positions usually remain static. The trading requirement for Q1 2012 was just one buy/sell transaction to get the model updated from Q4 2011— Motorola Solutions had to be replaced with VistaPrint.

Overall, the model is very satisfactory when used against value manager portfolios that keep concentrated positions.

Equal Allocation Largest New Positions

Table 14.3 indicates the alterations to Greenberg's portfolio from Q4 2011 to Q1 2012 and highlights the largest five additions (Data source: 13Fs for those two quarters). The model consists of the highlighted five rows with the $50,000 capital equally distributed.

The model succeeds in capturing the manager's sentiment, as all of the significant additions during the quarter are included. Greenberg's highest conviction position (Table 14.1), Valeant Pharmaceuticals, is a no-show, as it is not among the largest new purchases. Oracle Corporation, a position doubled as of Q1 2012, persevered. Although the stake is only 4 percent, the model picked up the manager's bullish sentiment.

A certain level of trading is involved to keep the portfolio updated on a quarterly basis: Per Greenberg's new additions for Q4 2011, the portfolio would have had Adobe Systems, Oracle Corporation, Primerica, Valeant Pharmaceuticals, and VistaPrint. In Q1 2012, the stakes of Oracle and VistaPrint were increased significantly, allowing them to retain their presence in the model. The other three positions were liquidated to make room for Google, Higher One, and Laboratory Corp.

Weighted Allocation Largest Positions

The model uses the top five positions highlighted in Table 14.1 but, instead of allocating each pick $10,000, position sizing aims to approximate the manager's allocation in a mechanical fashion. Cloning becomes exact if positions are established to mimic the manager's position and its size in the same ratio as it appears in his 13F.

Table 14.3 Sample Portfolio: Equal Allocation Largest New Positions

Entity	Price per Share (03/31/2012)	Share Count (03/31/2012)	Price per Share (12/31/2011)	Share Count (12/31/2011)	Market Value of New Positions (03/31/2012)
Adobe Systems Inc. (ADBE)	$34.31	1,441,656	$28.27	1,422,229	$666,540.37
Aon Corp. (AON)	$49.06	1,279,957	$46.80	1,508,051	$0.00
Comcast Corp. (CMCSA)	$29.51	4,276,864	$23.56	4,923,282	$0.00
Fiserv Inc. (FISV)	$69.39	2,050,188	$58.74	2,375,270	$0.00
Globe Specialty Metals Inc.			$13.39	249,400	$0.00
Google Inc. (GOOG)	$641.24	323,472	$645.90	299,084	$15,638,561.12
Higher One Hldgs Inc. (ONE)	$14.95	6,539,352			$97,763,312.40
Laboratory Corp Amer Hldgs (LH)	$91.54	892,050	$85.97	784,011	$9,889,890.06
Mastercard Inc. (MA)			$372.82	163,686	$0.00
Motorola Solutions Inc. (MSI)	$50.83	1,901,857	$46.29	2,156,663	$0.00
Oracle Corp. (ORCL)	$29.16	1,901,571	$25.65	1,027,695	$25,482,224.16
Primerica Inc. (PRI)	$25.21	1,702,581	$23.24	1,683,852	$472,158.09
US Bancorp (USB)			$27.05	2,959,375	$0.00
Valeant Pharmaceuticals Intl. (VRX)	$53.69	4,413,146	$46.69	4,359,658	$2,871,770.72
Visa Inc. (V)	$118.00	271,098	$101.53	273,734	$0.00
VistaPrint NV (VPRT)	$38.65	3,364,275	$30.60	2,085,592	$49,421,097.95

NOTE: The highlights in dark gray indicate the new additions in the model for Q1 2012 and the light gray highlights are those that carried over from Q4 2011.

For this illustration, a simple 3:2:1 weightage ratio is applied to Greenberg's top five positions:

- The largest position in the 13F is bestowed a weightage of 3
- The next two largest positions bags a weightage of 2
- The remaining two positions receive a weightage of 1

A variation on the weightage distribution is to base the weightage on the percentage allocations in the 13F portfolio rather than adopt a fixed number of positions for each weightage. For concentrated portfolios, using a fixed number achieves more distribution and hence that approach was adopted for this illustration.

Table 14.4 shows how the $50,000 capital gets spread among the top five picks using the weighted allocation. The model consists of the highlighted five rows with the $50,000 capital distributed in a weighted fashion.

A good look at the position sizing of the smallest and largest positions in the manager's portfolio in Table 14.4 gives a hint on how the weightage works: Valeant Pharmaceuticals, the highest stake in Greenberg's 13F for Q1 2012 with an allocation of 17.4 percent, scores a 3, thus this position gets 33 percent of the total capital of $50,000. On the other hand, Comcast Corp with a weightage of 1 gets only 11 percent of the capital.

Updating the portfolio every quarter is not rocket science. The lone change in the top five positions between Q4 2011 and Q1 2012 was the replacement of Motorola Solutions with VistaPrint. Both these positions had the same weightage of 1. The update involved liquidating Motorola Solutions and purchasing VistaPrint. At times, the weightages among the top five positions also change and then a little more trading is required to keep the positions up to date.

Weighted Allocation Largest New Positions

The highlighted stakes in Table 14.3 represent the largest five additions. The weightage ratio of 3:2:1 is then applied to allocate the $50,000 capital:

- The largest addition to the portfolio is given a weightage of 3
- The next two are each earmarked a weightage of 2
- The last two end up with a weightage of 1

Table 14.4 Sample Portfolio: Weighted Allocation Largest Positions

Entity	Market Value (03/31/2012)	Share Count (03/31/2012)	% of U.S. long portfolio (03/31/2012)	Weightage	Model Allocation
Adobe Systems Inc. (ADBE)	$49,463,000.00	1,441,656	3.63%		
Aon Corp. (AON)	$62,795,000.00	1,279,957	4.61%		
Comcast Corp. (CMCSA)	$126,210,000.00	4,276,864	9.27%	1	$5,555.56
Fiserv Inc. (FISV)	$142,263,000.00	2,050,188	10.45%	2	$11,111.11
Google Inc. (GOOG)	$207,423,000.00	323,472	15.23%	2	$11,111.11
Higher One Hldgs Inc. (ONE)	$97,763,000.00	6,539,352	7.18%		
Laboratory Corp Amer Hldgs (LH)	$81,658,000.00	892,050	6.00%		
Motorola Solutions Inc. (MSI)	$96,671,000.00	1,901,857	7.10%		
Oracle Corp. (ORCL)	$55,450,000.00	1,901,571	4.07%		
Primerica Inc. (PRI)	$42,922,000.00	1,702,581	3.15%		
Valeant Pharmaceuticals Intl. (VRX)	$236,942,000.00	4,413,146	17.40%	3	$16,666.67
Visa Inc. (V)	$31,990,000.00	271,098	2.35%		
VistaPrint NV (VPRT)	$130,029,000.00	3,364,275	9.55%	1	$5,555.56
Total	**$1,361,579,000.00**				

NOTE: The highlights in dark gray indicate the new additions in the model for Q1 2012 and the light gray highlights are those that carried over from Q4 2011.

Table 14.5 illustrates how the capital gets allocated across the largest five additions using this model. The model consists of the highlighted five rows with the $50,000 capital distributed in a weighted fashion.

The model allocates one-third of the capital to Higher One, the largest new addition for Greenberg in Q1 2012. VistaPrint, a stake being built by the manager, is represented well in the model with a 22 percent allocation. Overall, the model succeeds in capturing the manager's current sentiment reasonably well, with the major new additions featuring in the portfolio in a weighted fashion.

A fair amount of trading is required to keep this model current. Similar to the equal allocation variant, three positions (Adobe, Primerica, and Valeant) had to be liquidated to make room for Google, Higher One, and Laboratory Corp in Q1 2012. Besides, the weightage shift for VistaPrint required another buy/sell.

10–5–2 Allocation Largest Positions

The model aims to establish a common manager trait of allocating over 10 percent of assets each to a very small number of the highest conviction bets, over 5 percent each to an average number of high conviction stakes, and around 2 percent each for the rest. To shadow this allocation, the portfolio will need to have upwards of twenty positions. This illustration approximates the model by restricting the number of positions to five and allocating the $50,000 capital based on a 10:5:2 ratio. The five positions are divided into three groups: the best, the better, and the good:

1. The best position command a weightage of 10
2. The better two positions are each given a weightage of 5
3. The good two positions end up with a weightage of 2

Table 14.6 represents how the $50,000 capital gets allocated among the top five picks using this model. The model consists of the highlighted five rows with the $50,000 capital distributed in a 10:5:2 ratio.

Greenberg runs a very concentrated portfolio: Even the lowest allocation (Comcast Corp) among his top five accounts for close

Table 14.5 Sample Portfolio: Weighted Allocation Largest New Positions

Entity	Market Value of New Positions (03/31/2012)	New Additions as % of Portfolio (03/31/2012)	Weightage	Model Allocation
Adobe Systems Inc. (ADBE)	$666,537.44	0.05%		
Aon Corp. (AON)	$0.00	0.00%		
Comcast Corp. (CMCSA)	$0.00	0.00%		
Fiserv Inc. (FISV)	$0.00	0.00%		
Google Inc. (GOOG)	$15,638,547.15	1.15%	1	$5,555.56
Higher One Holdgs Inc. (ONE)	$97,763,000.00	7.18%	3	$16,666.67
Laboratory Corp Amer Hldgs (LH)	$9,889,853.53	0.73%	1	$5,555.56
Motorola Solutions Inc. (MSI)	$0.00	0.00%		
Oracle Corp. (ORCL)	$25,482,311.31	1.87%	2	$11,111.11
Primerica Inc. (PRI)	$472,157.35	0.03%		
Valeant Pharmaceuticals Intl. (VRX)	$2,871,773.04	0.21%		
Visa Inc. (V)	$0.00	0.00%		
VistaPrint N V (VPRT)	$49,421,011.01	3.63%	2	$11,111.11
Total				**$50,000.00**

NOTE: The highlights in dark gray indicate the new additions in the model for Q1 2012 and the light gray highlights are those that carried over from Q4 2011.

Table 14.6 Sample Portfolio: 10–5–2 Allocation Largest Positions

Entity	Market Value (03/31/2012)	Shares (03/31/2012)	% of U.S. Long Portfolio (03/31/2012)	Weightage	Model Allocation
Adobe Systems Inc. (ADBE)	$49,463,000.00	1,441,656	3.63%		
Aon Corp. (AON)	$62,795,000.00	1,279,957	4.61%		
Comcast Corp. (CMCSA)	$126,210,000.00	4,276,864	9.27%	2	$4,166.67
Fiserv Inc. (FISV)	$142,263,000.00	2,050,188	10.45%	5	$10,416.67
Google Inc. (GOOG)	$207,423,000.00	323,472	15.23%	5	$10,416.67
Higher One Hldgs Inc. (ONE)	$97,763,000.00	6,539,352	7.18%		
Laboratory Corp Amer Hldgs (LH)	$81,658,000.00	892,050	6.00%		
Motorola Solutions Inc. (MSI)	$96,671,000.00	1,901,857	7.10%		
Oracle Corp. (ORCL)	$55,450,000.00	1,901,571	4.07%		
Primerica Inc. (PRI)	$42,922,000.00	1,702,581	3.15%		
Valeant Pharmaceuticals Intl. (VRX)	$236,942,000.00	4,413,146	17.40%	10	$20,833.33
Visa Inc. (V)	$31,990,000.00	271,098	2.35%		
VistaPrint NV (VPRT)	$130,029,000.00	3,364,275	9.55%	2	$4,166.67
Total	**$1,361,579,000.00**				**$50,000.00**

NOTE: The highlights in dark gray indicate the new additions in the model for Q1 2012 and the light gray highlights are those that carried over from Q4 2011.

to 10 percent of the overall allocation. The highest stake, Valeant Pharmaceuticals, is at over 17 percent. On the other hand, the model highlighted in Table 14.6 has the highest allocation at just over 40 percent and the lowest allocation at around 8 percent. Increasing the number of positions in the model can take care of the very high allocation to a single position.

Updating the portfolio every quarter is not all that cumbersome. Between Q4 2011 and Q1 2012, replacement of Motorola Solutions with VistaPrint was the only change in the top five positions. It is worth mentioning again, the possibility for the percentage allocation to shift among the top five positions between quarters cannot be ruled out. Given our penchant for value-oriented managers that tend to hold on to positions for long periods of time, it should happen only rarely. When it does happen, a little more trading will be necessary to keep the positions up to date.

10–5–2 Allocation Largest New Positions

The five positions highlighted in Table 14.3 are the largest new additions. The weighted ratio of 10:5:2 is applied to allocate the $50,000 capital among these positions:

- The largest new addition is given the lion's share, with a weightage of 10
- The next two new additions each get a weightage of 5
- The last two new additions have to be content with a weightage of 2

Table 14.7 shows how the capital gets allocated across the largest five additions using this model. The model consists of the highlighted five rows with the $50,000 capital distributed in a 10:5:2 ratio.

The model allocates over 40 percent of the capital to Higher One, the largest new addition for Q1 2012 compared to less than 8 percent in the 13F. The very high allocation to individual positions can be avoided by increasing the number of positions in the model portfolio and correspondingly adjusting the number of positions for each weightage. Overall, the model succeeds in approximating the manager's expected allocations and capturing the sentiment.

Table 14.7 Sample Portfolio: 10–5–2 Allocation Largest New Positions

Entity	Market Value of New Additions (03/31/2012)	New Additions as % of Portfolio (03/31/2012)	Weightage	Model Allocation
Adobe Systems Inc. (ADBE)	$666,537.44	0.05%		
Aon Corp. (AON)	$0.00	0.00%		
Comcast Corp. (CMCSA)	$0.00	0.00%		
Fiserv Inc. (FISV)	$0.00	0.00%		
Google Inc. (GOOG)	$15,638,547.14	1.15%	2	$4,166.67
Higher One Hldgs Inc. (ONE)	$97,763,000.00	7.18%	10	$20,833.33
Laboratory Corp. Amer Hldgs (LH)	$9,889,858.93	0.73%	2	$4,166.67
Motorola Solutions Inc. (MSI)	$0.00	0.00%		
Oracle Corp. (ORCL)	$25,482,311.31	1.87%	5	$10,416.67
Primerica Inc. (PRI)	$472,157.35	0.03%		
Valeant Pharmaceuticals Intl. (VRX)	$2,871,773.04	0.21%		
Visa Inc. (V)	$0.00	0.00%		
VistaPrint NV (VPRT)	$49,421,011.01	3.63%	5	$10,416.67
Total				**$50,000.00**

NOTE: The highlights in dark gray indicate the new additions in the model for Q1 2012 and the light gray highlights are those that carried over from Q4 2011.

The trading requirements of this model is the same as the weighted allocation variant; three positions (Adobe, Primerica, and Valeant) had to be liquidated to make room for Google, Higher One, and Laboratory Corp in Q1 2012. Also, the weightage shifted for VistaPrint, prompting another buy/sell.

Notes

1. Mary Margaret Myers, James Poterba, Douglas Shackelford, and John Shoven, "Copycat Funds: Information Disclosure Regulation and the Returns to Active Management in the Mutual Fund Industry," Massachusetts Institute of Technology, Department of Economics, 10/2001.
2. Marno Verbeek and Yu Wang, "Better than the Original? The Relative Success of Copycat Funds," Rotterdam School of Management, Erasumus University, 11/2/2010.
3. Randy Cohen, Christopher Polk, and Bernhard Silli, "Best Ideas," 03/15/2010, http://papers.ssrn.com/sol3/papers.cfm?abstract_id=1364827.
4. Sara Eisen and Mazin Jadallah, "Cloning Hedge Fund Strategies," Bloomberg Money Moves, 07/24/2012, www.bloomberg.com/video/cloning-hedge-fund-strategies-UWkSvAZ1TiGX7pMe_e9EYw.html.
5. Gerald Martin and John Puthenpurackal, "Imitation Is the Sincerest Form of Flattery: Warren Buffett and Berkshire Hathaway," American University & University of Nevada, 05/15/2008, http://papers.ssrn.com/sol3/papers.cfm?abstract_id=806246.
6. Mebane Fabert and Eric Richardson, *The Ivy Portfolio: How to Invest Like the Top Endowments and Avoid Bear Markets* (Hoboken, NJ: John Wiley & Sons, 2009).
7. Blerina Reca, Richard Sias, and Harry Turtle, "Hedge Fund Herding and Crowded Trades: The Apologists' Evidence," The University of Toledo, 06/24/2012, http://papers.ssrn.com/sol3/papers.cfm?abstract_id=1906932.
8. Russ Wermers, "Is Money Really 'Smart'? New Evidence on the Relation Between Mutual Fund Flows, Manager Behavior, and Performance Persistence," Robert H. Smith School of Business University of Maryland, 05/2003, http://papers.ssrn.com/sol3/papers.cfm?abstract_id=414420.
9. George Aragon, Michael Hertzel, and Zhen Shi, "Why Do Hedge Funds Avoid Disclosure? Evidence From Confidential 13F Filings," Arizona State University, 05/16/2011, www.public.asu.edu/~goaragon/Papers/ahs_JFQA_01jun2012.pdf.

10. Adam Aiken, Christopher Clifford, and Jesse Ellis, "Out of the Dark: Hedge Fund Reporting Biases and Commercial Databases," Quinnipiac University, University of Kentucky, and University of Alabama, 03/03/2012, http://papers.ssrn.com/sol3/papers.cfm?abstract_id=1519914.

11. Burton Malkiel and Atanu Saha, "Hedge Funds: Risk and Return," *Financial Analysts Journal* 61, no. 6, November/December 2005.

Chapter 15

Equal Allocation Models

T he primer in the preceding chapter looked at the work involved in selecting managers to shadow and mechanically assembling portfolios based on their stock picks. Such portfolios are pieced together from a set number of stock picks based on some criteria, and the assets are distributed equally or in a ratio among the selections. Models founded on the equal allocation method are the simplest to implement and are discussed in this chapter.

This chapter focuses on managing and analyzing model portfolios of the three shortlisted managers: Bill Ackman, Warren Buffett, and David Einhorn. They are presented individually and combined, using the Equal Allocation method. For illustration purposes, these portfolios employ minimal three-stock models based on their largest positions. The three managers chosen are known to run concentrated portfolios making reasonable coverage possible with three-stock models. The combined models use one selection each from the three managers for the largest positions and the largest new positions portfolios to bring to the table a taste of real-life implementation with multiple managers.

The tables track the evolution of the model portfolios over a period of three years and indicate back-tested performance for the same time period.

The models offer no recommendation as to when to rebalance. Rebalancing on a fixed schedule can result in unnecessary trades, even when the components of the portfolio have not diverged much. Here, rebalancing is applied when the largest position is 50 percent greater than the smallest position.

Portfolio Management and Performance Analysis

A portfolio of $100,000 and an inception date of August 17, 2009 (the first trading day following the deadline for filing 13Fs for Q2 2009) were the assumptions for building these models. At launch time, the $100,000 was distributed evenly among the manager's largest (or largest new) position(s), as indicated in their Q2 2009 13F forms. Spreadsheets captured the updates performed forty-five days after every quarter, and rebalancing when the largest position went over 50 percent of the smallest position. Dividend income was ignored to provide a precise comparison with the S&P 500 Index performance.

Bill Ackman: Largest Three

Table 15.1 (A&B) illustrates the model portfolio based on Ackman's largest three positions with an inception date of August 17, 2009, and its progression for the next three years.

The columns display the portfolio allocation on the date indicated in the header row. The second column (8/17/2009) represents the allocation of the $100,000 portfolio across the largest three positions of Ackman's Q2 2009 13F and the following columns depict the mechanics of the portfolio progression on a quarterly basis per the corresponding 13F.

As mentioned earlier, the second column in Table 15.1A indicates the initial allocations made on 08/17/2009. The next column (11/16/2009) indicates the portfolio progression and reallocation

Table 15.1 Bill Ackman: Three Largest Positions Model

(A)

Ticker	8/17/2009	11/16/2009	2/15/2010	5/17/2010	8/16/2010	11/15/2010	2/15/2011
ADP	$33,333						
C					$46,369	$51,754	
CXW			$38,486				
EMC	$33,333	$38,876					
Fortune							$49,668
GGP							$49,668
H			$38,486				
KFT				$46,595		$46,955	
MCD		$38,933			$44,911		
JCP							$49,668
TGT	$33,333	$40,534	$39,204	$45,176	$40,880	$43,653	
YUM				$46,595			
Total	**$100,000**	**$118,343**	**$116,175**	**$138,367**	**$132,160**	**$142,361**	**$149,005**

(B)

Ticker	5/16/2011	8/15/2011	11/15/2011	2/15/2012	5/15/2012	8/15/2012
CP				$56,246	$56,698	$64,888
Fortune	$50,997	$52,438	$44,562			
GGP	$52,148	$46,627	$46,465	$54,409	$56,960	$60,221
JCP	$51,387	$37,370	$44,537	$58,347	$46,015	$32,688
Total	**$154,533**	**$136,535**	**$135,564**	**$169,002**	**$159,673**	**$157,797**

after the 13F for Q3 2009 was released. The largest positions almost remained intact save for the replacement of Automatic Data Processing (ADP) with McDonald's Corporation (MCD). The changes in dollar figures reflect the increase or decrease in the corresponding stock price between those two dates.

- EMC Corporation (EMC) and Target Corporation (TGT) held their spots in the top three for 11/16/2009. The new values for these holdings are obtained by multiplying the new price per share by the number of shares of the holding.
- The value realized by selling Automatic Data Processing (ADP) as of 11/16/2009 was used to acquire the new stake in McDonald's Corporation (MCD).

The next quarter (2/15/2010) saw shifts in the largest positions again, which in its turn called for more buy/sell trades: EMC Corporation (EMC) and McDonald's Corporation (MCD) were given the ax, and the proceeds equally split between Corrections Corporation of America (CXW) and Hyatt Hotels Corporation (H). Though rebalancing was never a concern during the entire three-year period, it was in the cards as of 08/15/2012—Canadian Pacific Railway (CP), the largest position, was 50 percent over JCPenney (JCP), the smallest position. A portion of each of the three stocks held will need to be either bought or sold so as to make the allocation equal across the holdings.

As of 8/15/2012, the total value of the portfolio improved to $157,797 (excluding dividends) for a total return of 57.80 percent. The S&P 500 Index return during that time period was 43.46 percent.

Warren Buffett: Largest Three

Table 15.2 (A & B) illustrate the model portfolio based on Buffett's largest three positions with an inception date of August 17, 2009, and its progression over the next three years.

The columns display the portfolio allocation on the date indicated in the header row. The second column (8/17/2009) represents the allocation of the $100,000 portfolio across the largest three

Table 15.2 Warren Buffett's Largest Three Positions Model

(A)

Ticker	8/17/2009	11/16/2009	2/15/2010	5/17/2010	8/16/2010	11/15/2010	2/15/2011
AXP	$33,333	$38,810		$45,395	$45,736	$47,013	$50,855
KO	$33,333	$35,742	$36,922	$36,532	$38,222	$43,065	$43,222
WFC	$33,333	$36,163	$34,057	$40,506	$32,537	$35,033	$42,673
BNI	$33,333		$44,675				
Total	**$100,000**	**$110,715**	**$115,654**	**$122,434**	**$116,494**	**$125,110**	**$136,750**

(B)

Ticker	5/16/2011	Rebalance	8/15/2011	11/15/2011	2/15/2012	5/15/2012	8/15/2012
AXP	$55,127	$45,607	$41,742				
KO	$46,396	$45,607	$45,380	$45,696	$45,965	$51,455	$52,886
IBM				$45,504	$46,332	$47,969	$47,814
WFC	$35,229	$45,607	$40,958	$41,400	$49,388	$52,777	$55,609
Total	**$136,821**	**$136,821**	**$128,530**	**$132,600**	**$141,685**	**$152,201**	**$156,310**

positions of Buffett's Q2 2009 13F, and the following columns depict the mechanics of the portfolio progression on a quarterly basis per the corresponding 13F.

Warren Buffett was never one to mince words when it comes to stating his favorite holding period: It is forever. As many of his larger positions are very long-term holdings, the largest position models work superbly with his portfolio as the long-term sentiment is captured in all its glory. Over the three-year tracking period, just five stocks were utilized by the model and the allocations were altered only twice.

- Burlington Northern Santa Fe (BNI) gave up its position to American Express Company (AXP) on 5/17/2010, following Buffett's Q1 2010 13F filing. Berkshire Hathaway bought BNI outright and, during that quarter, BNI became a wholly owned subsidiary.
- American Express (AXP) pulled out for International Business Machines Corp. (IBM) on 11/15/2011. The huge IBM stake disclosed in the filing easily found its place among the top three positions.

Rebalancing was required once, after the Q1 2011 13F filing (05/16/2011). American Express (AXP) had returned around 70 percent by then, compared to the marginal returns for Wells Fargo (WFC), thus meeting the rebalancing criteria. To rebalance, a portion of American Express (AXP) and Coca-Cola (KO) holdings were sold to buy shares of Wells Fargo (WFC), bringing the allocations equal at $45,607 apiece. In all, over the three-year period, trading activity was limited to just seven transactions:

- Sale of BNI to buy AXP with its proceeds on 5/17/2010
- Trade of AXP to purchase IBM on 11/15/2011
- Three buy/sell activities of portions of each stock in the portfolio on 05/16/2011 for rebalancing

As of 8/15/2012, the total value of the portfolio improved to $156,310 (excluding dividends) for a total return of 56.31 percent. The S&P 500 Index return during that time period was 43.46 percent.

David Einhorn: Largest Three

Table 15.3 (A&B) illustrate the model portfolio based on Einhorn's largest positions, with an inception date of August 17, 2009, and its progression over the next three years.

The columns display the portfolio allocation on the date indicated in the header row. The second column (8/17/2009) represents the allocation of the $100,000 portfolio across the largest three positions of Einhorn's Q2 2009 13F and the following columns depict the mechanics of the portfolio progression on a quarterly basis per the corresponding 13F.

Einhorn sports a much more actively traded portfolio and the bustle was mirrored in the model. At inception, the top three holdings in the model were Pfizer Inc. (PFE), Teradata Corporation (TDC), and URS Corporation (URS). Only PFE maintained its status quo in the top three holding for any length of time, as both TDC and URS were bumped in the following quarter and replaced with Cardinal Health (CAH) and CareFusion (CFN). Two quarters later, those two positions made way for CIT Group (CIT) and Ensco PLC (ESV) (8/16/2010). The model portfolio value taxied quite a bit before taking off—the portfolio remained under break even at the one-year mark. The PFE position barely budged and despite the trading activity the other two positions also shared a similar fate. From the second year on, the portfolio gathered momentum, revving with the entry of Apple Inc. (AAPL) as a top three holding in Q1 2011 (5/16/2011). Three quarters later (2/15/2012), rebalancing criteria was met; the AAPL holding had already returned close to 50 percent, while the others continued to post anemic returns.

The portfolio progression pattern of this model offers a tutorial on the risks associated with the limited implementation of the models.

- When the number of stocks is reduced to just three, a large increase or decrease in the share price of a single holding over a period of time can make or break the performance of the model. Einhorn's model was literally carried by the vast outperformance of the AAPL position. The lackluster returns provided throughout by the other two positions did not help at all. While this model

Table 15.3   David Einhorn's Largest Three Positions Model

(A)

Ticker	8/17/2009	11/16/2009	2/15/2010	5/17/2010	8/16/2010	11/15/2010	2/15/2011
BSX			$36,545				
CAH		$35,149		$34,442			
CFN		$35,149	$34,684				
CIT				$34,442	$35,006	$39,856	$42,081
ESV					$31,020	$33,757	$37,439
PFE	$33,333	$37,656	$37,362	$33,815	$33,647	$35,158	$39,986
TDC	$33,333						
URS	$33,333						
Total	**$100,000**	**$107,955**	**$108,591**	**$102,699**	**$99,672**	**$108,772**	**$119,506**

(B)

Ticker	5/16/2011	08/15/2011	11/15/2011	2/15/2012	Rebalance	5/15/2012	8/15/2012
AAPL	$37,920	$43,709	$44,327	$56,734	$44,084	$49,232	$56,144
CIT	$39,633						
GM				$36,423	$44,084	$37,871	
GDX			$41,707				
MSFT		$33,181					$35,608
PFE	$44,037	$38,496	$34,789	$39,095	$44,084		
STX						$44,319	$48,266
Total	**$121,590**	**$115,385**	**$120,822**	**$132,253**	**$132,253**	**$131,422**	**$140,017**

was buoyed by the returns of one position, the reverse can also be a very real scenario. An enormous drop in the share price over a period of time will cause the performance of the model to sink, should the position continue as a top three holding. To alleviate this problem, the number of positions should be increased for a genuine implementation. Then, the portfolio impact due to an increase or decrease in the share price of a single position can be contained.

• It is entirely possible for individual managers to have periods of underperformance. Einhorn's model seemingly started its innings with a dull group of top picks, explaining the depressing performance early on. Following a group of value-oriented managers over prolonged time periods can lessen this problem.

As of 8/15/2012, the total value of the portfolio improved to $140,017 (excluding dividends) for a total return of 40.02%. However, the S&P 500 Index return during that time period was 43.46%.

Combined Portfolio: Largest Positions

Table 15.4 (A&B) illustrate the model portfolio based on the largest position from each of the three managers with an inception date of August 17, 2009, and its progression over the next three years:

The columns display the portfolio allocation on the date indicated in the header row. The second column (8/17/2009) represents the allocation of the $100,000 portfolio across the three largest positions per their Q2 2009 13Fs, and the following columns depict the mechanics of the portfolio progression on a quarterly basis per the corresponding 13Fs.

The combined portfolio had just 11 positions overall during the tracking period. The trading activity was also fairly low, with average buy/sell activity per quarter hovering under one. Rebalancing was a one-time event following the Q2 2011 13F update on 08/15/2011; JCPenney (JCP) dropped about 25 percent in the preceding two quarters. The largest position, Coca-Cola, (KO) became 50 percent over the smallest position, JCP, resulting in the model meeting the rebalancing criteria. Buffett's largest position (KO) held

Table 15.4 Combined Model: Largest Positions

(A)

Ticker	8/17/2009	11/16/2009	2/15/2010	5/17/2010	8/16/2010	11/15/2010	2/15/2011
KO	$33,333	$38,810	$36,922	$36,532	$38,222	$43,065	$43,222
TGT	$33,333	$40,534	$39,204	$39,204	$45,176		
KFT						$40,880	
JCP							$40,721
PFE	$33,333	$37,656					
CIT				$34,430	$34,968	$39,813	
BSX			$37,362				
ESV							$42,036
Total	$100,000	$117,000	$113,488	$110,166	$118,366	$123,758	$125,979

(B)

Ticker	5/16/2011	8/15/2011	Rebalance	11/15/2011	2/15/2012	5/15/2012	8/15/2012
KO	$46,396	$46,649	$38,164	$38,080	$38,304	$42,879	$44,072
JCP	$42,122	$30,632	$38,164				
Fortune				$45,484			
CP					$57,410	$57,878	$66,238
PFE	$42,577	$37,212	$38,164				
AAPL				$41,348	$52,753	$58,636	$66,868
Total	$131,094	$114,493	$114,493	$124,912	$148,467	$159,393	$177,178

steady throughout the tracking period, and the other two managers had the same stock as their top holding for more than a year multiple times. The portfolio had some volatility early on, although overall the returns were always upbeat. After the first two years, the model returned just under 15 percent, as the top positions of Ackman and Einhorn failed to energize the portfolio sufficiently. However, in the final year, the model spiked 55 percent, as the top holdings of all three managers posted handsome returns: Coca-Cola (KO), Canadian Pacific (CP), Fortune Brands, and Apple Inc. (AAPL) formed their largest holdings during those four quarters. Going forward, a rebalancing is in the cards, as the relative performance of KO failed to match the returns of CP, Fortune, and AAPL, thereby meeting the rebalancing criteria: AAPL, the largest position, became 50 percent over the smallest position, KO, at that point.

As of 8/15/2012, the total value of the portfolio improved to $177,178 (excluding dividends) for a total return of 77.18 percent. The S&P 500 Index return during that time period was 43.46 percent.

Combined Portfolio: Largest New Positions

Table 15.5 illustrates the model portfolio based on the largest new position from each of the three managers, with an inception date of August 17, 2009 and its progression over the next three years.

The columns display the portfolio allocation on the date indicated in the header row. The second column (8/17/2009) represents the allocation of the $100,000 portfolio across the three largest new positions per their Q2 2009 13Fs, and the following columns depict the mechanics of the portfolio progression on an annual basis per the corresponding 13Fs.

As the managers being tracked are value oriented with fairly long-term holding periods, the change in positions between two consecutive quarters is mostly insignificant. Since the selected managers fail to make significant changes every quarter, a paradigm shift is due for this model. Instead of performing portfolio updates to maintain conformance every quarter, the updates are done only annually. Usually the portfolio gets a clean slate, as it is very rare for a manager

Table 15.5   Model of Largest New Positions on the Combined Portfolio

Ticker	8/17/2009	8/16/2010	8/15/2011	8/15/2012
COP	$33,333			
WMT		$40,010		
WFC			$41,569	
IBM				$52,395
EMC	$33,333			
KFT		$40,010		
JCP			$41,569	
PG				$52,395
PFE	$33,333			
CIT		$40,010		
S			$41,569	
STX				$52,395
Total	**$100,000**	**$120,030**	**$124,708**	**$157,186**

to continue having the same stock as the largest new position. In the model, it never happened at all. The fringe benefit is that rebalancing is eliminated: When the positions are all sold to buy new positions for the updates, rebalancing is automatic. The equal allocations to the three positions on every column in the spreadsheet, without doing any explicit rebalancing, make this clear.

As of 8/15/2012, the total value of the portfolio improved to $157,186 (excluding dividends) for a total return of 57.19%. The S&P 500 Index return during that time period was 43.46%.

Summary

The chapter charted the course of five portfolios over three years. They served to illustrate how to manage and mechanically maintain equal allocation based model portfolios on an ongoing basis. Relatively straightforward spreadsheets are sufficient to guide the implementation of the portfolios in a real-life situation. To reiterate, the individual models used three stock positions for each portfolio for easier illustration. For the same reason, the combined portfolios stayed in the comfort zone of single picks from each manager.

The frequency of trading is a genuine concern with mechanically cloned portfolios. The equal allocation models fared outstandingly well in this regard: On average, for the largest positions-based models, less than one buy/sell trade was required per quarter to echo the manager's positions. Rebalancing involves buying or selling a portion of the shares for every holding but, per our criteria, rebalancing was required far less frequently compared to the quarterly reallocations: The average for the portfolios over the three-year tracking period was less than one.

The largest new positions model for the combined portfolio display some distinct characteristics:

- Numerous trades are necessary to maintain the model. In the portfolio illustrated earlier, all the positions had to be replaced with new positions to keep conformance with the model.
- Unlike the other models, in which trades were done to maintain conformance every quarter, the buy/sell activity for this model was limited to once a year: For one, activity was insufficient among the managers to warrant updates every quarter and, for another, the portfolio turnover would have ended up being around 400 percent as the positions would have to be replaced every quarter.
- The model needs to use a larger group of managers to have significant new activity every quarter.

While the models were more for illustration than for actual application, two of the single-manager models (Buffett and Ackman) showed very strong results, and one had an equitable result (Einhorn). It was Einhorn's model that laid bare the risks associated with limiting the number of positions to three, and the single-manager risk:

- A large rise or fall in the share price of a single position over a period of time can have a significant impact on the performance of the model.
- Single-manager risk is very real, even value managers with long-term track records are not spared. Einhorn had awful runs during the tracking period, which was reflected in the model based on his portfolio. The risk can be mitigated by modeling based on a set

of such managers. This is confirmed by our combined largest positions model that strongly outperformed the S&P 500 Index.

To conclude, the small window of three years is obviously way too small to prove the mettle of these models; the sharpest tool in the arsenal for the kind of money managers followed is undoubtedly time. The illustrations bring to the fore single-manager risk and concentration risk. Real cloning models should employ at least ten positions. They should also consider using the combined portfolio approach with upward of five managers.

Chapter 16

Weighted Allocation Models

W eighted allocation brings character to cloning. Models based on weighted allocation attempt to draw benefit from the relative size of the stock picks held in source managers' portfolios.

The process of assembling the models from a determined number of stock picks from a single manager or a group of managers based on selection criteria is similar to the equal allocation model described in chapter 15. The weighted model takes wing when it comes to allotting assets: Distribution is done based on a weightage associated with each pick. This weightage is derived from the percentage allocation in the source manager portfolios.

This chapter presents the evolution of five different weighted allocation model portfolios from the three shortlisted managers: Bill Ackman, Warren Buffett, and David Einhorn. The different types are:

- Three single-manager weighted allocation models demonstrating the manager's largest three positions individually.
- A combined weighted allocation portfolio displaying the largest position of the three managers.
- A combined weighted allocation portfolio based on the largest new position of the selected three managers.

Applying quarterly updates to get the portfolios to conform to the models involve significant trading activity. As with the equal allocation model, a buy/sell trade is necessary whenever the stock picks change. Things can get cranking if, in the weighted allocation model, the weightage of the new pick is different from the weightage of the previous quarter's pick it replaced. In such cases, to restore the weightages, rebalancing becomes necessary. Rebalancing can also come calling when the weightage changes for any of the stock picks. As the odds are good for at least one of these events to happen, rebalancing trades are done every quarter.

Portfolio Management and Performance Analysis

A portfolio of $100,000 and an inception date of August 17, 2009 (the first trading day following the deadline for filing 13Fs for Q2 2009) were the assumptions for building these models. At launch time, the $100,000 was distributed among the positions chosen from the manager's portfolio, as indicated in their Q2 2009 13F using preset weightage ratios. Depending on the model, the picks could be the manager's largest or largest new position(s). The updates are made (including rebalancing) 45 days after every quarter for each model. Dividend income is ignored to provide a precise comparison with the S&P 500 Index performance.

The weighted allocation model does not provide guidance as to what weightages to use or how to map the source portfolio percentage allocations. To make the illustrations easy to understand, a minimalist three-term ratio of 1:2:3 is used for all five models. The following conventions are used for mapping the largest position(s) based models:

- Weightage 1, if the value of the holdings for the stock pick in the source portfolio is less than 10 percent of the corresponding 13F total portfolio value.
- Weightage 2, if the value of the holdings for the stock pick in the source portfolio is between 10 percent and 20 percent of the corresponding 13F total portfolio value.
- Weightage 3, if the value of the holdings for the stock pick in the source portfolio is above 20 percent of the corresponding 13F total portfolio value.

Bill Ackman: Largest Three

Table 16.1 (A&B) illustrates the model portfolio based on Ackman's largest three positions with an inception date of August 17, 2009, and its progression for the next three years.

The second column (8/17/2009) represents the initial allocation of the $100,000 portfolio across the largest three positions of Ackman's Q2 2009 13F. The following columns depict the mechanics of the portfolio's progression on a quarterly basis per the corresponding 13F on the date indicated in the header row after updates and rebalancing.

At the time of initial allocation, Automatic Data Processing (ADP) qualified for 2 points, while EMC Corporation (EMC) and Target Corporation (TGT) both claimed eligibility for 3 points. These weightages were justified by their allocations in Ackman's 13F filing for Q2 2009: 11.34 percent for ADP, 33.89 percent for EMC, and an unbelievable 43.28 percent for TGT. The assets were spread in the ratio 2:3:3 among ADP, EMC, and TGT respectively as represented in second column (08/17/2009). The next column (11/16/2009) is the portfolio progression after the Q3 2009 13F filing and reflects the score after updates and rebalancing. EMC and TGT retained their top rankings but McDonald's (MCD), which replaced ADP as a top three holding, had to be content with

Table 16.1 Bill Ackman: Three Largest Positions Model

(A)

Ticker	8/17/2009	11/16/2009	2/15/2010	5/17/2010	8/16/2010	11/15/2010	2/15/2011
ADP	$25,000						
C					$31,852	$39,008	
CXW			$38,772				
EMC	$37,500	$44,443					
Fortune							$47,137
GGP							$47,137
H			$19,386				
KFT				$50,313	$47,779		
MCD		$29,629					
JCP						$58,512	
TGT	$37,500	$44,443	$58,158		$47,779	$39,008	$47,137
YUM				$33,542			
Total	**$100,000**	**$118,516**	**$116,317**	**$134,169**	**$127,410**	**$136,528**	**$141,411**

(B)

Ticker	5/16/2011	8/15/2011	11/15/2011	2/15/2012	5/15/2012	8/15/2012
CP				$70,466	$67,386	$67,084
Fortune	$36,673	$36,277	$43,925			
GGP	$55,010	$36,277	$43,925	$46,977	$44,924	$44,722
JCP	$55,010	$54,416	$43,925	$46,977	$44,924	$44,722
Total	**$146,693**	**$126,971**	**$131,774**	**$164,421**	**$157,233**	**$156,529**

a weightage of 2 (15.04 percent of assets in Ackman's 13F). The updated total value of the portfolio as of 11/16/2009 ($118,516) was then distributed among EMC, MCD, and TGT respectively in the ratio 3:2:3 to arrive at the allocations shown.

The remaining columns denote the portfolio progression over the next three years. The portfolio experienced a significant 13.5 percent dip in Q3 2011 when JCP, a pick with a weightage of 3, dropped over 25 percent. Over the following two quarters, the total portfolio value saw a rebound as JCP had an about-face and appreciated over 55 percent in those two quarters. The volatility due to the vagaries of the market pricing of a single stock is clearly cautioning the concentration risk associated with the minimal three-stock model used for this illustration.

As of 8/15/2012, the total value of the portfolio improved to $156,529 (excluding dividends) for a total return of 56.53 percent. The S&P 500 Index return during that time period was 43.46 percent.

Warren Buffett: Largest Three

Table 16.2 (A&B) illustrates the model portfolio based on Buffett's largest three positions with an inception date of August 17, 2009, and its progression for the next three years.

The second column (8/17/2009) represents the initial allocation of the $100,000 portfolio across the largest three positions of Buffett's Q2 2009 13F. The following columns depict the mechanics of the portfolio progression on a quarterly basis per the corresponding 13F on the date indicated in the header row after updates and rebalancing.

The equal initial allocations in Table 16.2A to Coca-Cola (KO), Wells Fargo (WFC), and Burlington Northern Santa Fe (BNI) signal that they all fell into the same weightage category. The percentages allocated to KO, WFC, and BNI were 19.61 percent, 15 percent, and 11.53 percent respectively in Buffett's 13F filing for Q2 2009; they were all granted the weightage 2. The equal allocation of assets continued for two more quarters as evidenced by numbers in the next two columns. Change came knocking in Q1 2010 when American Express (AXP) replaced BNI. The allocation to KO went over

Table 16.2 Warren Buffett's Largest Three Positions Model

(A)

Ticker	8/17/2009	11/16/2009	2/15/2010	5/17/2010	8/16/2010	11/15/2010	2/15/2011
AXP				$35,275	$34,069	$36,938	$35,140
KO	$33,333	$36,925	$38,643	$52,912	$51,104	$55,407	$52,710
WFC	$33,333	$36,925	$38,643	$35,275	$34,069	$36,938	$52,710
BNI	$33,333	$36,925	$38,643				
Total	**$100,000**	**$110,775**	**$115,929**	**$123,462**	**$119,242**	**$129,282**	**$140,559**

(B)

Ticker	5/16/2011	8/15/2011	11/15/2011	2/15/2012	5/15/2012	8/15/2012
AXP	$34,568	$37,239				
KO	$51,852	$55,858	$57,399	$61,012	$51,292	$67,667
IBM			$38,266	$40,675	$51,292	$45,112
WFC	$51,852	$37,239	$38,266	$40,675	$51,292	$45,112
Total	**$138,273**	**$130,336**	**$133,930**	**$142,361**	**$153,876**	**$157,890**

20 percent, honoring it with a weightage of 3 while the others received a weightage of 2. The total value of the portfolio as of that quarter (05/17/2010) was distributed at a ratio of 2:3:2 across AXP, KO, and WFC.

The portfolio progression indicates a relatively steady ascent throughout with some minor dents (well under 10 percent) in a few quarters. The marvel of this portfolio is the remarkable stability it achieved with just five positions in the top three slots over three years, and all of them receiving a weightage of either 2 or 3.

As of 8/15/2012, the total value of the portfolio improved to $157,890 (excluding dividends) for a total return of 57.89 percent. The S&P 500 Index return during that time period was 43.46 percent.

David Einhorn: Largest Three

Table 16.3 (A&B) illustrates the model portfolio based on Einhorn's largest three positions with an inception date of August 17, 2009 and its progression for the next three years.

The second column (8/17/2009) represents the initial allocation of the $100,000 portfolio across the largest three positions of Einhorn's Q2 2009 13F. The following columns depict the mechanics of the portfolio progression on a quarterly basis per the corresponding 13F on the date indicated in the header row after updates and rebalancing.

The second column in Table 16.3A confirms Einhorn's portfolio also started out with equal allocations to Pfizer Inc. (PFE), Teradata Corporation (TDC), and URS Corporation (URS); they all were entitled to a weightage of 1. As Einhorn's portfolio is diversified over a larger number of positions, the majority of the stocks that made the top three list over the three years tracked represent less than 10 percent of the total 13F portfolio value for the corresponding quarter; needless to say, they earned a weightage of 1. There were a few two-point baggers, but there were no takers for the weightage of 3 during the tracking period. There was significant churn in the top three positions in the first few quarters, but the weightages held steady at 1 till Q4 2009 (5/17/2010) when CIT Group (CIT) and Pfizer (PFE) both received a weightage of 2.

Table 16.3 David Einhorn's Largest Three Positions Model

(A)

Ticker	8/17/2009	11/16/2009	2/15/2010	5/17/2010	8/16/2010	11/15/2010	2/15/2011
BSX			$36,213				
CAH		$35,985		$20,581			
CFN		$35,985	$36,213				
CIT				$41,162	$50,656	$44,685	$40,716
ESV					$25,328	$44,685	$40,716
PFE	$33,333	$35,985	$36,213	$41,162	$25,328	$22,342	$40,716
TDC	$33,333						
URS	$33,333						
Total	**$100,000**	**$107,956**	**$108,638**	**$102,905**	**$101,311**	**$111,712**	**$122,147**

(B)

Ticker	5/16/2011	08/15/2011	11/15/2011	2/15/2012	5/15/2012	8/15/2012
AAPL	$41,476	$29,673	$62,746	$71,483	$73,048	$78,717
CIT	$41,476					
GM				$35,741	$36,524	
GDX			$31,373			
MSFT		$29,673	$31,373	$35,741		$39,359
PFE	$41,476	$59,346				
STX					$36,524	$39,359
Total	**$124,427**	**$118,692**	**$125,493**	**$142,965**	**$146,095**	**$157,434**

The portfolio progression point to below-par performance during the first year—returns as of 8/16/2010 were just above breakeven. The value of the three positions steadily increased for the next two quarters and, by 5/16/2011, the portfolio reached a total value of $124,427. With its vast outperformance, Apple Inc. (AAPL) shouldered the portfolio for the rest of the tracking period. The weightage ratio method was an improvement over the equal-allocation model in this case, as AAPL received double the allocation compared to the other two positions during the last four quarters: AAPL in Einhorn's portfolio was well over 10 percent, thus receiving a weightage of 2, while the other two positions remained at a weightage of 1.

As of 8/15/2012, the total value of the portfolio improved to $157,434 (excluding dividends) for a total return of 57.43 percent. The S&P 500 Index return during that time period was 43.46 percent.

Combined Portfolio: Largest Positions

Table 16.4 (A&B) illustrates the model portfolio, based on the largest position from each of the three managers with an inception date of August 17, 2009, and its progression over the next three years.

The columns display the portfolio allocation on the date indicated in the header row. The second column (8/17/2009) represents the initial allocation of the $100,000 portfolio across the largest three positions of Ackman, Buffett, and Einhorn per their Q2 2009 13F. The following columns depict the mechanics of the portfolio progression on a quarterly basis per the corresponding 13F on the date indicated in the header row after updates and rebalancing.

The second column in Table 16.4A shows a weightage ratio of 2:3:1 applied across Coca-Cola (KO), Target Corporation (TGT), and Pfizer Inc. (PFE) respectively. The percentage allocations of these stocks in the 13F portfolios of Buffett, Ackman, and Einhorn as of Q2 2009 were 19.61 percent, 43.28 percent, and 6.34 percent in that order. The positions and the allocation ratios continued for one more quarter. In Q4 2009, Einhorn's top pick shifted—PFE was replaced with CIT Group (CIT) without any weightage change. Buffett's top pick did

Table 16.4 Combined Model: Largest Positions

(A)

Ticker	8/17/2009	11/16/2009	2/15/2010	5/17/2010	8/16/2010	11/15/2010	2/15/2011
KO	$33,333	$39,477	$38,138	$42,193	$45,503	$47,619	$64,372
TGT	$50,000	$59,216	$57,207	$42,193	$45,503		
KFT						$47,619	$42,915
JCP		$19,739					
PFE	$16,667						
CIT				$28,129	$30,336	$31,746	
BSX			$19,069				
ESV							$21,457
Total	**$100,000**	**$118,431**	**$114,414**	**$112,515**	**$121,342**	**$126,984**	**$128,745**

(B)

Ticker	5/16/2011	8/15/2011	11/15/2011	2/15/2012	5/15/2012	8/15/2012
KO	$57,960	$43,993	$54,887	$55,586	$45,550	$66,359
JCP	$57,960	$43,993				
Fortune			$36,591			
CP				$55,586	$68,326	$66,359
PFE	$19,320	$29,329				
AAPL			$36,591	$37,057	$45,550	$44,239
Total	**$135,239**	**$117,314**	**$128,069**	**$148,229**	**$159,427**	**$176,958**

not change throughout the three-year tracking period. However, the allocation hovered around 20 percent, causing the weightage to shift between 2 and 3 several times. The essence of Ackman's concentrated portfolio was soundly captured by the model as almost all his top picks (except two) were awarded a weightage of 3; they consistently had an allocation well over 20 percent in the source portfolio. Einhorn's diversification translated to his top picks always having an allocation less than 20 percent. Accordingly, the picks from his portfolio had to be content with a weightage of 1 or 2.

The portfolio progression indicated steady growth for the most part. One major disappointment occurred in Q2 2011, when JCP dropped over 25 percent. JCP at that time had a weightage of 3 and the allocation was ~43 percent in the model. All told, the model dropped by over 13 percent that quarter. The last three quarters demonstrated a huge bounce back as the top picks of Ackman (Canadian Pacific: CP) and Einhorn (Apple Inc.: AAPL) posted handsome returns.

As of 8/15/2012, the total value of the portfolio improved to $176,958 (excluding dividends) for a total return of 76.96 percent. The S&P 500 Index return during that time period was 43.36 percent.

Combined Portfolio: Largest New Positions

Table 16.5 illustrates the model portfolio based on the largest new position from each of the three managers with an inception date of August 17, 2009, and its progression over the next three years.

The columns display the portfolio allocation on the date indicated in the header row. The second column (8/17/2009) represents the initial allocation of the $100,000 portfolio across the three largest new positions of Ackman, Buffett, and Einhorn per their Q2 2009 13F. The remaining columns depict the mechanics of the portfolio progression on a quarterly basis per the corresponding 13F on the date indicated in the header row after updates and rebalancing.

Similar to the equal allocation model described in the previous chapter, the updates to this model are also performed only annually

Table 16.5   Model of Largest New Positions on the Combined Portfolio

Ticker	8/17/2009	8/16/2010	8/15/2011	8/15/2012
COP	$28,571			
WMT		$17,289		
WFC			$21,231	
IBM				$64,417
EMC	$42,857			
KFT		$51,868		
JCP			$63,692	
PG				$64,417
PFE	$28,571			
CIT		$51,868		
S			$42,462	
STX				$21,472
Total	**$100,000**	**$121,025**	**$127,385**	**$150,305**

and are immediately rebalanced. To obtain a better weightage distribution, the mapping is adjusted as follows:

- Weightage 1, if the value of the new holdings for the largest <u>new</u> stock pick in the source portfolio is less than 5 percent of the corresponding 13F total portfolio value.
- Weightage 2, if the value of the new holdings for the largest <u>new</u> stock pick in the source portfolio is between 5 percent and 10 percent of the corresponding 13F total portfolio value.
- Weightage 3, if the value of the new holdings for the largest <u>new</u> stock pick in the source portfolio is over 10 percent of the corresponding 13F total portfolio value.

The initial allocations, as represented by the second column in Table 16.4, were to Buffett's ConocoPhillips (COP), Einhorn's Pfizer Inc. (PFE), and Ackman's EMC Corporation (EMC). Of these, COP and PFE received a weightage of 2 and EMC bagged a weightage of 3. The value of the new holdings for those picks in the portfolios of Buffett, Einhorn, and Ackman were 5.54 percent, 6.34 percent, and 33.89 percent respectively for Q2 2009. Throughout the tracking period, the largest new positions changed avatars and weightages with the value of the new holdings representing a very wide range, from 0.85 percent (Buffett's largest new position for Q2 2011) to 33.89 percent (Ackman's largest new position for Q2 2009).

As of 8/15/2012, the total value of the portfolio improved to $150,305 (excluding dividends) for a total return of 50.31 percent. The S&P 500 Index return during that time period was 43.46 percent.

Summary

The chapter demonstrated how to manage and mechanically maintain weighted allocation based model portfolios. In general, such portfolios are trade intensive, as in every quarter both the weightage and the positions involved can change. In the models used, all positions were tweaked after applying updates every quarter bringing the number of trades involved equal to the number of positions. The number of trades can be reduced by choosing to rebalance only if the weightages shifted between quarters.

For actual implementation of the models, a more granular weightage ratio should be considered. The allocation mapping for a five-term weightage ratio of 1:2:3:4:5 can be worked out as: Weightage 1 for less than 5 percent, 2 for between 5 percent and 10 percent, 3 for between 10 percent and 15 percent, 4 for between 15 percent and 20 percent, and 5 for over 20 percent portfolio allocations respectively in the original source portfolios. Such an allocation allows effective capture of the manager's sentiment when the source portfolio is diversified over many positions and when using a combined model with a group of managers.

The three single-manager weighted allocation models demonstrated credit-worthy outperformance during the three-year tracking period. While it is easy to be bowled over by the performance of these models, it is worth recollecting that single-manager portfolios carry risks. In fact, if these models were based on the portfolios of some of the other managers introduced in Part I, the performance would have been an eye opener. Specifically, over the time tracked, John Paulson and Prem Watsa had some terrible picks among their top-three positions, and the models would have picked up those selections, causing significant underperformance. Manager selection has a role in mitigating this risk, but it is very normal for even reputable managers that fit the criteria of having a value-oriented bottom-up investment approach to have periods of vast underperformance compared to the market indexes.

The combined model using the largest positions showed the best performance among the five portfolio progressions illustrated. Since there were only three positions in these minimalist models, a large variation in the stock price of one or more of those positions will immediately be reflected in the model. The performance can fluctuate easily as it is entirely possible for the positions to underperform over a tracking period. To cushion that blow, it is best to employ more positions in a real cloning model implementation.

The models illustrated how applying weightages to stock picks can approximate the source portfolio allocations. While the weighted allocation models succeed in capturing the largest positions, a downside is that the other large positions are completely unheeded by the model. This is true with the equal allocation based model as well. On the other hand, limiting the number of positions makes the management of the cloned portfolios simpler. Overall, such models are a very good tool by which to implement cloning strategies.

Chapter 17

Ten-Five-Two (10–5–2) Allocation Models

Ten-five-two (10–5–2) allocation models endeavor to shadow a manager's portfolio as diligently as possible. The numbers 10, 5, and 2 represent the recommended percentage allocations of individual positions in a well-diversified portfolio. To put this model in perspective, the allocation distribution for a reasonably sized portfolio of twenty positions would be: 10 percent for the three highest conviction positions, 5 percent for the next twelve positions, and 2 percent for the remaining five positions. For a healthier diversification, the number of positions at the upper end of the allocation spectrum is reduced and the number at the lower end is increased. For example, if the number of positions in the portfolio is increased to thirty, the allocation percentages of this model could be: 10 percent for the two highest conviction positions, 5 percent for the next eight, and 2 percent for the remaining 20 positions.

The model can be used as is, provided the total number of positions in the source portfolio is within the range of 20 to 40. The technique can be adapted to accommodate those portfolios whose position size lie outside this range by adhering to the same allocation ratio but varying the percentage values. For example, an option to model a portfolio with 60 positions would be to assign 5 percent to four of the highest conviction positions, 2.5 percent for the next 16, and 1 percent for each of the remaining 40 positions.

The chapter focuses on applying the model to the selections of the shortlisted three managers: Bill Ackman, Warren Buffett, and David Einhorn, and presenting their progression over the last three years. As this model aims to closely approximate the manager's source portfolio, a comparison with exactly cloned versions of the manager portfolios from their corresponding 13Fs is also included.

Portfolio Management and Performance Analysis

In keeping with the models in the prior chapters, the portfolio size and the inception dates are set at $100,000 and August 17, 2009 (first trading day following the deadline for filing 13Fs for Q2 2009) for these models too. The number of positions used in the models is directly related to the diversification of the source portfolio. This number in turn determines the allocation ratios. The updated values, as well as the progression of the portfolios, including rebalancing (45 days after every quarter) are captured in the tables given. Dividend income is ignored to provide a precise comparison with the S&P 500 Index performance.

The model provides some leeway, as it does not mandate the number of positions for each percentage allocation. The guideline merely calls for a very small number of highest conviction positions for the 10 percent allocation, a good number of high conviction positions for the 5 percent allocation, and the rest for the 2 percent allocation. The intent is to capture the quintessence of the whole portfolio by eliminating tiny positions irrelevant to performance. A good rule of thumb to decide on the number of positions with portfolios that are not too diversified is to use the number after eliminating those position sizes below 1.5 percent or so in the source portfolio. The models will use this guideline to decide on the number of positions.

The largest new positions of value-oriented manager portfolios generally do not parallel the allocation guidelines of the 10–5–2 allocation model. As such, the largest new positions-based portfolios are not suited for this model and will not be considered.

Bill Ackman

Bill Ackman, who runs the most concentrated portfolio of the three managers, had around nine as the average number of positions over the three-year tracking period. Ackman also had the smallest number of overall positions for any quarter; in Q2 2009, the portfolio had just six positions. The portfolio rarely had any allocations below 1 percent. Given these factors, seven was chosen as the number of positions for the model portfolio. As this number was outside the working zone of 20 to 40 positions for the 10–5–2 model, it was adapted to seven positions by distributing the assets at the same ratio. The distribution details of the adapted model are:

- The largest position was allocated 30 percent.
- The next four largest positions were allotted 15 percent each.
- The last two positions were given 5 percent.

The allocation ratio closely matched the 10:5:2 ratio although the smallest position in this allocation (30:15:5) is slightly lower than the recommendation (30:15:6) of the model.

Table 17.1 (A&B) illustrates the model portfolio with an inception date of August 17, 2009 and the progression for the next three years. The columns display the portfolio allocation on the date indicated in the header row after updates and rebalancing. The second column (8/17/2009) represents the initial allocation across Ackman's positions as of Q2 2009 13F, and the following columns depict the mechanics of the portfolio progression on a quarterly basis per the corresponding 13F.

As of Q2 2009 (08/17/2009), Target Corporation (TGT) received the highest allocation of 30 percent as it was the largest position in the

Table 17.1 Bill Ackman: Adapted 10–5–2 Model

(A)

Ticker	8/17/2009	11/16/2009	2/15/2010	5/17/2010	8/16/2010	11/15/2010	2/15/2011
ADP	$15,000	$17,250	$5,229		$17,650	$6,509	
Borders	$15,000	$5,750	$15,686				
C				$6,064	$17,650	$19,527	$20,529
CXW		$17,250	$15,686	$18,192	$5,883		
EMC	$15,000	$17,250					
Fortune						$6,509	$20,529
GGP				$18,192	$17,650	$19,527	$20,529
GM							$6,843
GLRE	$10,000	$5,750	$5,229				
H			$15,686				
KFT				$18,192	$17,650	$39,054	$20,529
Landrys				$6,064			
MCD	$15,000	$17,250					
JCP						$19,527	$41,058
TGT	$30,000	$34,500	$31,372	$36,383	$35,299	$19,527	$6,843
YUM				$18,192	$5,883		
Total	**$100,000**	**$114,999**	**$104,575**	**$121,277**	**$117,664**	**$130,181**	**$136,860**

166

(B)

Ticker	5/16/2011	8/15/2011	11/15/2011	2/15/2012	5/15/2012	8/15/2012
ALEX	$6,882					$7,257
BEAM				$21,490	$21,355	$21,772
CP				$42,980	$42,710	$21,772
C	$20,645	$17,685	$18,054	$7,163	$21,355	
FDO		$5,895	$6,018	$7,163		
FBHS					$7,118	
Fortune		$17,685	$36,108			
GGP	$20,645	$17,685	$18,054	$21,490	$21,355	$21,772
HHC	$6,882	$5,895				$7,257
KFT	$20,645	$17,685	$18,054	$21,490	$7,118	$7,257
LOW			$6,018			
JCP	$41,291	$35,369	$18,054	$21,490	$21,355	$21,772
PG						$43,543
Total	**$137,637**	**$117,897**	**$120,362**	**$143,266**	**$142,366**	**$145,143**

source portfolio. The next four positions—Automatic Data Processing (ADP), Borders, EMC Corporation (EMC), and McDonald's (MCD)—each received 15 percent of the assets. As Ackman only held six positions then, the last position, Greenlight Capital Re (GLRE), received 10 percent of the assets instead of the 5 percent recommended by the model. The next column (11/16/2009) indicates the portfolio progression after Ackman's Q3 2009 13F filing (after updates and rebalancing). This time around, as the source portfolio had seven positions, the assets were distributed per the model. Though Target Corporation (TGT) continued as the highest position, there was churn in a couple of other positions—Corrections Corp. of America (CXW), a new position, received a 15 percent allocation while Borders slipped from 15 percent to a 5 percent allocation.

The tactic behind the values assigned to positions in the remaining columns is very straightforward: The updated total value of the portfolio for the corresponding quarter is distributed among the seven largest positions per the allocation ratio. For example, for Q4 2009 (2/15/2010), the largest seven positions in decreasing order of size in the source portfolio were Target Corporation (TGT), Corrections Corp. of America (CXW), Hyatt (H), Landrys, Borders, Greenlight Capital Re (GLRE), and Automatic Data Processing (ADP). The updated total portfolio value of $104,575 was distributed across those positions at 30 percent, 15 percent, 15 percent, 15 percent, 15 percent, 5 percent, and 5 percent respectively.

As of 8/15/2012, the total value of the portfolio improved to $145,143 (excluding dividends) for a total return of 45.14 percent. The S&P 500 Index return during that time period was 43.46 percent.

Warren Buffett

Over the tracking period, Buffett held a diversified portfolio with around 35 positions on average. From a mimicking standpoint, a number of his minute positions (less than 1 percent allocation) can be categorized as noise. For the model, 14 was the favored number as that comprised most positions with an allocation above 1.5 percent. As this number was outside the operating zone of 20 to 40 for the 10–5–2 model, it was adapted to 14 positions by distributing the assets at the same ratio. The distribution is detailed here:

- The largest two positions were issued 15 percent each.
- The next eight largest positions 7.5 percent each.
- The last four positions 2.5 percent.

The allocation ratio of 15:7.5:2.5 matched the 10:5:2 ratio almost exactly, although the smallest positions were granted a slightly lower allocation compared to the recommendation (15:7.5:3) of the model.

Table 17.2 (A&B) illustrates the model portfolio with an inception date of August 17, 2009 and the progression for the next three years. The columns display the portfolio allocation on the date indicated in the header row after updates and rebalancing. The second column (8/17/2009) represents the initial allocation across Buffett's positions as of Q2 2009 13F, and the following columns depict the mechanics of the portfolio progression on a quarterly basis per the corresponding 13F.

The model portfolio remained remarkably steady over the three-year tracking period. Only 22 different positions had a role in the portfolio in the 12 quarters—given the portfolio size of 14, this meant that only eight new stakes were introduced over the three years. The allocation percentages also held fairly firm. The progression spreadsheet brought to light a limitation with the model whereby under certain rare scenarios allocations are changed unnecessarily between quarters: Wells Fargo (WFC) had the highest allocation of 15 percent from inception till Q2 2011. During Q3 2011, Buffett initiated a very large position in International Business Machines Corporation (IBM), whose position size overtook Wells Fargo (WFC) by a slight margin for that quarter. This margin, though slim, knocked Wells Fargo (WFC) from its 15 percent pedestal to a 7.5 percent one. The allocation maintained status quo for one more quarter, but in Q1 2012 things took a U-turn; the position size for Wells Fargo (WFC) marginally exceeded that of International Business Machines (IBM) in Buffett's portfolio and the allocations had to be reversed in the model.

As of 8/15/2012, the total value of the portfolio improved to $149,418 (excluding dividends) for a total return of 49.42 percent. The S&P 500 Index return during that time period was 43.46 percent.

Table 17.2 Warren Buffett's Adapted 10–5–2 Model

(A)

Ticker	8/17/2009	11/16/2009	2/15/2010	5/17/2010	8/16/2010	11/15/2010	2/15/2011
AXP	$7,500	$8,391	$8,401	$8,973	$8,325	$9,129	$9,788
BNI	$7,500	$8,391	$8,401				
KO	$15,000	$16,781	$16,801	$17,945	$16,650	$18,258	$19,577
COP	$7,500	$8,391	$8,401	$8,973	$8,325	$9,129	$9,788
COST							$3,263
JNJ	$7,500	$8,391	$8,401	$8,973	$8,325	$9,129	$9,788
KFT	$7,500	$8,391	$8,401	$8,973	$8,325	$9,129	$9,788
MTB				$2,991	$2,775	$3,043	$3,263
MCO	$7,500	$2,797	$2,800	$2,991	$2,775	$3,043	$3,263
NKE			$2,800	$2,991	$2,775	$3,043	
PG	$7,500	$8,391	$8,401	$8,973	$8,325	$9,129	$9,788
USB	$2,500	$2,797	$2,800	$8,973	$8,325	$9,129	$9,788
UNP	$2,500	$2,797					
WMT	$2,500	$8,391	$8,401	$8,973	$8,325	$9,129	$9,788
WPO	$2,500	$2,797	$2,800	$2,991	$2,775	$3,043	$3,263
WFC	$15,000	$16,781	$16,801	$17,945	$16,650	$18,258	$19,577
Wesco	$7,500	$8,391	$8,401	$8,973	$8,325	$9,129	$9,788
Total	$100,000	$111,874	$112,008	$119,634	$110,998	$121,722	$130,513

(B)

Ticker	5/16/2011	8/15/2011	11/15/2011	2/15/2012	5/15/2012	8/15/2012
AXP	$9,914	$9,309	$9,686	$10,183	$10,519	$11,206
KO	$19,828	$18,618	$19,371	$20,366	$21,037	$22,413
COP	$9,914	$9,309	$9,686	$10,183	$10,519	$11,206
COST	$3,305	$3,103	$3,229			
DVA				$3,394	$3,506	$3,735
DTV					$3,506	$11,206
IBM			$19,371	$20,366	$10,519	$11,206
JNJ	$9,914	$9,309	$9,686	$10,183	$10,519	$3,735
KFT	$9,914	$9,309	$9,686	$10,183	$10,519	$11,206
MTB	$3,305	$3,103	$3,229	$3,394		
MCO	$3,305	$3,103	$3,229	$3,394	$3,506	$3,735
PSX						$3,735
PG	$9,914	$9,309	$9,686	$10,183	$10,519	$11,206
USB	$9,914	$9,309	$9,686	$10,183	$10,519	$11,206
USG		$3,103				
WMT	$9,914	$9,309	$9,686	$10,183	$10,519	$11,206
WPO	$3,305	$9,309	$3,229	$3,394	$3,506	
WFC	$19,828	$18,618	$9,686	$10,183	$21,037	$22,413
Wesco	$9,914					
Total	**$132,184**	**$124,119**	**$129,143**	**$135,770**	**$140,248**	**$149,418**

David Einhorn

Einhorn ran a more actively traded portfolio with over 40 positions on the average over the tracking period. The number of long stock holdings during the timeframe exceeded over 120 different positions, although many of them were quite small (less than 1 percent allocation). Given the large number of overall positions and their allocations, at least 20 positions were required to do justice to his significant holdings. With 20 positions, the 10–5–2 model can be applied directly. For a genuine implementation of this model against Einhorn's portfolio, a higher number of positions should be preferred, but 20 was chosen here to keep the illustrations simpler.

- The largest three positions were apportioned 10 percent each.
- The next 12 largest positions 5 percent each.
- The last five positions 2 percent each.

Table 17.3 shows the model portfolio with an inception date of August 17, 2009. To keep the table from getting unwieldy, the data presented is limited to the first two quarters and the last two quarters. The columns display the portfolio allocation on the date indicated in the header row after updates and rebalancing. The second column (8/17/2009) represents the initial allocation across Einhorn's positions as of Q2 2009 13F, and the next column depicts the portfolio progression for the following quarter, per the corresponding 13F. The data for the next 11 quarters are given a miss and the last two columns present the data for Q1 2012 and Q2 2012.

The model portfolio had 57 different positions over the three years, while Einhorn's 13F holdings over that tracking period easily doubled that. The average churn between quarters was around six, which was high compared to the model portfolios based on the other two managers. The allocations also shifted significantly between quarters reflecting Einhorn's more active trading philosophy—none of the top three initial positions that had an allocation of 10 percent retained their top allocation through the three-year tracking period. Pfizer (PFE), which had the longest run, was eliminated in Q3 2011. Apple

Table 17.3 Snapshot of David Einhorn's 10–5–2 Model

Ticker	8/17/2009	11/16/2009	...	Ticker	5/15/2012	8/15/2012
FE	$5,000		...	AET		$2,978
AHL	$5,000	$5,527	...	AAPL	$13,555	$14,892
ADP		$2,211	...	AHL	$2,711	
CAH	$5,000	$11,054	...	BBY	$6,778	
CFN		$11,054	...	CFN	$6,778	
EMC	$5,000	$5,527	...	CBS	$6,778	$7,446
BAGL	$5,000	$5,527	...	CI		$7,446
RE	$5,000	$5,527	...	CVH		$7,446
GE	$2,000		...	DELL	$6,778	
HAR	$2,000		...	DLPH	$6,778	$7,446
HMA	$5,000	$2,211	...	BAGL	$6,778	$7,446
HNT		$2,211	...	ESV	$6,778	$7,446
HLX	$2,000		...	GM	$13,555	$7,446
PC Hldgs	$5,000		...	HCA	$2,711	
GDX	$5,000	$5,527	...	HUM		$2,978
MDT	$5,000	$5,527	...	HII	$2,711	
WFR	$5,000		...	LM	$2,711	
MI Devs	$2,000	$5,527	...	GDX	$6,778	$7,446
MSFT		$5,527	...	MRVL	$6,778	$7,446
PTEN	$2,000	$2,211	...	MSFT	$6,778	$14,892
PFE	$10,000	$11,054	...	NCR	$6,778	$7,446
TDC	$10,000	$5,527	...	STX	$13,555	$14,892
TRV		$5,527	...	S	$6,778	$7,446
URS	$10,000	$5,527	...	UNH		$2,978
VR		$2,211	...	VMED		$2,978
Wyeth	$5,000	$5,527	...	WLP		$2,978
			...	XRX	$2,711	$7,446
Total	**$100,000**	**$110,539**	...	**Total**	**$135,553**	**$148,915**

Inc. (AAPL), a presence in the portfolio for five consecutive quarters, is the largest position as of Q2 2012.

As 20 positions were used for this model, updating and rebalancing every quarter implied 40 trades every quarter. The trading level can be optimized by choosing to rebalance only those positions whose allocations changed between quarters. Compared to models based on Ackman's and Buffett's 13Fs, this model is trade intensive, as Einhorn's positions change quite frequently.

As of 8/15/2012, the total value of the portfolio improved to $148,915 (excluding dividends) for a total return of 48.92 percent. The S&P 500 Index return during that time period was 43.46 percent.

Summary

The chapter illustrated how to clone and mechanically maintain single-manager–based model portfolios using 10–5–2 allocation techniques. Trading requirements for such models were influenced by the number of positions and the trading philosophy (active vs. passive) of the source managers. The three selections used above showed a diverse range of trading requirements. Ackman's model won effortlessly in minimal trading requirements, followed by Buffett, then Einhorn. As these managers run relatively concentrated value-oriented portfolios, with optimized rebalancing, the number of trades required becomes very manageable, even in the case of Einhorn. Applying the model to more active portfolios that chalk up hundreds of positions can be overwhelming. While that may come across as a limitation, the purpose of the 10–5–2 model is to match the source portfolio performance as closely as possible. This is practical only by replicating most of the positions after eliminating the noise. It is to be expected that, if the source portfolio manager has an active trading style and deals with hundreds of positions, the cloned portfolio will also reflect some of that behavior.

The model portfolios demonstrated strong outperformance during the three-year tracking period. Single-manager risk is inherent with this model, since its purpose is to clone a single manager's picks. The risk can be cushioned to a certain extent by proper manager selection. It is a fact of life that even the best value-oriented bottom-up managers go through phases during which they vastly underperform the indexes. Realistically speaking, the best way to combat this threat is by being loyal to a selected manager for the very long term. For real-life implementations, funds set aside for very long-term investments are good candidates to use for this purpose.

The aim of these model portfolios was to faithfully clone the source-manager portfolio performance. The fact that the model portfolios also outperformed the index was a pleasant outcome. Table 17.4

Table 17.4 10–5–2 Model versus Exact Cloning Comparison

Manager/Model	8/17/2009	11/16/2009	2/15/2010	5/17/2010	8/16/2010	11/15/2010	2/15/2011
Ackman/10–5–2	$100,000	$114,999	$104,575	$121,277	$117,664	$130,181	$136,860
Ackman/Exact	$100,000	$118,530	$113,615	$129,455	$123,697	$134,977	$142,759
Buffett/10–5–2	$100,000	$111,874	$112,008	$119,634	$110,998	$121,722	$130,513
Buffett/Exact	$100,000	$112,821	$113,159	$120,383	$112,651	$123,053	$131,759
Einhorn/10–5–2	$100,000	$110,539	$109,649	$111,902	$105,194	$114,783	$131,163
Einhorn/Exact	$100,000	$115,820	$114,070	$116,864	$109,710	$119,993	$136,758

Manager/Model	5/16/2011	8/15/2011	11/15/2011	2/15/2012	5/15/2012	8/15/2012
Ackman/10–5–2	$137,637	$117,897	$120,362	$143,266	$142,366	$145,143
Ackman/Exact	$144,190	$125,633	$126,533	$148,762	$148,425	$149,344
Buffett/10–5–2	$132,184	$124,119	$129,143	$135,770	$140,248	$149,418
Buffett/Exact	$133,192	$125,432	$129,849	$137,032	$144,466	$150,429
Einhorn/10–5–2	$132,155	$121,870	$128,764	$138,917	$135,553	$148,915
Einhorn/Exact	$136,839	$123,137	$130,350	$139,938	$135,014	$147,078

displays how the models fulfilled their objective of cloning the manager portfolios exactly. It is a comparative spreadsheet that illustrates the portfolio progression of the models compared to a portfolio that exactly clones the manager picks.

The three cases show very similar progressions of the three model portfolios and their corresponding exact clones over the three-year tracking period. The point of maximum divergence for Ackman's holdings was in Q4 2009 (2/15/2010) at 8.65 percent—the total value for the exact model at that point was $113,615 compared to $104,575 for the 10–5–2 model. The divergence narrowed in the latter part of the tracking period and by Q2 2012 (8/15/2012), it had closed in to around 2.89 percent. For Einhorn, the maximum divergence occurred in Q2 2009 at 4.78 percent—the total value for the exact model was at $115,820 versus $110,539 for the 10–5–2 model. Here again, the divergence narrowed in the latter half of the tracking period. In fact, by Q2 2012 (8/15/2012), the 10–5–2 model pulled ahead, with a slight outperformance of 1.25 percent as the total value at that point came in at $148,915, compared to $147,078 for the exact model. The two models based on Buffett's 13Fs showed the least divergence as the two portfolios were neck and neck every quarter; the divergence was less than 1 percent throughout the tracking period. At the end of the tracking period, the difference in performance was a mere 0.67 percent.

Although the differences were too small to create a ripple, it is good to analyze the reasons for the divergence at certain points. Ackman not only runs a very concentrated portfolio but keeps outsized positions. This results in the portfolio not matching the diversification assumptions made by the model. During the first four quarters, Ackman's 13F portfolio had an average allocation to Target Corporation (TGT) of close to 50 percent, with the allocation exceeding a whopping 70 percent in Q4 2009. Also, during several quarters, just three positions accounted for over 90 percent of the assets. In the case of Einhorn's models, 20 positions were chosen for the 10–5–2 model for illustrative purposes, although the prudent choice would have been a higher number. This resulted in some of the significant positions not figuring in the model in certain quarters, thus accounting for the slight divergence.

Chapter 18

Alternate Models

Alternate models serve to address some of the limitations encountered while cloning a money manager's portfolio based on 13Fs. The ten-five-two (10–5–2) allocation model (introduced in the previous chapter) is a very viable option when attempting to closely clone manager portfolios. But, if the source portfolio does not fit the allocation assumptions inherent in the model, the resulting portfolio performance will show divergence from the source portfolio. Bill Ackman's portfolio implementation model in the last chapter demonstrated this drawback. An alternate model whose allocations match the source portfolio positions and eliminates the noise introduced by very small positions can fix this drawback. The first model in this section presents such a portfolio, using Bill Ackman's 13F positions as the source.

The 13F based models are suitable only for the domestic-equity portion of an overall asset allocation plan as those reports show only such positions. This chapter goes beyond 13Fs to explore models suitable for use in an overall asset allocation setting. Some of the renowned managers have recommended asset classes and distributions for individual investors. Model portfolios that use the suggested allocations can be constructed using very liquid exchange traded funds (ETF) and certain other index mutual funds. Reasonably priced, decidedly liquid, ETF options and/or index mutual funds are almost always available for this purpose. Such model portfolios are amazingly simple to maintain. As the allocation is static and only a small set of ETFs are involved, periodic rebalancing is a breeze. The ease of maintenance aptly earns such portfolios the nickname *lazy portfolios.* David Swensen endorses such an asset allocation plan for individual investors in his classic book, *Unconventional Success: A Fundamental Approach to Personal Investment.*[1] A model portfolio constructed using his recommendation with progression over the last five years is presented along with an analysis on how the portfolio holds up over different market cycles.

Asset allocation in lazy portfolios requires a fixed allocation among different asset classes. The focus is on diversifying among a set of asset classes with uncorrelated risk profiles. Although such portfolios reduce risk and offer something of a safety net in a bear market, they are not very suitable for generating good absolute returns; they underperform the averages in bull markets, while failing to provide good positive returns in bear markets.

Techniques that incorporate market sentiment (judging direction from historical prices) can be used to generate good absolute returns in all market conditions. The chapter presents two such models (based on David Swensen's recommended asset allocation) with their progression over the last five years. Their performance in different market conditions is analyzed to demonstrate the absolute returns possible with such portfolios. These techniques can be adapted in combination with domestic-equity long-only portfolios constructed from 13Fs to arrive at an asset allocation that is dynamic and suitable for all market conditions.

Portfolio Management and Performance Analysis

The exact match approximation model eliminates the clutter introduced by very small positions, while keeping the relative position sizes for the rest of the portfolio to match the source portfolio. The size of the model portfolio and the inception dates are set at $100,000 and August 17, 2009 (first trading day following the deadline for filing 13Fs for Q2 2009) respectively in keeping with the assumptions made in the domestic-equity models presented in previous chapters. The portfolio progression is assembled from Bill Ackman's 13Fs, as his 10-5-2 model showed the most divergence.

The rest of the alternate models use the same initial portfolio size of $100,000 but, to illustrate the portfolio performance during the bear market that started in the latter half of 2008, the inception date is pushed back to August 15, 2007. The performance analysis during the bear market helps assess the suitability of the models for overall asset allocation.

David Swensen's recommended asset allocation model uses his suggested allocation percentages and maps them to the most liquid index ETFs available in the market. It is to be remembered that the actual percentages recommended are more of an expert opinion than those based on any proven theory. The intention here is to diversify among asset classes that have little correlation among them; the allocation recommendations individually carry higher risk, but the overall risk is reduced, as they all do not move in one direction.

For the two models that incorporate market sentiment, Swensen's asset allocation is used. The caveat is that the resources are channeled equally among the asset classes that the models recommend regardless of the relative ratios suggested by Swensen. This is done mainly for illustrative ease. Besides, going with the recommended relative ratios does not create a huge variance in performance.

Rebalancing is done every quarter and dividends ignored in all portfolios.

Bill Ackman: Exact Match Approximation Model

The exact match approximation model poses no restriction whatsoever on the number of positions in the portfolio. In fact, the only criterion is to ensure that the resulting portfolio covers all the significant positions in the source portfolio. This is achieved by ignoring positions in the source portfolio that have an allocation below a certain percentage number. The cutoff can be based on covering over 90 percent of the 13F source portfolio value. The higher the coverage the better the match, but then the number of positions also increase.

For Ackman's 13Fs, the cutoff was set at 1.5 percent. With a portfolio as concentrated as his, the model will have a limited number of positions, even if the entire portfolio were cloned verbatim. Despite this, the 1.5 percent cutoff was chosen to illustrate the workings of the model. The relative sizes of positions in the model were kept at the same ratio as in the source portfolio after eliminating the small positions that do not fit the model.

Table 18.1 (A&B) illustrates the model portfolio progression over three years, starting with an inception date of August 17, 2009. The columns display the portfolio allocation on the date indicated in the header row after updates, eliminations, and rebalancing.

The second column in Table 18.1A represents the initial allocations made on 08/17/2009. Ackman's portfolio had, at that time, a 0.19 percent allocation on Greenlight Capital RE (GLRE). With the 1.5 percent cutoff in effect, the model eliminated that position. The 0.19 percent allocation was then distributed among the rest of the positions in the same ratio as the positions in Ackman's Q2 2009 13F. This is best explained with an example. In the source portfolio, as of Q2 2009, Automatic Data Processing (ADP) was allotted 11.34 percent. However, the model assigned it 11.36 percent (column 08/17/2009). The calculation involved is:

- The portion of the GLRE allocation that goes to ADP's bucket per the model: 0.19% * 11.34 %/(100 − 0.19%) = 0.02%.
- This 0.02% is then added to the 13F allocation to ADP to obtain the ADP allocation in the model: 11.34% + 0.02% = 11.36%.

By Q3 2009 (11/16/2009), the total size of the portfolio increased to $117,385. The model for that quarter had to reject GLRE (0.15 percent) and Borders (1.05 percent) from the source portfolio. The total portfolio ($117,385) was allocated among the rest of the positions in the same ratio as in Ackman's 13F to arrive at the allocations shown in column 11/16/2009. The steps were repeated in a similar fashion to determine the distributions for the remaining columns.

Table 18.1 Bill Ackman: Exact Match Approximation Model

(A)

Ticker	8/17/2009	11/16/2009	2/15/2010	5/17/2010	8/16/2010	11/15/2010	2/15/2011
ADP	$11,361	$9,216			$11,980	$12,429	
Borders	$1,723						
C					$19,820	$19,416	$17,265
CXW		$6,386	$22,087	$8,648	$7,508	$9,174	$4,887
EMC	$33,951	$38,325					
Fortune						$12,492	$25,020
GGP				$15,345	$11,429	$12,701	$26,983
GM							$6,601
HHC							$4,838
H			$6,785				
KFT				$39,492	$33,903	$28,982	$15,284
Landrys			$2,722				
MCD	$6,094	$18,037					
JCP						$14,515	$31,454
TGT	$46,871	$46,543	$82,728	$43,321	$36,588	$25,690	$11,085
YUM				$23,197	$2,679		
Total	**$100,000**	**$118,507**	**$114,323**	**$130,003**	**$123,907**	**$135,398**	**$143,418**

(*Continued*)

Table 18.1 (Continued)

(B)

Ticker	5/16/2011	8/15/2011	11/15/2011	2/15/2012	5/15/2012	8/15/2012
ALEX	$4,436	$3,380	$2,742		$3,249	$3,838
BEAM				$20,861	$22,436	$25,729
CP			$4,094	$31,970	$33,763	$35,004
C	$17,688	$19,297	$14,105	$13,441	$17,569	
FDO		$11,489	$12,206	$9,456	$3,045	
FBHS				$6,935	$5,410	
Fortune	$28,141	$21,573	$23,726			
GGP	$30,320	$23,753	$18,419	$21,221	$22,581	$25,843
HHC	$6,875	$4,572	$3,166	$3,083	$4,193	$4,350
KFT	$19,024	$15,431	$17,821	$15,463	$10,845	
LOW			$8,657			
JCP	$38,277	$26,592	$22,052	$26,865	$25,474	$18,014
PG						$36,708
Total	**$144,762**	**$126,087**	**$126,987**	**$149,295**	**$148,566**	**$149,486**

The small number of positions eliminated and the matching allocations made to the rest of the positions clearly signal that the resulting portfolio performance will closely tag the returns for a portfolio that exactly cloned Bill Ackman's 13F positions. As of Q2 2012 (08/15/2012), the model showed a total value of $149,486 compared to $149,344 for a portfolio that clones exactly. In fact, the largest divergence over the three-year period was less than $1000.

David Swensen: Asset Allocation Model

Swensen's asset distribution recommendation calls for the following allocation percentages:

- Domestic equity: 30 percent
- Foreign developed equity: 15 percent
- Emerging markets equity: 5 percent
- Real estate investment trusts (REIT): 20 percent
- U.S. Treasury Bonds: 15 percent
- Treasury inflation protected securities: 15 percent

Accordingly, the allocations are mapped to the following Exchange Traded Funds:

- Domestic equity: Vanguard Total Stock Market ETF (VTI)
- Foreign developed equity: Vanguard FTSE All-World ex-US ETF (VEU)
- Emerging markets equity: Vanguard MSCI Emerging Markets ETF (VWO)
- Real estate investment trusts (REIT): Vanguard REIT ETF (VNQ)
- U.S. Treasury Bonds: iShares Barclays 20+ Yr Treasury Bond ETF (TLT)
- Treasury inflation protected securities: iShares Barclays TIPS Bond Fund ETF (TIP)

Table 18.2 illustrates the model portfolio with an inception date of August 15, 2007 and its progression over the next five years. The columns indicate the portfolio allocation on the date indicated in the header rows (highlighted) after updates and rebalancing.

Table 18.2 David Swensen: Asset Allocation Model

Ticker	8/15/2007	11/15/2007	2/15/2008	5/15/2008	8/15/2008	11/17/2008	2/17/2009
VTI	$30,000	$31,249	$30,034	$32,124	$29,593	$20,675	$19,665
VEU	$15,000	$15,625	$15,017	$16,062	$14,796	$10,337	$9,833
VWO	$5,000	$5,208	$5,006	$5,354	$4,932	$3,446	$3,278
VNQ	$20,000	$20,833	$20,023	$21,416	$19,728	$13,783	$13,110
TLT	$15,000	$15,625	$15,017	$16,062	$14,796	$10,337	$9,833
TIP	$15,000	$15,625	$15,017	$16,062	$14,796	$10,337	$9,833
Total	**$100,000**	**$104,165**	**$100,114**	**$107,080**	**$98,642**	**$68,916**	**$65,551**

Ticker	5/15/2009	8/17/2009	11/16/2009	2/15/2010	5/17/2010	8/16/2010	11/15/2010
VTI	$22,038	$24,392	$27,351	$26,220	$28,171	$28,284	$30,114
VEU	$11,019	$12,196	$13,676	$13,110	$14,086	$14,142	$15,057
VWO	$3,673	$4,065	$4,559	$4,370	$4,695	$4,714	$5,019
VNQ	$14,692	$16,262	$18,234	$17,480	$18,781	$18,856	$20,076
TLT	$11,019	$12,196	$13,676	$13,110	$14,086	$14,142	$15,057
TIP	$11,019	$12,196	$13,676	$13,110	$14,086	$14,142	$15,057
Total	**$73,459**	**$81,308**	**$91,171**	**$87,401**	**$93,903**	**$94,281**	**$100,379**

Ticker	2/15/2011	5/16/2011	8/15/2011	11/15/2011	2/15/2012	5/15/2012	8/15/2012
VTI	$31,435	$32,291	$31,030	$31,650	$33,312	$33,090	$34,112
VEU	$15,717	$16,145	$15,515	$15,825	$16,656	$16,545	$17,056
VWO	$5,239	$5,382	$5,172	$5,275	$5,552	$5,515	$5,685
VNQ	$20,956	$21,527	$20,686	$21,100	$22,208	$22,060	$22,741
TLT	$15,717	$16,145	$15,515	$15,825	$16,656	$16,545	$17,056
TIP	$15,717	$16,145	$15,515	$15,825	$16,656	$16,545	$17,056
Total	**$104,782**	**$107,636**	**$103,432**	**$105,499**	**$111,040**	**$110,301**	**$113,707**

As the portfolio consisted of a static list of six ETFs held at a steady allocation over five years, rebalancing every quarter required only minor adjustments to the six positions; as the total value of the portfolio changed from quarter to quarter, position sizes were increased or decreased to retain the recommended allocation.

During the three-year period (from August 17, 2009), the model appreciated from $81,308 to $113,707 for a total return of 39.85 percent. Even though the return underperformed the S&P 500 index, which had a return of 43.46 percent (increased from 979.73 to 1405.53), it was not a surprise, as the portfolio had a significant bond allocation of ~30 percent. Unlike Swensen's equity-oriented Yale portfolio, for reasons best known to him, his recommendation for individual investors has significant bond allocation.

During the five-year period (from August 15, 2007), the model improved in value from $100,000 to $113,707 for a total return of 13.71 percent. This compares favorably to the S&P 500 index which was flat for the period. At the low point of the bear market (2/17/2009), the model was down almost 35 percent. The only saving grace was that the S&P 500 index put on an even more dismal show, as it dropped from 1406.7 to 789.17, for a loss of almost 44 percent.

In general, the portfolio progression exhibits some protection from drawdowns in bear markets: The trade-off is that, in bull markets, the portfolio is likely to underperform compared to the S&P 500 index. The drawdowns during bear markets make the model unsuitable for an overall asset allocation plan focused on achieving absolute returns. Swensen's recommended portfolio for individual investors is beneficial only for passive investors; if the individual investor is ready to take on a more active role, there is potential for improvement.

Sector Rotation Model

Sector rotation, a timing model, attempts to trail market trends by allocating assets dynamically to a small subset of the market sectors. At any given time, certain sectors outperform, while others remain flat or underperform. The model endeavors to make allocation shifts periodically, as positive trends are recognized. In short, the approach can be considered a mechanical equivalent of George Soros's trading philosophy, as the idea is to identify trends and conduct trades to profit from them.

David Swensen's asset allocation recommendations from the previous section are used to construct this model, too. Trend-following strategies invariably involve heavy trading when the strategy is implemented based on technical triggers. The model uses a variation that evaluates trends in the individual asset classes every quarter and allocates assets equally among the two best-performing asset classes from the previous quarter. The strategy is to shadow the recently outperforming asset classes by allocating assets exclusively to them every quarter. Obviously, the disadvantage is the loss of diversification benefits.

Table 18.3 shows the model portfolio with an inception date of August 15, 2007, and the progression over the next five years. The model implementation is really simple as only two positions are maintained during any given quarter; two buy/sell trades are all that is necessary.

At inception (8/15/2007), the best performing asset classes for the quarter ending 8/15/2007 were foreign developed equity (VEU) and Treasury inflation protected securities (TLT). Those ETFs were flat during that quarter, while the funds representing the rest of the asset classes showed negative returns. Accordingly, the $100,000 initial portfolio value was equally distributed among those two positions. By the next quarter (11/15/2007), the portfolio increased in value to $102,486. The two best performing asset classes for that quarter were emerging markets equity (VWO) and US Treasury bonds (TLT). The existing positions (VEU and TLT) were liquidated, and the funds realized were equally distributed between TLT and VWO. The same procedure was used for the following 18 quarters to work out the allocations for the rest of the columns.

During the three-year period from August 17, 2009, the portfolio increased in value from $103,442 to $149,447, for a total return of 44.47 percent. The returns were satisfactory, for it marginally beat the 43.46 percent return of the S&P 500 index for the same period. Over the five-year period from August 15, 2007, the portfolio increased in

Table 18.3 Sector Rotation Model

Ticker	8/15/2007	11/15/2007	2/15/2008	5/15/2008	8/15/2008	11/17/2008	2/17/2009
VTI							
VEU	$50,000		$48,432	$51,058			
VWO		$51,243					
VNQ			$48,432	$51,058			
TLT		$51,243			$44,239	$42,662	$45,991
TIP	$50,000				$44,239	$42,662	$45,991
Total	**$100,000**	**$102,486**	**$96,864**	**$102,116**	**$88,478**	**$85,324**	**$91,982**

Ticker	5/15/2009	8/17/2009	11/16/2009	2/15/2010	5/17/2010	8/16/2010	11/15/2010
VTI				$59,105	$61,678		
VEU	$44,491						
VWO	$44,491	$51,721	$62,444			$59,080	$59,886
VNQ		$51,721	$62,444		$61,678		
TLT							
TIP				$59,105		$59,080	$59,886
Total	**$88,983**	**$103,442**	**$124,888**	**$118,210**	**$123,357**	**$118,160**	**$119,772**

Ticker	2/15/2011	5/16/2011	8/15/2011	11/15/2011	2/15/2012	5/15/2012	8/15/2012
VTI	$60,002			$69,924	$72,679		
VEU							$74,724
VWO							$74,724
VNQ	$60,002	$61,269	$65,591	$69,924	$72,679	$73,809	
TLT		$61,269	$65,591			$73,809	
TIP							
Total	**$120,003**	**$122,538**	**$131,181**	**$139,848**	**$145,357**	**$147,618**	**$149,447**

value from $100,000 to $149,447, for a total return of 49.45 percent. It handsomely beat the S&P 500 index, which was flat during that time frame. Even on an absolute basis, the five-year total return was respectable, considering the bear market during the early part of that period.

The model's performance from inception to the lowest point during the bear market, which was 02/15/2009, reveals its strength. The model lost only around 8 percent since inception at that point, compared to a stunning 44 percent loss for the S&P 500 index. There was little correlation between the returns of the model and that of the index; the low point for the model portfolio was Q3 2008 (11/17/2008) when it showed a loss of ~15 percent, compared to a ~40 percent loss for the S&P 500 index.

Simple Moving Average (SMA) Based Model

Moving averages are technical indicators used to identify bullish and bearish trends. Several variations exist but the underlying concept is the same—compare the current prices to prices of the positions over a period of time to identify trends. Two such popular averages are the Simple moving average (SMA) and the exponential moving average (EMA). In SMA the comparison relies on a simple average of the prices over a time-period, whereas in EMA the more recent prices are given more weightage. The 200-day SMA, one of the simplest such indicators, is the mainstay among technical traders. Its trading strategy in a nutshell is—if the position considered is above the 200-day SMA, go long, else liquidate the position and stay in cash.

A variation of the 200-day SMA based trading strategy that eliminates cash allocation is the root for this model. It applies the 200 day SMA to the asset classes recommended by David Swensen. As his recommendations are diversified and non-correlated, allocating assets among the identified longs is a better option than staying in cash. At inception, the model studies the 200 day SMA and gauges whether to go long on any of the six ETF positions. The $100,000 portfolio is then equally distributed among those assets identified as worthy of going long. At the end of each quarter, the rule is invoked again to decide which positions to go long in the following quarter. The assets are again distributed across the longs identified.

Table 18.4 shows the model portfolio with an inception date of August 15, 2007, and the progression over the next five years. The model implementation was very straightforward and the average number of positions per quarter was around three. The number of trades necessary to maintain the model quarterly is also fairly low.

At inception (8/15/2007), as only Vanguard MSCI Emerging Markets ETF (VWO) and iShares Barclays TIPS Bond Fund ETF (TIP) traded above its 200-day SMAs, the $100,000 portfolio was equally distributed among those two positions. By the next quarter (11/15/2007), the portfolio size swelled to $116,806 mainly due to a splendid ~30 percent return in VWO. As of 11/15/2007, in addition to these two existing positions iShares Barclays 20+ Year Treasury Bond Fund ETF (TLT) also traded above its 200-day SMA. Therefore, the portfolio assets were distributed among those three positions for the next quarter. The rest of the columns show the allocations for the subsequent quarters by applying the same procedure.

During the three-year period from August 17, 2009, the portfolio improved in value from $124,578 to $166,136, for a total return of 33.36 percent. The returns were not great because it underperformed the 43.46 percent return of the S&P 500 index during the same period. Over the five-year period from August 15, 2007, the portfolio increased in value from $100,000 to $166,136 for a total return of 66.14 percent. Now, this performance is stunning, as the S&P 500 index was flat during this timeframe.

This model showed stellar performance during the bear market that started in 2008. From inception to the lowest point for the S&P 500, which was on 02/15/2009, it returned 21.16 percent. The portfolio delivered very good absolute returns in the face of a bear market that saw drawdowns of 44 percent in the S&P 500 index. Here again, the returns are not correlated to the index return as the low point for the model was Q1 2009 (05/15/2009 column) when the model portfolio showed a positive return of 12.49 percent compared to ~37 percent loss for the S&P 500 Index.

Table 18.4 Simple Moving Average (SMA) Based Model

Ticker	8/15/2007	11/15/2007	2/15/2008	5/15/2008	8/15/2008	11/17/2008	2/17/2009
VTI							
VEU	$50,000			$23,550			
VWO		$38,935		$23,550			
VNQ			$37,836	$23,550			
TLT		$38,935	$37,836	$23,550	$106,751	$109,677	$121,162
TIP	$50,000	$38,935	$37,836	$23,550			
Total	**$100,000**	**$116,806**	**$113,507**	**$117,749**	**$106,751**	**$109,677**	**$121,162**

Ticker	5/15/2009	8/17/2009	11/16/2009	2/15/2010	5/17/2010	8/16/2010	11/15/2010
VTI		$24,916	$28,717	$34,110	$36,938		$30,726
VEU	$37,496	$24,916	$28,717	$34,110			$30,726
VWO	$37,496	$24,916	$28,717	$34,110	$36,938	$37,286	$30,726
VNQ		$24,916	$28,717	$34,110		$37,286	$30,726
TLT					$36,938	$37,286	
TIP	$37,496	$24,916	$28,717		$36,938	$37,286	$30,726
Total	**$112,488**	**$124,578**	**$143,584**	**$136,438**	**$147,754**	**$149,144**	**$153,628**

Ticker	2/15/2011	5/16/2011	8/15/2011	11/15/2011	2/15/2012	5/15/2012	8/15/2012
VTI	$39,746	$32,419			$32,888	$40,858	$27,689
VEU	$39,746	$32,419					$27,689
VWO	$39,746	$32,419			$32,888		$27,689
VNQ	$39,746	$32,419			$32,888	$40,858	$27,689
TLT			$76,361	$81,405	$32,888	$40,858	$27,689
TIP		$32,419	$76,361	$81,405	$32,888	$40,858	$27,689
Total	**$158,985**	**$162,095**	**$152,721**	**$162,811**	**$164,441**	**$163,433**	**$166,136**

Summary

The mechanical models introduced in this chapter presented a medley of portfolios suitable for different situations. Bill Ackman's 13F portfolio was used to demonstrate the effectiveness of the exact match approximation model when it comes to cloning manager portfolios with concentrated positions but seemingly random allocations. The rest of the chapter presented model portfolios appropriate for use with an overall asset allocation plan as opposed to just the domestic-equity portion.

David Swensen's asset allocation recommendation based portfolio progression over the three- and five-year periods demonstrated the strengths and weaknesses of lazy portfolios. The model underperformed the S&P 500 index during the three-year period, but showed a decent positive return for the five-year period when the S&P 500 Index remained flat. During the bear market, the portfolio outperformed the S&P 500 Index despite losing a third of its value.

Lazy portfolios are a very popular strategy among individual investors and this field is also swarmed with different recommendations. Rather than their demonstrated ability to generate good absolute returns, it is their ease of implementation that makes such portfolios a popular choice. They are good options only for individual investors seeking to invest on their own in a largely passive manner. The lazy portfolios use fixed allocations to the different equity and debt options, thereby recommending a diversified mix for distributing the assets. Although the diversification provides some protection against bear markets, it is not enough to provide good absolute returns.

The final two portfolios employed David Swensen's asset allocation recommendations but technical indicators decided the positions to go long in a given quarter. Overall, the results from these portfolios were quite agreeable in most market conditions. During the bear market, when the S&P 500 index experienced drawdowns in the 45 percent range, these portfolios significantly outperformed the index—that too, with positive returns during that timeframe. The excellent returns over the 3-year and 5-year timeframes demonstrated the potential of such portfolios to generate good absolute returns independent of market conditions.

The earlier chapters in Part Two, covered choices to construct cloned portfolios based on one or more manager's 13F positions. A carefully chosen mechanical model from the ones presented is a good choice for the domestic-equity portion of asset allocation for individual investors; such portfolios tend to outperform the market indexes, especially over the long term. Manager selection and model selection based on the investing styles of the managers involved are both central when following this approach.

For generating respectable absolute returns in an overall asset allocation setting, a strategy that combines a set of asset allocation choices with recommendations from a market-timing tactic is a marvelous option. The latter two models presented in this chapter are superb in that regard, given their relative ease of implementation and potential for good absolute returns. Even when using a mechanical cloning model for the domestic-equity portion of one's assets, a variation of the market timing strategy is a good route to consider. The market timing strategy mandates how much to allocate to each portion of the overall asset allocation mix. The portion of the total assets slated for the domestic-equity portion (implemented using the mechanical cloning model) for a particular time period is mandated by the market timing method. The size of the mechanically cloned portfolio is adjusted every quarter, based on the mandated asset allocation mix. The implementation of the strategy involves more trades: All positions are to be adjusted proportionally depending on the change to the domestic-equity portion of the asset allocation. Though the approach adds a little more complexity, it should be well worth the extra effort.

Note

1. David Swensen, *Unconventional Success: A Fundamental Approach to Personal Investment* (New York: Free Press, A Division of Simon & Schuster, 2005).

Part Three

LEARNING FROM THE MASTERS

Chapter 19

Introduction

S trategies for picking stocks and size positions from money manager trades and their investing techniques are the focus of Part Three. The techniques employed are a little bit more involved than the models presented so far. The mechanical models in Part Two work well for individual investors who prefer to stay relatively passive; they can still expect to realize superior long-term returns by adhering to proper manager and compatible model selection.

There are techniques that can be applied to the 13F stock picks to filter positions on the basis of money manager bias. Some models in Part Two charted this course to arrive at model portfolios based on filtering for the largest new positions. Obviously, those models were price-neutral, as they factored neither the price at which the manager traded, nor the price when the information became public. This is a glaring risk, as the purchase price of the stock involved in the model portfolio can be like apples and oranges from the manager's actual traded prices due to the time lag (i.e., the time period from when the manager traded the stock and when that information became public through a 13F filing). The actual time can vary anywhere from 45 days (if the trade was on the last day of the previous quarter) to as long as four-and-a-half months (if the trade was on the first day of the previous quarter). Many a proverbial slip lurks in that duration, in fact, more so with volatile stocks. Appraising price information is a way to optimize the entry and exit points of a stock pick. This approach calls for more analysis but the process is definitely worthwhile for it is a chance to trade positions at better prices than the manager.

The time of entry for stock picks from 13Fs can be optimized by monitoring a set of other regulatory SEC filings:

- **Schedule 13D and 13G:**[1] SEC filing requirements call for beneficial owners acquiring more than 5 percent of a voting class of a security to file one of these forms within ten days of such activity. The regulation applies to all securities registered under Section 12 of the Securities Exchange Act of 1934. 13G is an abridged version of 13D—passive investors holding between 5 percent and 20 percent of the security concerned can opt to file 13G instead of 13D. Material changes to the facts in the schedule require filing an immediate amendment.[2]
- **Forms 3, 4, and 5:**[3] Corporate insiders are required to file one or more of these forms periodically after they become affiliated with a company registered under Section 12 of the Securities Exchange Act of 1934.[4] Corporate insiders cover company officers, directors, and more than 10 percent owners.
  - Form 3 is the initial form required to be filed with the SEC, and that, too, within the ten days of a corporate insider becoming affiliated with a registered company. Also, when a company is registered under Section 12, Form 3 must be filed by all corporate insiders prior to the effective date of the registration statement.
  - Corporate insiders are required to file Form 4 (statement of ownership), when there is a material change in the ownership within two business days of the transaction that resulted in the change of ownership. Buy/sell activity in the open market along with company stock options activity are covered in this form.

- Form 5 is an annual filing to report transactions that are exempt from the Form 4 filing. It is due within 45 days after the company's fiscal year end.

From the perspective of tracking money managers, these forms cover only a fragment of their holdings and trading activity. For an activity to appear in one of these forms, ownership of more than 5 percent of the company's outstanding shares is required. Even so, monitoring these forms has certain advantages over monitoring 13F activity:

- **The information reported is very timely**: If the ownership in the company involved is between 5 and 10 percent, the 13D or 13G reports the activity within 10 days of the associated transaction. If it exceeds 10 percent ownership, Form 4 reports the activity within two days of the transaction, making the information even more valuable.
- **High conviction positions get reported**: As the reports are compulsory if the money manager owns more than 5 percent of the outstanding shares, by their very nature, the activity usually points to the manager's highest conviction positions.

These regulatory filings can also be a sign of activist involvement. Monitoring such filings can be particularly productive when applied against managers who specialize in activist investing. In general, their large ownership stakes in public companies are a means to effectively sway the executives and the board. As such positions are reported almost immediately in regulatory filings, it is possible to achieve very similar prices to those of the manager. There are a couple of caveats with this approach:

- With some of the celebrated activist managers, a price spike is inevitable as soon as the position is disclosed through regulatory filings. Giving a few days for the price to settle is a worthwhile plan to limit the damage, and
- Manager selection is critical; even with the best activist managers, there are no guarantees. Not all activist campaigns are successful, although the best managers have good track records.

The chapter introduces techniques to pick stocks from 13Fs by gauging pricing information and by analyzing corporate insider (Forms 3, 4, and 5) and beneficial owner (13D and 13G) regulatory filings.

Beating the Managers at Their Own Game

Arming oneself with a manager bias spreadsheet is the initial step towards developing a strategy to attain better pricing for money manager stock picks. The variables to be considered are:

- **Manager selection**: The short-listed managers from Part Two are used for these illustrations: Bill Ackman, Warren Buffett, and David Einhorn.
- **Assessing bullish/bearish bias**: The latest activity can be determined by comparing the positions in the 13F for the latest quarter with the same for the previous quarter. The bias is drawn out by filtering significant trading activity, via cutoffs, based on the size of positions and the size of the trades during the quarter relative to the overall 13F portfolio size.

Table 19.1 presents a bias spreadsheet that compares the 13Fs for Q2 2012 of the three managers with the corresponding 13Fs for Q1 2012. To capture this bias information, the positions were filtered using the following criteria:

- For a position to be considered, it should be, at minimum, 2 percent of the portfolio as of that quarter. This searches for trading activity among the significant positions.
- Only those positions that were increased or decreased by at least 1 percent of the portfolio were considered. This condition screens for positions that saw significant trading activity.

The relatively larger number of entries in this table is due to David Einhorn's frequent trading. Among the filtered positions, only Procter & Gamble (PG) had multiple showings. It was traded in opposite directions by Bill Ackman and Warren Buffett; Ackman added a very large position, while Buffett trimmed his position significantly. Given Buffett's proclivity for holding on to his larger positions over the very

Table 19.1   Bill Ackman, Warren Buffett, David Einhorn: Manager Bias Q2 2012

Holding	Manager	% Stake Q2 2012	% Stake Q1 2012	% Stake Traded in Q2 2012	Bias
C	Bill Ackman	0.40%	11.83%	(11.33%)	Bearish
FDO	Bill Ackman	0.00%	2.05%	(2.05%)	Bearish
FBHS	Bill Ackman	0.00%	3.64%	3.64%	Bearish
KFT	Bill Ackman	0.00%	7.30%	7.30%	Bearish
PG	Bill Ackman	24.46%	0.00%	24.46%	Bullish
JNJ	Warren Buffett	0.94%	2.54%	(1.64%)	Bearish
PG	Warren Buffett	4.91%	6.54%	(1.22%)	Bearish
BBY	David Einhorn	0.40%	3.30%	(2.78%)	Bearish
CFN	David Einhorn	1.86%	4.88%	(2.73%)	Bearish
CI	David Einhorn	4.46%	0.00%	4.46%	Bullish
CVH	David Einhorn	3.34%	0.00%	3.34%	Bullish
DELL	David Einhorn	0.00%	3.59%	(3.59%)	Bearish
HUM	David Einhorn	2.01%	0.00%	2.01%	Bullish
GDX	David Einhorn	4.24%	6.51%	(1.13%)	Bearish
MRVL	David Einhorn	4.55%	5.22%	1.29%	Bullish
MSFT	David Einhorn	6.10%	4.36%	2.49%	Bullish
STX	David Einhorn	9.04%	7.08%	3.37%	Bullish
UNH	David Einhorn	2.11%	0.00%	2.11%	Bullish
XRX	David Einhorn	3.22%	2.25%	1.32%	Bullish

long term, the significant stake reduction indicates a clear bearish bias. Ackman, on the other hand, initiated an activist stake to force operational changes in the company. When following multiple managers, conflicting trades needs further scrutiny.

Buying and selling based solely on a bias table also runs the risk that the pricing achievable may not have any bearing on what the manager attained. In most instances, by the time the information becomes public through the 13F, the stock will be trading at a very different price, making for incomparable entry/exit points with the manager's traded price. Analyzing the price to make buy/sell decisions can alleviate this problem. Table 19.2 is the bias spreadsheet expanded, with columns that indicate the price range the manager traded at and the price as of the date the latest trades became public (08/17/2012). The highlighted rows specify those positions that gave the public an edge over the manager's traded price range.

Table 19.2 Bill Ackman, Warren Buffett, David Einhorn: Manager Bias
Expanded with Pricing

Holding	Manager	% Stake Traded in Q2 2012	Bias	Traded Price Range Q2 2012	Price as of 08/15/2012
C	Bill Ackman	(11.33%)	Bearish	$24.82–$36.87	$28.74
FDO	Bill Ackman	(2.05%)	Bearish	$62.82–$73.26	$63.82
FBHS	Bill Ackman	3.64%	Bearish	$20.15–$24.04	$23.68
KFT	Bill Ackman	7.30%	Bearish	$36.87–$39.87	$40.70
PG	Bill Ackman	24.46%	Bullish	$59.27–$67.56	$66.64
JNJ	Warren Buffett	(1.64%)	Bearish	$61.78–$67.56	$68.35
PG	Warren Buffett	(1.22%)	Bearish	$59.27–$67.56	$66.64
BBY	David Einhorn	(2.78%)	Bearish	$18.02–$23.64	$19.36
CFN	David Einhorn	(2.73%)	Bearish	$23.98–$27.09	$26.79
CI	David Einhorn	4.46%	Bullish	$42.58–$49.43	$43.86
CVH	David Einhorn	3.34%	Bullish	$29.03–$35.00	$32.72
DELL	David Einhorn	(3.59%)	Bearish	$11.86–$16.77	$12.21
HUM	David Einhorn	2.01%	Bullish	$74.53–$91.85	$67.72
GDX	David Einhorn	(1.13%)	Bearish	$39.34–$50.37	$44.15
MRVL	David Einhorn	1.29%	Bullish	$11.02–$15.88	$11.94
MSFT	David Einhorn	2.49%	Bullish	$28.45–$32.42	$30.20
STX	David Einhorn	3.37%	Bullish	$21.74–$32.21	$34.11
UNH	David Einhorn	2.11%	Bullish	$53.99–$60.26	$52.82
XRX	David Einhorn	1.32%	Bullish	$6.94–$8.15	$7.24

As the filters are designed to be on the lookout for high conviction positions trading at a better price compared to the managers' trades, the resulting dataset may be too small or empty at times. In the bias spreadsheet for Q2 2012, only four of the nineteen positions traded at a better price than the manager's trading range. Even so, the information is hugely valuable, as it identifies better trading opportunities.

Two of Einhorn's stake increases in Q2 2012 offered better prices when the information became public (08/15/2012) through his 13F filing: Humana Inc. (HUM) at almost 10 percent below the low end of the Q2 2012 price range and UnitedHealth Group Inc. (UNH) at slightly below the low end of the Q2 2012 price range. Similarly, Kraft

Foods Inc. (KFT) and Johnson & Johnson (JNJ) offered better disposal opportunities than those at which Ackman and Buffett trimmed theirs.

Trading based on a bias spreadsheet works hand in hand with a strategy that buys/sells based on one or both of the long and short opportunities identified in that table. To take advantage of both the long (bullish bias) and short (bearish bias) opportunities, a long/short model is ideal but, for this illustration, a simpler long-only model is used. The strategy scans the 13Fs for significant stake increases using the following criteria:

- The position size must have been at least 2 percent of the portfolio in the quarter identified by the 13F (in Table 19.1).
- The position size must have improved by at least 1 percent of the portfolio (in Table 19.1).
- Scan for positions trading below the low end (within 1 percent) of the price range during the quarter.
- Retain the positions until the source manager sells a stake greater than 1 percent of the 13F portfolio value.

Table 19.3 shows the performance of the positions purchased using only the long opportunities identified from manager bias spreadsheets. For Seagate Technology (STX) and Sprint (S), where the Sale Date column shows NA, the strategy calls to hold on to the positions as of Q2 2012. The price as of 08/15/2012 was used for calculating the returns for those holdings.

Scanning the 13Fs of the three managers over the last three years using the filter criteria yielded only seven positions. Applying the strategy to a larger group of managers is one way to address the dearth of opportunities. The criteria can also be adjusted to net positions trading below the manager's price point at any time after the trade information becomes public. The approach is more involved, as constant surveillance is essential to isolate potential opportunities. The 13Fs have to be monitored as well for a shift in bias.

The filtered positions show very encouraging signs in terms of performance, for the most part; only Boston Scientific (BSX) posted negative returns and that by a very modest percentage. The performance of the remaining positions ranged from 11.26 percent (over six months) for Family Dollar (FDO) to a whopping 184.01 percent

Table 19.3 Bill Ackman, Warren Buffett, David Einhorn: Manager Bias Based Strategy

Holding	Manager	Purchase Date	Purchase Price	Sale Date	Sale Price	Percentage Return
CXW	Bill Ackman	2/15/2010	$19.57	2/15/2011	$25.01	27.80%
ADP	Bill Ackman	8/16/2010	$40.07	2/15/2011	$49.55	23.66%
FDO	Bill Ackman	8/15/2011	$50.27	2/15/2012	$55.93	11.26%
JNJ	Warren Buffett	8/16/2010	$58.01	2/15/2012	$64.65	11.45%
BSX	David Einhorn	2/15/2010	$7.39	5/17/2010	$6.81	(7.85%)
STX	David Einhorn	8/15/2011	$12.01	NA	$34.11	184.01%
S	David Einhorn	11/15/2011	$2.92	NA	$5.39	84.59%

(over a year) for Seagate Technology (STX). As for overall performance, equally sized positions over the time frames indicated would
have posted a total return of 47.85 percent. Given the average holding
period of the selections was 9.4 months, the annualized return would
have been a striking 61.09 percent.

Trading Alongside the Managers

Corporate insider (Forms 3, 4, and 5) and beneficial owner (13D and
13G) regulatory filings offer timely information when a manager takes
a sizable (>5 percent) ownership stake in a stock. The size of the stake
relative to the overall manager portfolio is not carried in the filing,
but the information can be derived from the latest 13F portfolio total
value. An educated purchase decision can be made by combining these
two pieces of information. A similar strategy as was used in the previous section can help with the sell decision: Sell a position when the
manager sells a stake greater than 1 percent of the 13F portfolio value.
The chief benefit compared to strategies that solely depend on 13F
data is the prospect of trading manager positions very close to their
trading timeline; with that reduced time delay, the odds of achieving
a price range similar to that which the manager attained are increased.

The strategy monitors corporate insider (Forms 3, 4, and 5) and
beneficial owner (13D and 13G) filings for a selected set of managers.
When a new stake is reported, the latest 13F is compared to determine
how large the new stake is, relative to the overall size of the 13F portfolio. To be considered for purchase, the following criteria are to be met:

- The total stakes (new and any existing stakes reported in the latest
  13F) must add up to more than 2 percent of the 13F portfolio total
  value. This nets significantly large positions that have the potential
  for positive portfolio impact.
- The new stake size should be 1 percent or more of the latest 13F
  portfolio total value. This confirms sizable trading activity in the
  position concerned.

Table 19.4 shows the performance of positions purchased using
this plan. The sale date for Fortune Brands is Various, as it was split

Table 19.4 Corporate Insider and Beneficial Ownership Filings Based Strategy

Holding	Manager	Regulatory Filing	Purchase Date	Purchase Price	Sale Date	Sale Price	Percentage Return
BNI	Warren Buffett	Form 3	4/6/2007	$81.18	2/15/2010	$100.00	23.18%
TGT	Bill Ackman	SC 13D	7/16/2007	$68.89	2/15/2010	$48.64	(29.39%)
Long's Drug Stores	Bill Ackman	SC 13D	8/5/2008	$48.56	10/30/2008	$71.50	47.24%
JCP	Bill Ackman	Form 3	10/8/2010	$32.49	NA	$23.67	(27.15%)
Fortune Brands	Bill Ackman	Form 3	10/8/2010	$51.00	Various	$83.02	62.78%
HHC	Bill Ackman	Form 3	11/19/2010	$42.23	NA	$64.24	52.12%
ALEX	Bill Ackman	SC 13D	3/31/2011	$45.65	NA	$55.28	21.10%
CP	Bill Ackman	SC 13D	10/28/2011	$64.57	NA	$84.38	30.68%

into Fortune Brands Home & Security Inc. (FBHS) and Beam Inc. (BEAM). Ackman significantly reduced his stake in FBHS during Q1 2012, but held steady his stake in BEAM. For the percentage return calculation, the stock price of FBHS ($23.62 on 05/15/2012) was added to the stock price of BEAM ($59.40 on 08/15/2012) to arrive at the sale price. Long's Drug Stores was acquired by CVS Caremark Corporation (CVS) at $71.50 per share in cash and that became the sale price, and the closing date of the transaction (10/30/2008) ended up as the sale date. The sale date for JC Penney (JCP), Howard Hughes Corporation (HHC), Alexander & Baldwin Inc. (ALEX), and Canadian Pacific Railway Limited (CP) is listed as NA, as the strategy calls for holding on to those stocks. For the percentage return calculation for those holdings, the sale price was taken as the price as of 08/15/2012.

Predictably, all the positions in the table except one came from Ackman's portfolio. This is because the strategy works very well against activist managers, as their stakes tend to be well ahead of the 5 percent cut-off for the beneficial owner regulatory filings (13D and 13G) and, in many cases, they acquire positions well above the 10 percent cut-off for the corporate insider regulatory filings (Forms 3, 4, and 5). Among the stock picks in Table 19.4, four came from Schedule 13D beneficial ownership filings, while the other four came from Form 3 corporate insider filings.

The selected stakes in the table gave respectable performances overall. However, two positions posted negative returns: Target Corporation (TGT) showed negative 29.39 percent, while JCPenney (JCP) returned negative 27.15 percent. The former is acknowledged as one of Ackman's rare activist investment failures, and the latter is yet to play out completely, although his position was also under water as of the date of the percentage return calculation (8/15/2012). The performance of the rest of the positions ranged from 21.10 percent over a 16-month period for Alexander & Baldwin (ALEX) to 62.78 percent over a 19-month period for Fortune Brands. In terms of overall performance, equally sized positions over the timeframes indicated would have posted a total return of 22.57 percent. Given that the average holding period of the selections was 19.5 months, the annualized return would have been 13.88 percent.

Summary

The chapter introduced the concept of money manager bias spreadsheets, and illustrated their use to unveil opportunities to trade stocks at better prices than those that the managers themselves achieved:

- **Manager bias spreadsheet:** The 13Fs from Q2 2012 of the three managers were used to illustrate the construction of a bias spreadsheet. This spreadsheet was then expanded to include price points the manager traded at and the price when the information became public. The exercise identified opportunities to trade at better price points compared to those that the manager achieved.
- **Performance analysis:** The approach was used for the portfolios of the three managers over the last three years to demonstrate its effectiveness. The ability to trade stocks at better price points compared to the manager trades has a very attractive ring to it, but a comparatively larger group of managers need to be followed for it to succeed when it comes to portfolio construction.

A strategy to use a set of beneficial ownership and corporate insider regulatory filings to trade stocks at almost the same timeline as the money managers involved was also introduced:

- **Beneficial ownership and corporate insider filings:** The beneficial ownership filings (Schedule 13D and 13G) disclose trading activity within ten days of managers taking more than a 5 percent ownership stake in a company while the corporate insider filings (Forms 3, 4, and 5) disclose trading activity within two days of managers initiating a more than 10 percent ownership stake. They offer very timely information, which allows individual investors an opportunity to trade alongside the managers.
- **Performance analysis:** The performance of stocks picked using this approach for the filings of the three selected money managers over the last few years were analyzed. While the performance was respectable, opportunities were minimal, as only activist managers favored stakes so large that they mandated disclosure in the filings. As such, the method is most suited for activist manager portfolios.

The next step in the evolution of an individual investor is learning the techniques the best money managers employ and applying them to one's own portfolio. That sets one on the road to being a super investor! The rest of the book presents primers on stock selection and position sizing, based on the techniques the super investors use.

Notes

1. U.S. Securities and Exchange Commission, "Schedule 13D," www.sec.gov/ answers/sched13.htm, 04/04/2008.

2. U.S. Securities and Exchange Commission, "Exchange Act Sections 13(d) and 13(g) and Regulation 13D-G Beneficial Ownership Reporting," www .sec.gov/divisions/corpfin/guidance/reg13d-interp.htm, 11/16/2009.

3. U.S. Securities and Exchange Commission, "Forms 3, 4, 5," www.sec.gov/ answers/form345.htm, 09/07/2011.

4. U.S. Securities and Exchange Commission, "Exchange Act Section 16 and Related Rules and Forms," www.sec.gov/divisions/corpfin/guidance/ sec16interp.htm, 08/11/2010.

Chapter 20

Fundamental Analysis

Whn it comes to selecting stocks, the best money managers bank on fundamental analysis. Countless articles, books, and courses have been devoted to this very extensive topic. The chief objective is to examine the publicly available facts about businesses to project their future performances. The outcome of this study helps one make educated judgment calls: fair value estimate (FVE), future price projections, analysis of potential credit risk, and so on. The data points used in fundamental analysis gleans information from or about:

- Historical and latest financial facts, such as quarterly and annual financial statements for public businesses
- Executives and boards of directors
- Competitors, along with their strengths and weaknesses
- Competitive advantages, such as patents and brands
- Target markets
- Industry in which the company operates
- The overall economy

Evaluating each of these items to compile future performance pro-jections is a monumental undertaking, but investors need not be fazed. There are tools aplenty. The two basic approaches are top-down and bottom-up analysis.

1. Top-down: From the overall economy, industries and markets with the best prospects are determined, and the top businesses among them chosen.
2. Bottom-up: Stocks are selected based on individual business merit, and underweights any analysis of the broader market conditions.

Before forging ahead, it is best to take a breather and explore why money managers are such avid fans of fundamental analysis. Efficient market hypothesis (EMH) asserts that it is impossible to consistently outperform average market returns on a risk-adjusted basis, as the markets are efficient. The Nobel Prize winning work, modern portfolio theory (MPT) and capital asset pricing model (CAPM) forms the seminal research in this area:[1]

- MPT emphasizes the benefits of diversification when constructing an investment portfolio.
- CAPM describes the relationship between nondiversifiable risk, risk-free rate, and expected return in terms of a single variable Beta (β), where β is a measure of correlated volatility of the asset compared to the overall market as a whole.

CAPM cautions against diversifiable risk, as it is not rewarded with a higher return. In the context of a portfolio, this can be achieved by carefully combining assets that cancel out the diversifiable risk. Despite its elevated standing, CAPM is not without faults. It can account for only about 70 percent of returns. Moreover, β is not a good measure of nondiversifiable risk, as it overlooks the macro environment, business fundamentals, and current price. Efforts to extend CAPM to account for the remaining 30 percent of the returns have been decidedly mixed:

- The Fama-French Three Factor Model incorporated measures for two other factors into the CAPM formula, which succeeded in explaining 90 percent of the returns.[2] The model was based on the observation that value stocks (those with a high book-to-market ratio), and small-cap stocks were among those stocks that have traditionally shown excess returns. This finding was later refuted as the historic outperformance was attributed to the assumptions made about the type of stocks and the nature of their trades, not to their ability as a group to provide excess returns without a corresponding increase in nondiversifiable risk. For value stocks, studies showed value trumped growth over short holding periods (up to a few years) while the reverse was true for longer-term holding periods.[3] Similarly, a study of small-cap stocks (1981) presented evidence that the CAPM model was off on its specifics, as a non-linear size effect on returns over at least 40 years was observed.[4] Later studies further stoked suspicion as to whether a small-cap premium actually existed.[5]

• An array of multifactor models have appeared since, each attempting to provide the right mix of factors to explain the unaccounted returns in CAPM. Success eluded them all.

The inability to pinpoint precisely the reason for a sizable portion of the returns nails the fact that significant inefficiencies exist in the market, and that excess returns are available to stock pickers. Indeed, this is the area that many of the best managers focus on to create good absolute returns!

Value investing, a fundamental analysis-based philosophy, is the quest to identify stocks that are trading at a large discount from their intrinsic values. A sizable percentage of contemporary investment gurus have stamped their seal of approval on this approach and many among them are firm believers in the bottom-up methodology. The core ideas on value investing were first conceived by Benjamin Graham and David Dodd, and were presented in their classic investment book *Security Analysis* (1934).[6] This book is regarded as the bible of value investing.

Money manager bias spreadsheets, insider ownership, corporate insider filings, and so on, provide the investor with the advantage of realizing price points better than, or very close to, that which the manager paid. The downside, though, is that it does not offer insight as to why a money manager might be trading a particular position. A way to second guess the manager would be to partake in a value-oriented fundamental analysis exercise. The chapter focuses on the techniques the best managers are known to employ, and investors attempting to shadow them surely stand to benefit from doing an analysis based on these methods.

Margin of Safety

Benjamin Graham and David Dodd coined this phrase in 1934 to describe value investing, and defined it as the difference between intrinsic value and market price. Intrinsic value can be estimated by fundamental analysis. Purchasing securities with a good margin of safety allows safeguarding capital, should an estimate prove erroneous. Preservation of capital is crucial to value investing. Normal to frothy market conditions rarely make it easy for value investors to snag securities with a reasonable margin of safety. They, therefore, are left holding cash. While the concept of investing in securities with a margin of safety is easy to grasp, there are obstacles in following through and implementing the strategy:

- For the margin of safety to have validity, there needs to be confidence in the intrinsic value estimate. This can be achieved only through thorough fundamental research into the securities involved. Obviously, this calls for a significant time commitment; it takes experience to excel in this sort of analysis.
- Staying on the sidelines until opportunities materialize is easier said than done. Holding significant cash based on market conditions is a hard concept for most individual investors to digest, as they instinctively reason their money isn't working, as though it is akin to the familiar stuffed money under the mattress.
- Arriving at what is a reasonable margin of safety is more art than science. The type of security plays a large role; the objective of capital preservation can be achieved with a lower margin of safety when purchasing stable growing businesses compared to lower-quality issues.

Although substantial impediments exist when it comes to successfully investing with a good margin of safety, the techniques can be applied at different levels, based on experience. For investors new to value investing, a foolproof option would be to purchase securities of high-quality businesses (a back of the envelope definition would be steady dividend payments over ten years or so). Preserving capital is easier to achieve this way, more of a sandbox approach while getting to speed on intrinsic value estimates. Committing capital only when finding those securities that offer a respectable margin of safety (10 percent to 15 percent for high-quality issues) can do wonders to a portfolio's performance; patience is indeed a virtue. An investor is better off erring on the side of conservative intrinsic value estimation when starting out. That translates to holding on tightly to one's cash until a clear opportunity arises, following an overall market correction. In any given year, corrections upward of 3 percent occur often, but its frequency decreases as the percentage figure increases.

Fundamental analysis is by definition imperfect, for not all facts about a security are made public. In addition, unavailable information often causes a security to trade at a lower price; waiting for the uncertainty to pass can cost investors the opportunity to invest with a margin of safety. Therefore, fundamental analysis should be regarded as a quest to obtain a reasonably accurate intrinsic value estimate with the available information, rather than seeking the absolutely accurate intrinsic value. Better fund managers wait patiently for a market correction before deploying capital on a large scale. They also scout meticulously for securities mispriced by the market. Situations where mispricing of securities is prevalent include:

- **Spin-offs**: Institutional investors are inclined to dispose of such securities, as they do not fit into the general scheme of mutual fund investment philosophy. Besides, the information is time delayed; stock-selection screens do not acknowledge these securities immediately after the spin-off. These factors can lead to a significant margin of safety in the wake of the spin-off. Small-cap spin-offs generally get very little spotlight but, regrettably, sometimes management is responsible for this intentional anonymity: Stock options received as part of the spin-off can have the unfortunate side effect of management being incentivized to keep the first day's trading price low, as the exercise price is usually the first day's closing price. Spin-off through a rights offering can sometimes result in the rights trading at a discount to its value. *Rights* *offering* is an option for original shareholders to keep their relative ownership intact after the transaction. The rights end up trading at a discount, as the original shareholders may not be motivated to commit more capital for purchasing the new entity. A recent example best illustrates this: Sears Holdings (SHLD) conducted a spin-off of Sears Hometown Outlet Stores (SHOS) through a rights offering in mid-2012, whereby SHLD holders received the right (SHOSR) to purchase 0.218091 shares of SHOS at $15 per share. During the period till the spin-off date, the rights traded in the $2.50 price range on the average, implying a market price of $2.50*1/0.218091+$15=$26.46. SHOS started trading at around $30 in early October netting a quick 10 percent profit for anyone who exercised the right. The lack of interest in SHOSR kept the rights prices down, allowing an opportunity to invest with a margin of safety.

- **Liquidations**: There occur situations in which management decides the best course to adopt for a business is to liquidate its assets and return the equity to shareholders. Such announcements can cause the stock to slide due to certain behavioral factors: demand for such issues decrease as some prefer investing in ongoing businesses, while others shy away, given the uncertainties regarding the value that will be realized and the timing of the process. The lack of demand sometimes opens up a margin of safety for value investors to exploit.

- **Dividend eliminations**: Businesses generally reduce or eliminate dividends when they are in dire need of preserving cash, which is usually a sign that the business is going through some sort of distress. Dividend eliminations can cause the alienation of an entire class of shareholders who rely on dividend income. Consequently, it is not unusual for the shares to sink significantly in the days and months following a dividend elimination announcement. The price plunge can, in turn, open a margin of safety.

- **Window dressing**: Many mutual funds are famous for replacing stocks that had large losses with stocks that showed recent outperformance as they approach the end of the quarter/year. It is a familiar tactic to misguide prospective shareholders: The quarterly reports to shareholders show the mutual funds as holding outperforming securities instead of positions with losses. The activity can result in stocks that underperformed during the quarter to further dip by the end of the quarter, offering value investors a margin of safety.

- **Insider hints**: Significantly large net insider buys can point to securities that have a margin of safety. The idea is to follow the smart money; while insiders can sell for any reason, they buy significant stakes in the open market if and only if they can hear the charging bull.

- **Acquisitions, thinly traded securities, businesses in distress, and so on**: Huge margins of safety may lurk in these areas but, to unearth them, very specialized skills are required. It is best to tread with caution. A relatively safe opportunity can materialize in the risk-arbitrage area with respect to large announced acquisitions. The spread can still be attractive, despite professional arbitrage traders vying for the same pie.

For investing in mispriced securities to be worthwhile, the margin of safety also needs to be fairly high. Successful investments in such opportunities is a consequence of the accuracy of intrinsic value estimates—as the estimates get better with experience, the chance of success increases.

Basic Checklist

Those responsible for complex tasks appreciate the safety net that checklists offer. Checklists have figured in areas in which the tasks are so complex that great attention to detail and teamwork are required to complete them successfully. Missing an item can be disastrous. (Examples include aviation safety[7] and hospital safety,[8] emergency care, surgery, etc.). Checklists ensure that all pieces of the puzzle are accounted for. They have since been adapted for use in many industrial operations to limit errors and to mitigate risk of negligence lawsuits (the checklist is evidence of following proper procedure in such situations).

In the investment arena, fundamental analysis is a complex and imperfect process in which the game is won by those who make fewer mistakes overall. A checklist can better conceptualize the nature of the business. It can also help prevent mistakes induced primarily due to one's inherent emotional flaws. For example, it is a confirmed theory that whenever the market crashes, mutual fund redemptions increase and inflows go down and vice-versa. This bizarre phenomenon occurs because humans are wired to flee from distress.

The items that should constitute a basic investment checklist can be divided into several categories, each of which is a series of checklist items. For most of the items, the financials and other publicly available information of the business have to be studied at some level; supporting documentation can be used to substantiate them. Once completed, going through the checklist should clearly indicate the basic characteristics of the investment. Unlike checklists employed in other industries, there are no standard investment checklists; money managers who do use them consider them a competitive advantage and hence are hesitant to make the details public.

Presented here is a basic starter checklist divided into several categories.

Business Understanding

This category is aimed at filtering out businesses that are just too complicated to correctly arrive at an investment decision.

- ❑ The business is easy to follow.
- ❑ The business is comfortably contained within my circle of competence.
- ❑ Understands just how the business brings in revenue.
- ❑ The business operation does not entail highly specialized skills.

Business Sector and the Company's Standing

This set seeks to capture a clear picture of the sector the company operates in and its standing within that sector.

- ❑ Identify the type of business.
  - ❑ Cyclical
  - ❑ Cutting edge with excellent growth prospects
  - ❑ Stable growth
  - ❑ Mature
  - ❑ Declining
  - ❑ Financials
  - ❑ Large intangible asset–laden
- ❑ The sector has good growth prospects.
- ❑ The company has good prospects for growth in market share.

- ❏ Understands the overall impact of inflation on the business.
- ❏ General awareness of the impact of recession on the business.
- ❏ The company is among the top players in the industry.
- ❏ The products have pricing power.
- ❏ The company constantly introduces innovative and improved products.
- ❏ The business has the flexibility to demand better pricing from suppliers.
- ❏ Current operational requirements can be met with minimal spending.

Management Integrity and Competency

As management has the power to increase shareholder value, their integrity and competency is critical.

- ❏ Executives are honest.
- ❏ Management interest is aligned with that of the shareholders.
- ❏ Executive biography displays an impressive track record.
- ❏ Executive compensation is reasonable.
- ❏ Employee stock options and compensation are tied to individual performance.
- ❏ Management is competent.
- ❏ Management prefers organic growth over expensive acquisitions.
- ❏ Executives have demonstrated a keen interest in showing strong shareholder returns in the form of dividends and share buybacks.

Valuation

No matter how glorious a business is from a value investment perspective, allocating capital makes sense only if it is trading at a good discount to fair value.

- ❏ Discern the intrinsic value of the business with a high degree of confidence.
  - ❏ Downside is minimal, as the margin of safety is substantial.
- ❏ The business has one or more competitive advantages (moats).
  - ❏ The moats are strong, and should provide consistent earnings growth.

❑ Temporary tailwinds were not a factor in the business results.
❑ Temporary headwinds lowered the business results.
❑ Awareness of the current state of the industry within the business cycle (cyclical businesses only).
    ❑ Overall outlook of the industry
    ❑ General market trends that affect the company
    ❑ Current financials indicate boom-time numbers
    ❑ Current financials indicate midcycle numbers
    ❑ Current financials indicate depressed numbers
❑ Intangible assets generate respectable returns.
❑ The business has no significant regulatory constraints.
❑ The asset base of the business is relatively safe (financials only).
❑ The business maintains a capital buffer well above regulatory requirements (financials only).
❑ The company's bonds are trading near par value while the stock has crashed.
❑ Identify the business leverage.
    ❑ Refinancing schedule is manageable.
    ❑ Debt covenants are reasonable.
❑ Catalysts that can lift the share price exist.

Emotional Stance

Every investment has an emotional element associated with it. This can be gauged only from the behavioral aspects of an investor.

❑ Know whether the investment is at least partly speculative.
    ❑ Capital allocation is such that portfolio impact will be minimal even if the stock dips to zero.
    ❑ The best scenario is a return of multiple times the money allocated.
❑ Know the course to pursue (if any), should the stock drop 50 percent.
❑ Confidence level on this investment is high.
❑ Know the bias that can affect judgment.

The objective of a checklist is to gather an overall picture of the characteristics of the business. It should also offer hints as to how to value the business and the reasons behind money manager positions in the business. No business is expected to score on all items but, from a portfolio construction perspective, better diversification can be achieved if some effort goes into ensuring that the same items are not checked for all holdings.

Quantitative Measures

Quantitative measures focus on presenting an overall financial picture of the business. Conceptually, it is similar to a basic checklist, as they too pull together a clearer picture about the business.

The primary methods employed are indicator ratios and rating/scoring. These numeric values fall within a set range of values, and indicate the company's standing with respect to a composite metric. Composite measures typically evaluate several key financial data points before making an intelligent guess about the suitability of investing in a company based on criteria including bankruptcy risk, downside protection, upside potential, and so on. The section introduces several key measures that the best money managers are known to use.

Profitability Indicators

Profitability indicators are exactly that. They aim to paint an overall picture of how profitable the business is. Key indicators and characteristics are:

- **Return on equity (ROE)**: The ratio of net income to average shareholder's equity expressed as a percentage. The average for businesses is ~12 percent; upward of 30 percent over the last five years or so would be considered excellent.
- **Return on assets (ROA)**: The ratio of net income to total assets expressed as a percentage. Since ROA is regarded as a relative profitability measure, the figure should be compared with the sector average and the company's own historical track record. A rule of thumb would be to filter for numbers above 5 percent, although for financial companies that number can be much lower.

Table 20.1 Profitability Indicators (IBM)

Measure	Value	Source/Formula
Net Income (NI)	$15,855,000,000.00	2011 Income Statement
Shareholder's Equity (SE)	$20,138,000,000.00	2011 Balance Sheet
Total Assets (TA)	$116,433,000,000.00	2011 Balance Sheet
Debt Liabilities (DL)	$31,322,000,000.00	2011 Balance Sheet
Return on Equity (ROE)	78.73%	$ROE = NI \div SE$
Return on Assets (ROA)	13.62%	$ROA = NI \div TA$
Return on Capital Employed (ROCE)	30.81%	$ROCE = NI \div (DL + SE)$

- **Return on capital employed (ROCE)**: The ratio of net income to debt liabilities and shareholder's equity. ROCE measures the returns achieved on the capital employed to run the business. Ensure this figure is well above the company's net borrowing rate.

Table 20.1 displays these indicators for International Business Machines (IBM). From 2011, Buffett started investing a large portion of Berkshire Hathaway's investment portfolio in IBM. The indicators suggest that Buffett must have been well and truly impressed with IBM's profitability.

Management Effectiveness

Effective management is vital to the success of businesses over the long term. Value investing stresses a long-term focus, and measures to indicate management effectiveness are a key part of the research undertaken by the best value-oriented managers. Indicators and their characteristics in this area include:

- **Return on retained earnings (RORE)**: The measure of the increase in earnings from retained earnings over a period of time expressed as a percentage. Double-digit RORE over a period of five years or so are favorable values.
- **Cash conversion cycle (CCC)**: The measure of the average number of days required for the business to convert its inventory into cash. It is calculated by subtracting the days payable outstanding

Table 20.2 Management Effectiveness (IBM): Return on Retained Earnings
(A) and Cash Conversion Cycle (B)

(A)

Measure	Value	Source/Formula
Cumulative Earnings Per Share (CEPS$_5$): 2007–2011	$50.63	2007–2011 Income Statements
Cumulative Dividends Per Share (CDPS$_5$): 2007–2011	$11.40	2007–2011 Income Statements
Cumulative Retained Earnings (CRE$_5$): 2007–2011	$39.23	$CRE_5 = CEPS_5 - CDPS_5$
2011 Earnings Per Share (EPS$_{2011}$)	$13.06	2011 Income Statement
2007 Earnings Per Share (EPS$_{2007}$)	$7.15	2007 Income Statement
Increase in Earnings Per Share (IEPS$_5$): 2007–2011	$5.91	$IEPS_5 = EPS_{2011} - EPS_{2007}$
Return on Retained Earnings (RORE)	**15.07%**	$RORE = IEPS_5 \div CRE_5$

(B)

Measure	Value	Source/Formula
Cost of Sales per Day (CSD)	$155,556,164.38	2011 Income Statement: Cost of Sales/365
Average Inventory (AI)	$2,523,000,000.00	2010 & 2011 Balance Sheets: (BOY Inventory + EOY Inventory)/2
Days Inventory Outstanding (DIO)	16.22	$DIO = AI \div CSD$
Net Sales per Day (NSD)	$292,920,547.95	2011 Balance Sheet: Net Sales/365
Average Accounts Receivable (AAR)	$28,893,000,000.00	2011 Balance Sheet: (BOY Accounts Receivable + EOY Accounts Receivable)/2
Days Sales Outstanding (DSO)	98.64	$DSO = AAR \div NSD$
Average Accounts Payable (AAP)	$7,283,500,000.00	2011 Balance Sheet: (BOY Accounts Payable + EOY Accounts Payable)/2
Days Payable Outstanding (DPO)	46.82	$DPO = AAP \div CSD$
Cash Conversion Cycle (CCC)	**68.03**	$CCC = DIO + DSO - DPO$

from the days inventory outstanding and days sales outstanding. The lower the CCC, the better, but the number can vary widely across business sectors. For example, a pure point-of-sale retail outlet will have very low CCC (few days) while a manufacturing business will have a much higher number (few months). A low CCC compared to the competition is an indication of the business being managed well, while an increasing trend in CCC is a clear red flag.

Table 20.2 (A&B) presents the return on retained earnings (RORE) and cash conversion cycle (CCC) calculations for IBM. As illustrated, the base numbers are taken directly from the balance sheets and income statements. RORE over the last five years for IBM was very strong at over 15 percent, indicating that management was very successful in using retained earnings effectively. CCC for 2011 came in at 68.03 days. To get a good feel for this measure, a competitive comparison of CCCs, along with how the number progressed over the years, needs to be performed.

Liquidity Indicators

In worst-case scenarios, a liquidity crunch can throw a monkey wrench in the business by forcing it into bankruptcy. Liquidity indicators clues one in on how prepared a business is to pay its debt and other bills now and in the future. Key indicators and characteristics include:

- **Current ratio (CR):** The ratio of total current assets to total current liabilities, and indicates the ability of a business to fulfill its short-term obligations. Confirm CR is above 1.5.
- **Quick ratio (QR):** The ratio of cash and equivalents, short-term investments, and accounts receivable to total current liabilities. QR is similar to CR, but more conservative, as it ignores the less liquid assets such as inventory, prepaids, etc., from the numerator. Make certain QR is above 1.
- **Altman Z-score (AZS):** A composite measure used to predict bankruptcy. The original formula, specific to manufacturing companies, used multiple financial ratios to obtain a numeric value

Table 20.3 Liquidity Indicators (IBM): Current Ratio and Quick Ratio (A) and Z-score (B)

(A)

Measure	Value	Source/Formula
Current Assets (CA)	$50,928,000,000.00	2011 Balance Sheet
Current Liabilities (CL)	$42,126,000,000.00	2011 Balance Sheet
Cash & Equivalents (CE)	$11,922,000,000.00	2011 Balance Sheet
Short-term Investments (STI)	$0.00	2011 Balance Sheet
Accounts Receivable (AR)	$29,561,000,000.00	2011 Balance Sheet
Current Ratio (CR)	**1.21**	$CR = CA \div CL$
Quick Ratio (QR)	**0.98**	$QR = (CE + STI + AR) \div CL$

(B)

Measure	Value	Source/Formula
Current Assets (CA)	$50,928,000,000.00	2011 Balance Sheet
Current Liabilities (CL)	$42,126,000,000.00	2011 Balance Sheet
Total Assets (TA)	$116,433,000,000.00	2011 Balance Sheet
Retained Earnings (RE)	$104,857,000,000.00	2011 Balance Sheet
Earnings Before Interest & Taxes (EBIT)	$21,003,000,000.00	2011 Income Statement
Book Value of Equity (BVE) Shareholder's Equity	$20,138,000,000.00	2011 Balance Sheet
Total Liabilities (TL)	$96,297,000,000.00	2011 Balance Sheet
First Z-score Component Ratio (Z_1)	0.08	$Z_1 = (CA - CL) \div TA$
Second Z-score Component Ratio (Z_2)	0.90	$Z_2 = RE \div TA$
Third Z-score Component Ratio (Z_3)	0.18	$Z_3 = EBIT \div TA$
Fourth Z-score Component Ratio (Z_4)	0.21	$Z_4 = BE \div TL$
		$\mathbf{Z = 6.56 \times Z_1 + 3.26}$ $\mathbf{\times Z_2 + 6.72}$ $\mathbf{\times Z_3 + 1.05}$
Z-Score (Nonmanufacturing)	**4.86**	$\mathbf{\times Z_4}$

indicating the likelihood of bankruptcy. Since then, the work has been enhanced to apply to nonmanufacturing businesses as well. The result relates to one of three zones: safe zone (above 2.6), gray zone (between 1.1 and 2.6), and distress zone (below 1.1).

Table 20.3 (A&B) shows the current ratio (CR), quick ratio (QR), and Altman Z-score (Z) calculations for IBM. The CR and QR for IBM came in just below healthy ranges while the Z-score was in the safe zone. However, a closer look at the balance sheet will reveal that the CR and QR numbers are skewed because of huge buybacks: IBM reduced outstanding shares by over 65 million during the year, which resulted in a total cash outlay of well over $10 billion.

Valuation Indicators

Valuation Indicators signal a stock's price assessment, whether it is under- or overvalued, and the relative level of such under- or overvaluation. Several such indicators exist; many of them were introduced by value investment gurus.

- **Price/earnings to growth (PEG) ratio**: Introduced in 1969 by Mario Farina[9] and popularized decades later by Peter Lynch[10] and Jim Slater,[11] PEG ratio quantifies that a high P/E ratio does not mean a stock is overvalued if the expected growth rate is correspondingly high. Broadly speaking, stocks with PEG ratios below 1 are considered undervalued. PEG is most suitable for growing businesses; for mature businesses, an adaptation where dividends are included in the calculation is used.
- **Price-to-book (P/B) ratio**: This compares the market price of the stock to its book value. Value stocks sport low P/B ratios and growth stocks high P/B ratios. Book-to-market (BTM) ratio, the inverse of P/B ratio, was used by Fama French in the three-factor model introduced previously. Historically, low P/B stocks have provided excess returns compared to high P/B stocks.
- **Initial rate of return (IRR)**: This is a percentage value that indicates the trailing-12-month (TTM) net earnings-per-share (EPS) of a business in terms of the market price of the stock. For

example, the IRR is 5 percent for a stock ABC trading at $20 with a trailing-twelve-month-EPS of $1. To obtain a respectable valuation reading, the IRR has to be combined with the expected earnings growth rate over the medium term (five years or so).

- **Piotroski F-score**: A rating scale for value stocks (high BTM) introduced by Joseph D. Piotroski in 2002.[12] It is not a valuation measure per se, but rather a way to avoid weak companies in the value space, as their risk of bankruptcy is higher. The score can be used to filter out weaker companies from the universe of value stocks. F-scores can vary between 0 and 9; higher numbers (8 and 9) indicate strength. Piotroski's major finding was that high BTM stocks (value stocks) that scored high (strong stocks) outperformed a broad portfolio of value stocks by 7.5 percent over a 20-year period.

Table 20.4 (A&B) demonstrates the price-earnings-to-growth ratio (PEG), the price-to-book ratio (PB), the initial rate of return (IRR), and the Piotroski F-score (F) calculations for IBM. The PEG ratio came in just slightly above 1, indicating fair valuation. The very high PB ratio means IBM should be viewed as a growth stock, rather than as a value stock. The IRR for IBM was 7.10 percent. Warren Buffett is known to use IRR by looking at the stock concerned as a bond with an initial rate of return and an expanding coupon.[13] The last three rows in Table 20.4A illustrate that approach: The initial rate of return of 7.1 percent expands to a rate of return of 12.97 percent in five years (last row), assuming IBM's earnings growth rate (CAGR) for the previous five years will continue for the following five years.

The F-score is to be used with value stocks (high BTM) but IBM, a growth stock (low BTM), was retained in Table 20.4B, as it was used for the rest of the indicators. IBM came in as a strong stock, scoring 8 (column 2) on the F-score. The gauges were all derived from 2010 and 2011 financial statements (income, balance sheet, and cash flow), and the condition in the fourth column was applied to arrive at a value of 0 or 1 for each line item. To demonstrate the usefulness of the F-score in rating value stocks, Research in Motion (RIMM) was also included in the table. (RIMM is a value stock Prem Watsa started buying in Q3 2010. The position has since been increased to a very large

Table 20.4   Valuation Indicators: PEG, P/B, and IRR of IBM (A) and
Piotroski F-score of IBM, RIMM (B)

(A)

Measure	Value	Source/Formula
Price per Share (P)	$183.88	EOY 2011
2011 Earnings per Share (EPS$_{2011}$)	$13.06	2011 Income Statement
Price-to-Earnings (PE) Ratio	14.08	$PE = P \div EPS_{2011}$
2007 Earnings per Share (EPS$_{2007}$)	$7.15	2007 Income Statement
Compounded Annual Growth Rate (CAGR) in Earnings 2007–2011	12.80%	$(EPS_{2011} \div EPS_{2007})^{(1 \div 5)} - 1$
Book Value of Equity (BVE)— Shareholder's Equity	$20,138,000,000.00	2011 Balance Sheet.
Shares Outstanding (SO)	$1,163,180,000.00	2011 Balance Sheet.
Book Value (BV)	$17.31	$BV = BVE/SO$
Price-Earnings-to-Growth (PEG) Ratio	**1.10**	$PEG = PE \div CAGR$
Price-to-Book (PB) Ratio	**10.62**	$PB = P \div BV$
Initial Rate of Return (IRR)	**7.10%**	$IRR = EPS_{2011} \div P$
Projected EPS in 5 Years (PEPS$_5$)	$23.85	$EPS_{2011} \times (1 + CAGR)^5$
Projected Rate of Return in 5 years (PRR$_5$)	12.97%	$PRR_5 = PEPS_5 \div P$

(B)

Measure	IBM	RIMM	Source/Formula
Net Income (NI) Gauge	1	1	If NI$_{2011}$ > 0 then 1 else 0
Operating Cash Flow (OCF) Gauge	1	1	If OCF$_{2011}$ > 0 then 1 else 0
Return on Assets (ROA) Gauge	1	0	If ROA$_{2011}$ > ROA$_{2010}$ then 1 else 0
Quality of Earnings (QE) Gauge	1	1	If OCF$_{2011}$ > NI$_{2011}$ then 1 else 0
Long-Term Debt (LTD) vs. Total Assets (TA) Gauge	0	1	If (LTD = 0 or (LTD$_{2011}$/ TA$_{2011}$) < (LTD$_{2010}$/TA$_{2010}$)) then 1 else 0
Current Ratio (CR) Gauge	1	1	If CR$_{2011}$ > CR$_{2010}$ then 1 else 0
Shares Outstanding (SO) Gauge	1	1	If SO$_{2011}$ <= SO$_{2010}$ then 1 else 0
Gross Margin (GM) Gauge	1	0	If GM$_{2011}$ > GM$_{2010}$ then 1 else 0
Asset Turnover (AT) Gauge	1	0	If Percentage Sales Increase > Percentage Assets Increase then 1 else 0
Piotroski F-score (F)	**8**	**6**	**Sum of the nine gauges**

~10 percent stake, despite the decline in the stock price.) The F-score for RIMM came in at 6, a middle-ground rating, meaning it was neither a strong or weak stock in the value terrain, as of EOY 2011.

For investors attempting to follow money manager trades, valuation indicators provide an insight into how the manager views the business.

Fair Value Estimates

Fair value estimates (FVE) are procedures aimed at associating a reasonable valuation with a business. FVEs provide an overall sense about the range in the margin of safety (if any) when investing in a business. The unknowns make it impossible to come up with an absolute FVE. In short, the process gives analysts an idea as to how varied the valuations can be, depending on different assumptions.

As the value of any business is the present value of future payouts from the business until dissolution, the life cycle of the business and the variability of the parameters during the life cycle are key factors for a proper FVE. Even then, FVE's accuracy is highly dependent on the assumptions made to arrive at future payouts.

FVE's complexity is subject to the number of parameters, and also whether the calculation factors in the variability of those parameters over time. The section presents several FVE calculation methods with different assumptions and levels of complexity. The decision to follow a particular money manager position is easier if there is a sense of what the business might be worth under varying assumptions.

Risk-Free Equivalent Fair Value

The *risk-free equivalent fair value* determines the price-per-share (PPS) that would result in the current earnings-per-share (EPS) equaling the risk-free interest rate. This extremely simple fair value estimate (FVE) has several limitations:

- Unlike risk-free (U.S. government bonds) debt-coupon rates, the EPS for all corporations fluctuate. Moreover, only a portion of the EPS is actually paid out (as dividends) to shareholders every year. This

Table 20.5 Risk-Free Equivalent Fair Value Estimate (FVE) for IBM

Parameter	Value	Source/Formula/Description
Earnings per Share (EPS)	13.06	2011 income statement
10-Year Treasury Rate (TTR)	1.89%	EOY 2011—treasury.gov
Fair Value Estimate (FVE)	**$691**	*FVE = EPS ÷ TTR*

FVE assumes EPS as a constant with the entire amount paid out every year.

- Any stock investment has risks, and the risk-free equivalent FVE disregards the risk premium that stock holders would demand.
- Business evaluation is completely overlooked.

Despite the limitations, the FVE has its merits: It allows comparison of the investment with the risk-free asset class. If the FVE exceeds the current market price, it is safe to consider the investment as not overvalued relative to government bonds. To allocate capital, an estimate of the present value of its future payouts, and the likelihood that such payouts will materialize, should be undertaken.

Table 20.5 represents the risk-free equivalent FVE calculation for IBM. The estimate came in at $691, which is well above the $200 range that the stock is trading at. The historically low treasury rates are responsible for that number to be so promising. The low rates mean a negative economic outlook for the United States as a whole, which should be seen in a negative light when valuing IBM stock.

Fair Values Based on Earnings Growth

Peter Lynch proposed a growth stock to be fairly valued if the price-earnings-to-growth (PEG) ratio is 1. The formula for a fair value estimate (FVE) based on this observation is:

$$FVE_1 = GR \times EPS$$

Where,
  GR = Earnings growth rate
  EPS = Trailing 12-month earnings-per-share

By including dividends the formula can be adjusted to suit mature dividend paying companies as:

$$FVE_2 = (GR + DY) \times EPS$$

Where,

DY = Current dividend yield as a percentage of current price

This formula, although very simple, does not distinguish between a business that pays a stable dividend and one that pays an increasing dividend. To accommodate businesses that offer dividend growth the formula can be adjusted further:

$$FVE_3 = (GR + 2 \times DY) \times EPS$$

The number 2 used in the formula is arbitrary; the idea here is to include a weightage for expected dividend growth. If that growth rate is very high, a higher number instead of the number 2 in the formula can be used. (The formula does not specify how to get to the growth rate number.) For relatively stable businesses, a conservative assumption is to employ the compounded annual growth rate (CAGR) for the last five years.

Table 20.6 indicates the earnings-growth-based fair value estimates (FVE) for IBM. The dividends per share (D) for IBM increased from \$1.50 in 2007 to \$2.90 in 2011 for a CAGR of 14.09 percent. Given the level of dividend growth, it is reasonable to go with FVE_3 (\$208.44). The growth rate (GR), taken as the CAGR for the last five years, is a reasonable assumption for steadily growing businesses. The earnings grew at a much higher CAGR for the previous five years (2002 to 2006), compared to the most recent five years (2007 to 2011). An argument can be made that the CAGR is slowing for IBM and, hence, the growth rate should be more conservative.

Earnings growth based FVEs ignore all business evaluations: A static value for the growth rate is used to project a fair value. The simplicity of the basic formula applicable to growth stocks and extensions to make the basic approach applicable to other types of businesses (mature dividend stocks and dividend growth stocks) account for the appeal of this formula.

Table 20.6   Earnings-Growth-Based Fair Value Estimates (FVE) for IBM

Parameter	Value	Source/Formula/Description
Growth Rate (GR): five-year CAGR for IBM	12.80%	See Table 20.4A for calculation of 2007–2011 CAGR for IBM
Dividends per Share (D)	$2.90	2011 income statement
Price per Share (P)	$183.88	EOY 2011 market quote
Dividend Yield (DY)	1.58%	$DY = D \div P$
Earnings per Share (EPS)	$13.06	2011 income statement
FVE_1	$167.17	$FVE_2 = GR \times EPS$
FVE_2	$187.80	$FVE_2 = (GR + DY) \times EPS$
FVE_3	$208.44	$FVE_3 = (GR + 2 \times DY) \times EPS$

Fair Values Based on Benjamin Graham's Teachings

Benjamin Graham first taught the value-oriented investment approach at Columbia Business School in 1928 and has to his credit several published books and papers on value investing. The most famous among them were *Security Analysis*, (1934) with David Dodd, and *The Intelligent Investor* (1949).[14] Over the years, several formulas have been derived from his ideas. Leading that list are the Graham number, Benjamin Graham intrinsic value formula, net current asset value (NCAV), and net net working capital (NNWC).

Graham Number

Graham categorized investors as either *defensive* (passive) or *enterprising* (aggressive). The primary goal of defensive investors is safety of principal, and the freedom from having to supervise and analyze investments constantly, as an investment professional would do. For them, Graham's recommendation is to either index or follow a set of canned criteria when selecting stocks. The criteria included sufficiently strong financial condition, earnings stability, dividend record, earnings growth, moderate P/E ratio, and moderate P/B ratio. Of these, the latter two criteria were quantified: The P/E ratio times the P/B ratio should not exceed 22.5. The fair value estimate (FVE) derived from this condition,

Table 20.7 Graham Number for IBM

Parameter	Value	Source/Formula/Description
Earnings per Share (EPS)	13.06	2011 income statement
Book Value of Equity (BVE) Shareholder's Equity	$20,138,000,000.00	2011 balance sheet
Shares Outstanding (SO)	$1,163,180,000.00	2011 balance sheet
Book Value (BVPS)	$17.31	$BV = BVE \div SO$
FVE_{gn}	**$71.32**	$FVE_{gn} = \sqrt{22.5 \times EPS \times BVPS}$

is termed the *Graham number*, which is the maximum price a defensive investor should pay for a particular stock:

$$FVE_{gn} = \sqrt{22.5 \times EPS \times BVPS}$$

Where,

EPS = Earnings per share for the trailing twelve months
BVPS = Book value per share from the latest financial report

Table 20.7 points out the Graham number calculation for IBM. As the FVE is an order of magnitude below the current share price, Graham would not recommend IBM stock for the defensive investor. The formula uses just two parameters, each of which is significant in the valuation: IBM's low book value was reflected in the FVE. For a defensive investor, for whom safety is paramount, book value is an important measure to consider.

Benjamin Graham Intrinsic Value Formula

According to Graham, growth stocks are those stocks with per share earnings that increased well above the rate for common stocks and are expected to do so in the future. Growth stocks are not advised for the defensive investor, as they are uncertain and risky. For the enterprising investor, valuing growth stocks involve estimating future earnings and analyzing the worth of the stock in terms of general long-term prospects, management, financial strength and capital structure, dividend record and current rate, and so on. In place of this full-fledged process,

Table 20.8   Benjamin Graham's Growth Stock Valuation for IBM

Parameter	Value	Source/Formula/Description
Earnings per Share (EPS)	$13.06	2011 income statement
Expected Growth Rate (EGR)— Half of the Five-Year CAGR for IBM	6.40%	See Table 20.4A for calculation of 2007–2011 CAGR for IBM
AAA Corporate Bond Yield (Y)	3.85%	EOY 2011—research.stlouisfed.org
FVE$_1$	**$278.18**	*FVE*$_1$ = *EPS* × (8.5 + 2 × *EGR*)
FVE$_2$	**$317.92**	*FVE*$_2$ = *EPS* × (8.5 + 2 × *EGR*) × 4.4 ÷ *Y*

the end result of which would depend on the accuracy of the assumptions, Graham proposed a simple formula for valuing growth stocks based on a solitary key variable—expected annual earnings growth rate. The original formula is:

$$FVE_1 = EPS \times (8.5 + 2 \times EGR)$$

Where,

EPS = Current (normal) earnings per share

EGR = Expected annual earnings growth rate for the next 7 to 10 years

The formula was since modified to allow for changes in the basic rate of interest.[15] The expanded version is:

$$FVE_2 = EPS \times (8.5 + 2 \times EGR) \times 4.4 \div Y$$

Where,

Y = Current yield on AAA corporate bonds

Table 20.8 describes the fair value estimates (FVE) for IBM based on Graham's growth stock valuation formulas. For the expected growth rate (EGR), which is defined as the estimated earnings growth for the next seven to ten years, half of IBM's earnings growth rate for the last five years was used. With that assumption, the FVEs were well above the current market price for IBM. For a more conservative estimate, the average U.S. long-term GDP growth rate of 3.5 percent for the EGR can be substituted; the result would be an FVE of $231.35 for IBM, still above the current market price.

Benjamin Graham's Net-Current-Asset-Based Valuation

One of the very successful investment strategies of the Graham-Newman Corporation between 1926 and 1956 was to purchase as many stocks as possible below two-thirds of net current asset value. Net current asset value means zero value is associated with items such as property, plant and equipment, intangibles, goodwill, and so on. Total liabilities are removed from current assets to obtain net current assets (NCA)— the valuation is a conservative estimate of what a shareholder will receive in case of immediate liquidation at fire-sale prices. Two-thirds of net current asset value condition makes the valuation even more conservative. Under normal market conditions, not many stocks will qualify; the ones that do make the cut need scrutiny, as some of them will be declining companies on the way to bankruptcy. The fair value estimate (FVE) derived is:

$$FVE_{nca} = (CA - TL) \times 2 \div (3 \times SO)$$

Where,

CA = Current Assets
TL = Total Liabilities
SO = Shares Outstanding

A variation of this formula uses the net net working capital (NNWC). It does not rely on the two-thirds discounting of net current assets to build in a margin of safety, as is used in the NCA model. Instead, it bases the FVE on the estimated liquidation value of current assets by including some level of discounting based on how liquid the current assets are: Cash and short-term investments are counted at 100 percent, accounts receivable (AR) is discounted at 75 percent, and inventory (I) is discounted at 50 percent. The formula is:

$$FVE_{nnwc} = (CSI + (0.75 \times AR) + (0.5 \times I) - TL) \div SO$$

Where,

CSI = Cash and short-term investments
AR = Accounts receivable
I = Inventory

Table 20.9 Benjamin Graham's Net-Current-Assets-Based Valuation for IBM & RIMM

Parameter	IBM	RIMM	Source/Formula/Description
Current Assets (CA)	$50.93B	$7.06B	2011 balance sheets
Total Liabilities (TL)	$96.30B	$3.63B	2011 balance sheets
Shares Outstanding (SO)	1.16B	515.45M	2011 balance sheets
Cash and Short-Term Investments (CSI)	$11.92B	$1.78B	2011 balance sheets
Accounts Receivable (AR)	$29.56B	$3.06B	2011 balance sheets
Inventory (I)	$2.60B	$1.03B	2011 balance sheets
FVE_{nca}	NA	$4.43	$FVE_{nca} = (CA - TL) \times 2 \div (3 \times SO)$
FVE_{nnwc}	NA	$1.85	$FVE_{nnwc} = (CSI + (0.75 \times AR) + (0.5 \times I) - TL) \div SO$

Table 20.9 demonstrates the fair value estimates (FVE) calculations for IBM and RIMM, based on Graham's net-current-assets-based valuation method. For IBM, total liabilities (TL) exceeded current assets (CA), making the valuation meaningless. For RIMM, the FVE came in at $4.43, using the net current asset (NCA) method, and $1.85 using the more conservative net net working capital (NNWC) method. The stock never traded that low in 2011, as the 52-week low was well over $10.

Fair Values Using Present Discounted Value

Present discounted value is a popular method used to value a series of future cash flows. The calculation takes into account two factors: the time value of money and the risk that future cash flows do not always materialize. The two basic approaches to this discounting are:

- **Perpetual discounting**: This assumes future cash flows grow at a constant rate in perpetuity. The essence of this simple approach is defining a reasonable rate of growth for the cash flows that extends in perpetuity. The dependency on a single variable is a downside, as fair values are very sensitive to the actual rate used.

- **Two-step discounting**: This admits that accurately associating a constant growth rate for the cash flows in perpetuity is a lost cause. Instead, the focus is on calculating a constant growth rate for the cash flows for a short period (five years or so), and using a different constant growth rate for the cash flows from that point on.

For common stocks, the most conservative cash flow to use is dividend payments; the logic being that the value of any business can be viewed as the present value of all its future dividend payouts. However, businesses that do not currently issue dividends cannot be valued in this way. For such businesses, the base approach is still applicable, that is, assuming dividends will be initiated at a future point, once the growth phase is over. The approach is termed *growth discounting*. Similar but less conservative approaches to discounting involve using net earnings or free cash flows instead of dividends for discounting.

The section looks at the different discounting models along with their strengths and weaknesses.

Dividend Discount Model

The dividend discount model (DDM) considers the fair value of a stock as the present value of all its future dividends. The formula for DDM, termed the Gordon model is:[16]

$$FVE_{dm1} = D_1 \div (DR - DG_p)$$

Where,
D_1 = Dividend per share expected next year
DR = Estimated cost of equity of the business (discount rate)
DG_p = Dividend growth rate in perpetuity

The dividends per share expected in the next year (D_1) are the announced dividends for the following year. In the absence of such announcements, a reasonable assumption is to use the growth in dividends for the previous year to calculate a value for the following year. Weighted average cost of capital (WACC), calculated from the company's current financials, is a practical substitute for the discount rate (DR). The dividend growth rate in perpetuity (DG_p) assumes a

Table 20.10 Dividend Discount Model Valuation for IBM

Parameter	Value	Source/Formula/Description
Next Year Dividends per Share (D_1)	$3.30	2011–2012 quarterly reports
Discount Rate (DR)	7.26%	WACC for IBM calculated from 2011 financials
Dividend Growth Rate in Perpetuity (DG_p)	5%	Best guess!
FVE_{dm1}	$146.02	$FVE_{dm1} = DY_1 \div (DR - DG_p)$

constant perpetual growth rate in dividends. As this is untrue for businesses, this is a weakness of the model.

Table 20.10 presents the fair value estimate (FVE) calculations for IBM using the dividend-discount-model- based valuation method. IBM grew dividends at an impressive rate of well over 10 percent recently, but as DG_p is a constant rate in perpetuity, it should be much lower. Also, the dividend growth rate cannot be more than the discount rate (DR), as that leads to a negative value. For Table 20.10, DG_p was chosen to be 5 percent, which resulted in a FVE of $146.02, well below the current share price. The sensitivity of the FVE on this measure is to be noted: The valuation ranges from a low of $77.46 (3% DG_p) to a high of $1269 (7% DG_p).

Two-Step Dividend Discount Model

The two-step dividend discount model (DDM_2) addresses the limitation of having to come up with a dividend growth rate in perpetuity (DG_p), as in the previous model. For businesses, the near-term (five years or so) dividend growth rate is easier to estimate and, in some instances, management drops hints on their near-term dividend growth plans. A constant dividend growth rate for the period beyond that can then be used as in the DDM model to compute what is called a *terminal value* (TV). The fair value estimate (FVE) would then be the sum of the present values (PV) of the near-term dividends and the PV of the TV. The formula is:

$$FVE_{dm2} = \sum_{i=1}^{n} PV_i + PV_{tv}$$

Table 20.11   Two-Step Dividend Discount Model Valuation for IBM

Parameter	Value	Source/Formula/Description
Number of years considered as near Term (n)	5	
Expected near-term dividend growth rate (dg_5)	10%	Conservative estimate
Dividends per share paid in the current year (D_0)	$2.90	2011 Income statement
Discount rate (DR)	7.26%	WACC for IBM calculated from 2011 financials
Present value of expected dividends in the near term ($\Sigma_{i=1}^{5} PV_i$)	$15.65	$\Sigma_{i=1}^{5}(D_0 \times (1 + DG_n)^i \div (1 + DR)^i)$
Dividend growth rate in perpetuity (DG_p)	5%	Expected dividend growth rate after the near-term in perpetuity
Expected dividends per share in the last year of the near term (D_5)	$4.67	$D_0 \times (1 + DG_5)^5$
Expected dividends per share in the first year after the near term (D_6)	$4.90	$D_5 \times (1 + DG_p)^1$
terminal value of dividends paid in the years following near term in perpetuity (TV)	$216.99	$D_6 \div (DR - DG_p)$
Present value of terminal value (PV_{tv})	$142.50	$TV \div (1 + DR)^6$
FVE$_{dm2}$	**$158.15**	$\Sigma_{i=1}^{5} PV_i + PV_{tv}$

Where,

n = Number of years considered as the near-term

PV_i = Present value of the expected dividends in the ith year

PV_{tv} = Present value of the terminal value

The formula for the present value of dividends (any future year) is:

$$PV_i = D_i \div (1 + DR)^i$$

Where,

D_i = Expected dividends paid in the ith year.

It is calculated from the dividends paid in the current year and expected near-term dividend growth rate as:

$$D_i = D_0 \times (1 + DG_n)^i$$

Where,

DR = Estimated cost of equity of the business (Discount Rate)

D_0 = Dividends paid in the current year

DG_n = Expected dividend growth rate in the near term

Table 20.11 exemplifies the fair value estimate (FVE) calculations for IBM, using the two-step-dividend-discount-model-based valuation method. The formula is still very sensitive to the dividend growth rate in perpetuity (DG_p)—FVE drops to \$113.50 (4% DG_p), while the FVE moves to \$273.68 (6%. DG_p). The sensitivity will be reduced if the number of years in the near term is increased; if the business is well understood, it should be possible to come up with a reasonable dividend growth rate for the next ten years or so, and the formula becomes a lot less sensitive to the DG_p. The what-if analysis, based on different assumptions about the near term, near-term growth rate, and growth rate in perpetuity can be easily accomplished by substituting the altered values.

Growth Discounting Model

The growth discounting model, a variation of the dividend discount model, addresses the problem of valuing growth companies that currently do not pay dividends. The calculation is multitiered:

- From the current earnings per share (EPS), an EPS is projected for a future point when dividends are expected to be initiated using an estimate for the expected near-term earnings growth rate.
- The initial expected dividend payment is projected to be a percentage (say 50 percent) of the earnings then.
- The DDM calculation is then applied, based on that expected dividend and the expected growth to those dividends in perpetuity to arrive at a terminal value (TV).
- The TV is discounted to the present value (PV) to arrive at a fair value estimate for the business.

The formula is:

$$FVE_{dm3} = TV_n \div (1 + DR)^n$$

Where,

n = Expected year of first dividend payment,

DR = Estimated cost of equity of the business (discount rate), and

TV_n = Terminal value of dividends paid after near-term in perpetuity.

This can be calculated using the DDM formula as:

$$TV_n = D_n \div (DR - DG_p)$$

Where,

D_n = Expected dividend in year n.

Assuming, 50 percent of the earnings that year will be paid in dividends, the expected dividend can be calculated as:

$$D_n = EPS * (1 + EGR_n)^n \div 2$$

Where,

EPS   = Earnings per share for trailing twelve months

EGR_n = Expected near-term earnings growth rate

DG_p = Dividend growth rate from year n in perpetuity

Table 20.12 calculates the fair value estimate (FVE) for RIMM using the growth discount model based valuation method; this calculation is not meaningful for IBM, as they already issue dividends. RIMM currently doesn't dole out dividends and its business has been

Table 20.12   Growth Discount Model Valuation for RIMM

Parameter	RIMM	Source/Formula/Description
Discount rate (DR)	15.56%	WACC for RIMM calculated from 2011 financials
Dividend growth rate in perpetuity (DG_p)	5%	Expected dividend growth rate in perpetuity
Expected year of first dividend payment (n)	6	
Trailing twelve months earnings per share (EPS)	$2.22	2011 Income statement
Expected near term earnings growth rate (EGR_6)	10%	
Expected earnings per share in year six (EPS_6)	$3.93	$EPS * (1 + EGR_n)^n$
Expected dividends per share in year six (D_6)	$1.97	$EPS_6 \div 2$
Terminal value of dividends paid after near term in perpetuity (TV_6)	$18.62	$D_6 \div (DR - DG_p)$
FVE_{dm3}	$7.82	$TV_6 \div (1 + DR)^6$

deteriorating with earnings dwindling sharply in the last several years. The following is assumed:

- RIMM will turn around and post earnings-per-share growth of 10 percent over the next five years.
- In the sixth year, RIMM will initiate a dividend payment equal to 50 percent of that year's earnings per share.
- Perpetual dividend growth rate of 5 percent from the sixth year.

Under these assumptions, RIMM's fair value came in at $7.82. Here again, the validity of the assumptions is critical to the accuracy of the FVE.

Summary

The chapter introduced a set of fundamental analysis (FA) techniques that the best money managers use. The purpose of this exercise is to determine the motives behind money manager trading activity. This is useful for a number of reasons:

- Following a manager trade blindly is being value agnostic.
- The best managers do not always adhere to a strict bottom-up, value-oriented investment approach. A selection might make sense only in an overall diversified portfolio context. Hence, there is no guarantee that a particular pick is a good standalone choice.
- Some managers use positions as hedges, rendering such picks useless, even when they appear in bias spreadsheets or in the insider ownership and corporate insider filings.

Adopting the FA techniques should enhance the investor's stock selection skills. Valuing businesses using FA techniques calls for both effort and practice. Performing the analysis on money manager positions is an excellent way to get ahead of the game. By analyzing a number of such positions, eventually skills will be honed, and one will gain confidence in analyzing stocks, independent of whether a manager has taken a position.

That way, investors can identify mispriced businesses on their own, instead of waiting for a manager to initiate a position. In other words, *adieu* to following, hello to stock picking!

Notes

1. Harry Markowitz, Merton Miller, and William Sharpe, "Pioneering Work in the Theory of Financial Economics," Nobel Prize, 1990.

2. Eugene Fama and Kenneth French, "Multifactor Explanations of Asset Pricing Anomalies," *Journal of Finance* 51, no. 1, March 1996.

3. Jakub Jurek and Luis Viceira, "Optimal Value and Growth Tilts in Long-Horizon Portfolios," Harvard Business School, 2005, www.hbs.edu/faculty/Publication%20Files/06–012.pdf.

4. Rolf Banz, "The Relationship between Return and Market Value of Common Stocks," Northwestern University, 1981.

5. Gabriela Bis, "Theory and Evidence . . . Small Cap Premium: Does Liquidity Hold Water?" Leonard N. Stern School of Business, New York University, May 2007.

6. Benjamin Graham and David Dodd, *Security Analysis* (York, PA: McGraw-Hill, 1934).

7. John Schamel "How the Pilot's Checklist Came About," Mike Monroney Aeronautical Center, Oklahoma City. www.atchistory.org/History/checklst.htm.

8. Atul Gawande, *The Checklist Manifesto: How to Get Things Right* (New York: Henry Holt and Company, 2009).

9. Mario V. Farina, *A Beginner's Guide to Successful Investing in the Stock Market* (Palisades Park, NJ: Investors' Press, 1969).

10. Peter Lynch and John Rothchild, *One Up on Wall Street: How to Use What You Already Know to Make Money in the Market* (New York: Penguin Books, 1990).

11. Jim Slater, *The Zulu Principle. Making Extraordinary Profits from Ordinary Shares* (London: Orion Business Books, 1994).

12. Joseph Piotroski, "Value Investing: The Use of Historical Financial Statement Information to Separate Winners from Losers," University of Chicago Graduate School of Business, January 2002, www.chicagobooth.edu/~/media/FE874EE65F624AAEBD0166B1974FD74D.pdf.

13. Mary Buffett and David Clark, *Buffettology: The Previously Unexplained Techniques That Have Made Warren Buffett the World's Most Famous Investor* (New York: Fireside, 1999).

14. Benjamin Graham, *The Intelligent Investor* (New York: Harper & Brothers, 1949).

15. Benjamin Graham, "The Decade 1965–1974: Its Significance for Financial Analysts," The Renaissance of Value, 1974.

16. Myron Gordon, "Dividends, Earnings, and Stock Prices." *Review of Economics and Statistics* 41, no. 2, Part 1, May 1959.

Chapter 21

Types of Positions and Sizing

Manager bias spreadsheets go a long way toward constructing the equity portion of an overall asset allocation plan. Fundamental analysis techniques (introduced in the previous chapter) provide a general appraisal of business characteristics, as well as the market valuation of the security concerned. Assessing whether the security fits neatly with the equity portion of one's own portfolio and, if so, what would be an appropriate allocation size can be puzzling questions.

The strategy of owning equities in different market areas is sound, as it reduces both security and area-specific risks, which is the essence of *diversification*. A pair of securities can move along a similar path, go opposite ways, or be totally independent of one another. These movements are statistically represented by the correlation coefficient. Applying this observation to portfolio construction by combining negatively correlated assets to reduce overall risk is called *hedging*.

In the context of the overall asset allocation plan, the details of the different types of assets used by managers are not part of their 13F filings. However, most of their strategies can be drawn from other public disclosures. The common thread that binds many of the best managers is their reliance on diversification and hedging techniques to optimize portfolio risk and reward. This is the core message of modern portfolio theory (MPT) and the capital asset pricing model (CAPM). While it may seem as though the best money managers operate with the purpose of exploiting market inefficiencies, the concept of risk reduction without compromising return potential is not lost on them: They are fully cognizant of the need to reduce risk by choosing different assets with varied risk profiles and allocating among them in an optimized fashion. This chapter is a primer on diversification and hedging, the key attributes of risk management. It also introduces other techniques that managers employ to reduce the total risk in the equity portion and in asset allocation for the overall portfolio.

Diversification and Hedging

The primary objective of portfolio diversification is to reduce or eliminate diversifiable risk. It is best explained through the concept of correlation coefficient between any given pair of securities. The correlation coefficient can range from −1 to +1.

- −1 indicates perfect negative correlation: When one security goes up, its pair always goes down and vice-versa.
- 0 implies complete disconnection: The movement of one security has no bearing on the other.
- +1 denotes perfect positive harmony: When one security goes up, its pair always goes up and vice-versa.

The diversification objective is achieved when securities with low positive correlation are combined in a portfolio. The returns of random n-asset portfolios were studied to determine the optimal number of positions and the actual benefit gained through diversification.[1] Its conclusion was that the variability of returns reduced by almost 50 percent, when the portfolio held eight positions compared to the variability of returns for an average single-stock portfolio. Adding further positions had benefits, but there was less reduction in variability.

The variability of returns, a key representation of risk, is measured using standard deviation (σ). Standard deviation (σ) can be presented in terms of expected return probabilities for any given year. Assuming normal distribution for security returns, 1σ represents variability with 68.27 percent probability, 2σ denotes variability with 95.45 percent probability, 3σ signifies variability with 99.73 percent probability, and so on. For example, if portfolio ABC has a standard deviation (σ) of 20 percent, and is expected to return 10 percent, it implies:

- For seven out of ten years (1σ), returns will be in the range of -10% to $+30\%$. (Subtract or add 20% to the expected return of 10% for ABC.)
- For 19 out of 22 years (2σ), returns will be in the range of -30% to $+50\%$. (Subtract or add 2 $\star$ 20% to the expected return of 10% for ABC.)
- For 369 out of 370 years (3σ), returns will be in the range of -50% to $+70\%$. (Subtract or add 3 $\star$ 20% to the expected return of 10% for ABC.)

In terms of risk of loss, the standard deviation (σ) of 20 percent suggests:

- The probability of a loss greater than 10 percent (1σ negative cutoff point) as around 16 percent
- The probability of a loss greater than 30 percent (2σ negative cutoff point) as around 2 percent
- The probability of a loss greater than 50 percent (3σ negative cutoff point) as around 0.15 percent

Note that the odds are halved compared to the probability outside the range of σ, as only the left half of the normal distribution (traditional bell curve) of returns needs to be considered: The probability that returns are outside the range of 1σ is ~32% (i.e., $100\% - 68.27\%$), so the risk of loss greater than 10% is half that or ~16%. Similarly, the probability that returns are outside the range of 2σ and 3σ are ~4% and ~0.3% respectively. The corresponding risk of loss greater than 30% and 50% are ~2% and ~0.15% respectively.

The investment decision thus hinges on this variance in return for any given year being acceptable for the expected return of 10 percent in the equity portion of the overall asset allocation plan.

The expected return (ER) is a key variable and CAPM has a means by which to measure it:

$$ER = RFR + \beta * (EMR - RFR)$$

Where:

ER   = Expected return
RFR   = Risk free rate
EMR   = Expected market return
Beta (β) = a measure of the systematic risk or market risk

β can be negative, zero, or positive, with the overall market beta of 1.0 as the base. Negative β measures movement opposite to the overall market, zero indicates absolutely no correlation, and positive β measure movement with the market. The β is calculated by dividing the covariance in past prices of the security, compared to overall market prices by the variance in past prices of the overall market.

The beauty of CAPM is its simplicity. The expected return is represented in terms of a single variable: the nondiversifiable risk (β). Investing based on the principles of CAPM is very straightforward; the steps are listed here:

1. Calculate β for the portfolio.
2. Substitute the β value, risk free rate (RFR), and expected market return (EMR) to obtain the expected return (ER) of the portfolio from the CAPM formula.
3. Make the decision based on the portfolio's expected return (ER) and standard deviation (σ).

For example, consider portfolio ABC with a β of 1.20. The expected market return (EMR) is 10 percent. Assuming a risk free rate (RFR) of 4%, the expected return (ER) of the portfolio using the CAPM formula can be calculated as:

$$ER = 4\% + 1.2 * (10\% - 4\%) = 11.2\%$$

In the above discussion, beta (β) and standard deviation (σ) are key variables that are calculated from historical prices and returns. While σ

may be viewed as representing both nondiversifiable and diversifiable risks, β only represents nondiversifiable risk. Therefore, the CAPM formula is better suited to an already diversified portfolio.

Portfolio optimization maximizes expected return for a given level of overall risk. Minimizing overall risk for a given level of expected return is the other side of the coin. The optimization can be made both at the portfolio level and at the overall asset allocation level.

Both *diversification* and *hedging* help reduce overall risk (σ) in a portfolio. The reduction in σ will not shrink the expected return, provided that the expected return of the new security at least equals that of the equity portfolio. At the equity portfolio level, reduction in overall risk (σ) without a corresponding reduction in expected return is accomplished by combining securities with low positive or negative correlations. In the context of overall asset allocation, the same concept applies: Combine negatively correlated asset classes with positive expected returns to reduce overall risk (σ). Once the securities involved are identified through this process, further tuning is achieved by adjusting the weightages.

The concepts are best explained via an illustration. (Note: The stock[s] used in the examples for this chapter are chosen randomly. As the purpose of the examples is to comprehend risk reduction through diversification, the actual stocks used are irrelevant.)

Table 21.1 displays the key measures for Goodrich Petroleum Corporation (GDP). The beta (β) was taken from an online source; it could have been derived by applying the formula for β against *n*-years of price and return data for Goodrich (GDP) and the overall market (S&P 500 Index). The expected return (ER) is calculated from the CAPM formula as 10.30 percent, and standard deviation (σ) is 81.62 percent. The σ is a direct application of the formula against ten years (2002–2011) of yearly return data.

To demonstrate the benefits of diversification, seven random stocks with low positive correlation are added in equal amounts. (Note: Equal allocation is used for ease of illustration.)

Table 21.2 indicates the key measures for each of the eight stocks in the equity portion of the portfolio, along with the measures for the combined equity portfolio. Beta (β) for the portfolio is the average of the β for the individual stocks. Standard deviation (σ) of the portfolio is obtained by applying the formula against historical yearly returns of

Table 21.1 CAPM Measures for Goodrich Petroleum (GDP)

Parameter	Value	Description/Formula
Risk Free Rate (RFR)	4%	
Expected Market Return (EMR)	10%	
Beta (β)	1.05	
Expected Return (ER)	**10.30%**	$ER = RFR + \beta * (EMR - RFR)$
Standard Deviation (σ)	**81.62%**	**From ten years of historical annual return data through 2011**

Table 21.2 CAPM Measures for Random Eight Stock Equity Portfolio

Security	Beta (β)	CAPM-Expected Return (ER)	Standard Deviation (σ)
Goodrich Petroleum Corporation (GDP)	1.05	10.30%	81.62%
Owens & Minor, Inc. (OMI)	0.52	7.12%	17.97%
The McClatchy Company (MNI)	3.35	24.10%	127.94%
AFLAC Incorporated (AFL)	1.82	14.92%	20.42%
First Cash Financial Services (FCFS)	0.94	9.64%	51.24%
Mosaic Company (MOS)	1.29	11.74%	112.76%
Tejon Ranch Company (TRC)	0.92	9.52%	26.36%
Bank of Hawaii Corporation (BOH)	0.81	8.86%	15.24%
Averages	1.34	12.03%	**56.69%**
Equity Portfolio (EP)	1.34	12.03%	**28.07%**

the portfolio as a whole over ten years (2002–2011). It could also be derived from the correlation matrix and the yearly returns of the eight stocks in the portfolio over the same timeframe.

The benefits of diversification is clearly evident: Randomly adding a set of stocks that had low positive correlation resulted in a ~50% reduction in the overall risk: The standard deviation (σ) of the equity portfolio (EP) came in at 28.07 percent, compared to 56.69 percent for the average of the standard deviations of the eight securities.

Table 21.3 indicates the key measures for the overall portfolio when the equity portfolio is combined with certain ETFs (some have a negative correlation with the equity portion). Again, equal allocation across the five asset classes is used to make the illustration simpler. The overall risk (standard deviation, σ) diminished 50 percent further by incorporating the four asset classes into the equity portfolio in equal

Table 21.3   CAPM Measures for Combined Portfolio

Security	Beta (β)	CAPM-Expected Return (ER)	Standard Deviation (σ)
Equity Portfolio (EP)	1.34	12.03%	28.07%
iShares Treasury Inflation Protected ETF (TIP)	0.10	4.60%	5.28%
iShares 20-Year Treasury Bond ETF (TLT)	−0.29	2.26%	15.60%
Vanguard REIT ETF (VNQ)	1.41	12.46%	25.54%
Vanguard MSCI Emerging Market ETF (VWO)	1.35	12.10%	41.12%
Averages	0.78	8.69%	**23.12%**
Combined Portfolio (CP)	0.78	8.69%	**14.33%**

amounts—the σ for the combined portfolio came in at 14.33 percent compared to 28.07 percent for the Equity Portfolio (EP). It is interesting to note that the number 14.33 percent is well below 23.12 percent, which is the average of the σ for the five asset classes that was combined to form the portfolio. Although there was a reduction in σ, a drop in the expected return (ER) was also seen, as some of the asset classes added had lower expected returns (ER) compared to the equity portfolio.

When picking stocks from money manager bias spreadsheets and using fundamental analysis to make purchase decisions, it pays to remember the beneficial effects of diversification and hedging in the portfolio. The decision to include a particular security into the portfolio should also be based on how seamlessly it fits within the overall risk-reduction context. Building a correlation matrix with the securities in one's portfolio can come in handy in this regard.

Table 21.4 is the correlation matrix for the overall portfolio. The grayscale coding in each cell indicates the level of correlation between the pair of securities represented by the cell:

- Light gray indicates a low positive correlation.
- Gray indicates a high positive correlation.
- Dark gray indicates a low negative correlation.
- Black indicates a high negative correlation.

Table 21.4 Correlation Matrix of Combined Portfolio

	GDP	OMI	MNI	AFL	FCFS	MOS	TRC	BOH	TIP	TLT	VNQ	VWO
GDP	1.00	0.41	0.45	0.12	0.06	0.12	0.30	0.43	−0.57	−0.80	−0.18	0.56
OMI	0.41	1.00	0.27	0.33	0.42	0.34	0.51	0.14	−0.02	−0.28	0.15	0.56
MNI	0.45	0.27	1.00	0.40	0.32	−0.08	0.59	0.45	0.02	−0.55	0.15	0.58
AFL	0.12	0.33	0.40	1.00	0.76	0.62	0.59	0.20	0.28	−0.28	0.37	0.74
FCFS	0.06	0.42	0.32	0.76	1.00	0.65	0.81	0.34	0.55	−0.09	0.67	0.70
MOS	0.12	0.34	−0.08	0.62	0.65	1.00	0.45	0.33	0.19	−0.03	0.47	0.55
TRC	0.30	0.51	0.59	0.59	0.81	0.45	1.00	0.62	0.43	−0.26	0.69	0.73
BOH	0.43	0.14	0.45	0.20	0.34	0.33	0.62	1.00	0.17	−0.23	0.64	0.45
TIP	−0.57	−0.02	0.02	0.28	0.55	0.19	0.43	0.17	1.00	0.65	0.76	−0.01
TLT	−0.80	−0.29	−0.55	−0.29	−0.09	−0.03	−0.25	−0.22	0.65	1.00	0.34	−0.63
VNQ	−0.18	0.15	0.15	0.37	0.67	0.47	0.69	0.64	0.76	0.34	1.00	0.30
VWO	0.56	0.56	0.58	0.75	0.70	0.56	0.72	0.45	−0.01	−0.63	0.30	1.00

The values were taken from an online source, although they could have been derived by applying the formula for correlation coefficient. The grayscale coding in the row corresponding to a security in the correlation matrix signals whether it is a good fit in the portfolio: For example, in the correlation matrix (Table 21.4), with the equity portion (first eight rows and columns), the objective is diversification, as long as the individual cells within that portion are shaded something other than gray (high positive correlation), the objective is met. Looking at the matrix, the equity portion of the portfolio is fairly diversified, although the fit of TRC, with five cells that are gray (equity portion is columns 2 through 9), is questionable. By the same token, the pairs shown by dark gray and black cells indicate pairs that are hedged well (negative correlation).

Keeping Your Powder Dry

Holding cash is not easy for investors, as the whole world is only too aware of its falling purchasing power. This begs the question: Why do the money managers keep large amounts of cash in their overall portfolio? Or, to put it candidly, why do money managers hold on to the cash that investors entrusted them to put to work so that it can earn good absolute returns?

The best explanation for super investors preferring significant cash on their side was given by Alice Schroeder, in her 2008 book, *The Snowball: Warren Buffett and the Business of Life.*[2] Essentially, cash can be considered as a call option on every asset class, with no expiry and no strike price. In reality, there is no such thing as an option without expiry and strike price. The concept, however, allows investors to view cash from the context of the upfront cost they might be willing to forgo to gain the right to own a particular asset class at a price that will provide a worthy margin of safety.

Ms. Schroeder went on to claim that, when Buffett thinks that the option is inexpensive compared to the margin of safety (if any) provided by purchasing assets right now, he is more than willing to hold cash. This appears true from empirical evidence; Buffett held plenty of cash during the financial crisis and bought like there was no tomorrow when most others were unloading. It is difficult to prove this strategy, as the fund inflows and outflows at different times make it impossible to gauge the relative cash holdings of the best money managers.

Table 21.5 illustrates the concept through an example. The SPDR S&P 500 index ETF (SPY) traded at ~$135 per share in mid-November 2012. Purchasing 100 shares of SPY at $135 would require a cash outlay of $13,500. Instead of buying 100 shares, the investor chooses to wait until the margin of safety increases. The columns show the calculations to arrive at the time value of a call option with two different strike prices; those levels are a proxy for the margins of safety sought.

Scenario 1: Through fundamental analysis (FA), the investor has determined SPY to be fairly valued at $135, and is hence seeking a small increase to the margin of safety, shooting to purchase SPY at $125 instead of the market price of $135. The right to purchase SPY shares at $125 within the next one year has a market price associated with it: the time value of the call option that expires in one year at strike 125. That option was trading at $17.73, implying a time value of $7.73 or 6.18 percent (the second column shows the values and the fourth column shows the formulas). In other words, the cost of the right to purchase SPY with an increase in margin of safety of 7.41

Table 21.5 Cash as Call Option

Parameter	Scenario with SPY Fairly Valued	Scenario with SPY in a Bubble	Description/Formula
Current Price (CP)	$135	$135	
Strike Price (SP)	$125	$85	
Percentage Increase to Margin of Safety (PIM)	7.41%	37.04%	$PIM = 1 - (SP \div CP)$
Price of Call Option One Year Out (PCO)	$17.73	$53.63	Price of this option as of mid-November 2012
Time Value of Call Option (TV)	$7.73	$3.63	$TV = PCO - (CP - SP)$
TV as a Percentage Value (TV$_p$)	6.18%	4.27%	$TV_p = TV \div SP$

percent is 6.18 percent. The right is expensive; it makes better business sense to invest in SPY at 135 rather than hold on to the cash.

Scenario 2: The investor believes SPY to be in a bubble, that is, way too overvalued, and wants a much larger increase in the margin of safety, and is looking to purchase SPY at $85, instead of the market price of $135. The SPY call option at strike 85 one year out traded at $53.63, implying a time value of $3.63 or 4.27 percent. Decoded, the cost of the right to purchase SPY with an increase in margin of safety of 37.04 percent is 4.27 percent. The right is very economical and makes perfect sense to own; hold on to cash rather than invest in SPY at $135.

Building and Sizing Positions

The sizing of positions in a portfolio is a genuine puzzle in the diversification process. The 13F filings of money managers fail to enlighten us in this regard, as the sizing can appear very random. Many managers adjust positions on a quarterly basis, and comparing consecutive 13Fs will also provide a haphazard picture in terms of the adjustments made. This unpredictability has to do with several factors.

- Fund inflows and outflows, a regular portfolio feature of the best managers, result in changes to allocation amounts as they attempt to keep the overall ratios intact.
- Weightage adjustments (allocation) of assets in a portfolio along with periodic rebalancing to improve risk-adjusted returns can result in allocations to individual positions to appear unsystematic.
- Depending on market conditions and certain other parameters, managers are known to have a strategy in place that builds positions gradually. Therefore, quarter-to-quarter comparison of positions can show random changes to position sizes as managers rely on mechanically following the allocation mandated by the strategy.

When constructing a personal investment portfolio, inflows and outflows are not as much of a concern, but the other two factors play a role. The portfolio optimization illustration (Tables 21.1 through 21.4) in "Diversification and Hedging" assumed equally weighted assets.

Adjusting the weightages offer more opportunities to optimize the portfolio further.

Table 21.6 shows the CAPM measures for the combined portfolio (as in Table 21.3) with different weightages applied to the asset classes. To arrive at an appropriate risk-reward ratio, experimenting with different weightages is essential. For this illustration, a ratio of 1:1 between equity-like asset classes (EP, VNQ, and VWO) and the rest (TIP and TLT) was chosen. An even better risk-reward ratio resulted with this weightage adjustment: The overall risk (standard deviation or σ) reduced by almost a third from 14.33 percent to 10.81 percent. On the other hand, the expected return (ER) went down less than 1 percent. (Note: Adjusting the weightages this way will also require the allocation of the individual components within the equity portfolio to be adjusted proportionally as well).

Table 21.6   CAPM Measures for Combined Portfolio Using Weighted Allocation

Security	Beta (β)	CAPM-Expected Return (ER)	Standard Deviation (σ)	Allocation Percentages (Weightages)
Equity Portfolio (EP)	1.34	12.03%	28.07%	16.67%
iShares Treasury Inflation Protected ETF (TIP)	0.10	4.60%	5.28%	25%
iShares 20-Year Treasury Bond ETF (TLT)	−0.29	2.26%	15.60%	25%
Vanguard REIT ETF (VNQ)	1.41	12.46%	25.54%	16.67%
Vanguard MSCI Emerging Market ETF (VWO)	1.35	12.10%	41.12%	16.67%
Combined Portfolio (CP) Equal Weightage	**0.78**	**8.69%**	**14.33%**	
Combined Portfolio (CP) Weight Adjusted	**0.64**	**7.81%**	**10.81%**	

Periodic rebalancing involves regular adjustments to the weightages of the asset classes to retain the asset allocation for the target portfolio. (Note: Here, too, adjusting the asset classes implies adjusting the weightages of the individual components within the equity portfolio as well). A study on the optimal frequency for rebalancing determined rebalancing quarterly or yearly had some benefits in terms of risk adjusted returns; increasing the frequency is detrimental to portfolio returns, while decreasing it yielded marginally better returns, but with increased risk.[3]

Building stock positions over a period of time as opposed to buying the targeted allocation in one shot is a strategy many money managers use, especially with volatile securities. The logic behind this approach is to mitigate the risk due to price volatility by spreading the purchase over time. This can be done in different ways:

- **Share cost averaging (SCA)**: With SCA, independent of the share price, the same number of shares is purchased periodically. This is the most passive method to allocate money in a security over a period of time. Investors can purchase shares mechanically after determining the duration over which purchases should be spread out, the frequency of periodic purchases, and the number of shares to be purchased each time. The approach guarantees the average purchase price to be equal to the average of the share prices of the periodic purchases. The obvious disadvantage is that a ceiling cannot be placed on the capital required to purchase shares each period.
- **Dollar cost averaging (DCA)**: Here, the capital allocation for each period is determined and kept constant. Compared to SCA, the approach achieves a lower cost basis as more shares are purchased when prices are lower.
- **Value averaging (VA)**:[4] VA aims to increase the market value of the shares owned at a constant rate each period. The concept was originally introduced as a means by which to allocate a lump sum into a portfolio in an efficient manner over time using what is termed a *value path*. Rather than determining the number of shares to be purchased (SCA) or the amount to be allocated (DCA) each period, VA determines the target amount to be reached for each time interval and the entire allocation period. The approach achieves a lower cost basis than DCA, and has the distinct

feature that it mandates selling shares when prices rise rapidly. As a formula-based capital allocation method, VA is a more active strategy compared to SCA or DCA.

Table 21.7 illustrates how dollar cost averaging (DCA) works compared to share cost averaging (SCA). The table uses the month-end pricing for Bank of America (BAC) over a period of one year, ending October 31, 2012.

The values for DCA: Shares Purchased (fourth column) is obtained by dividing the cash outlay of $1,000 per month (third column) by the price per share at the end of the month (second column). The values for SCA: Cash Outlay Each Period (last column) is obtained by multiplying the number of shares purchased each period (183.82: fifth column) by the price per share at the end of the month (second column). The table illustrates the following:

- DCA purchased shares at an average cost basis of $7.51, compared to the average share price of $7.73 with SCA.

Table 21.7   Dollar Cost Averaging (DCA) versus Share Cost Averaging (SCA)

Purchase Date	BAC: Price per Share	DCA: Cash Outlay Each Period	DCA: Shares Purchased	SCA: Shares Purchased	SCA: Cash Outlay Each Period
11/30/2011	$5.44	$1,000.00	183.82	183.82	$1,000.96
12/30/2011	$5.66	$1,000.00	179.86	183.82	$1,023.04
1/31/2012	$7.13	$1,000.00	140.25	183.82	$1,311.92
2/29/2012	$7.97	$1,000.00	125.47	183.82	$1,466.48
3/30/2012	$9.57	$1,000.00	104.49	183.82	$1,760.88
4/30/2012	$8.11	$1,000.00	123.30	183.82	$1,492.24
5/31/2012	$7.35	$1,000.00	136.05	183.82	$1,352.40
6/29/2012	$8.18	$1,000.00	122.25	183.82	$1,505.12
7/31/2012	$7.34	$1,000.00	136.24	183.82	$1,350.56
8/31/2012	$7.99	$1,000.00	125.16	183.82	$1,470.16
9/28/2012	$8.83	$1,000.00	113.25	183.82	$1,624.72
10/31/2012	$9.32	$1,000.00	107.30	183.82	$1,714.88
Totals		$12,000.00	1,597.45	2,205.84	$17,073.36
Average Share Price (ASP)	$7.73		$7.51		$7.73

- Cash outlay with DCA is known up front: $1,000 invested in BAC shares every month end for a total of $12,000. With SCA, the total cash outlay over a given period is unknown. If the share price of the security concerned is increasing through the period, the cash outlay required will be well above $12,000; this was the scenario with BAC, and the strategy required a cash outlay of $17,073.36. On the other hand, if the share price had trended down over the period, the cash outlay would have been well below $12,000.

- SCA allocates more capital when the price per share is increasing and vice-versa. This goes against the value investing philosophy of trying to purchase shares at low prices. The issue can be clearly seen by comparing the row when the share price was highest (purchase date: 3/30/2012) with the row when the share price was lowest (purchase date: 11/30/2011). The capital allocated when the share price was at the highest value of $9.57 was $1,760.88, compared to just $1,000.96 allocated when the share price was at its lowest value of $5.44.

401K and other retirement account planners tout DCA as advantageous, as it fits in naturally with the periodic investment theme of such plans: Employees generally opt for a percentage of their paychecks to be taken out for investing in their retirement accounts. The same amount is allocated each period across their set investment choices (usually mutual funds) at a selected ratio, ensuring DCA allocation. The passive nature of DCA and its promise of automatically buying more shares of the assets concerned at lower prices make the strategy very appealing. When managing an investment portfolio where periodic cash flows is not a given, the strategy still has sway among value investors. This has to do with significant cash allocation in their portfolios. As previously mentioned, if asset classes are overvalued, holding cash is a more sensible option. DCA allows passive allocation of a part of that cash over a period of time at a low average cost. Again, the strategy is best suited for use with volatile securities.

Although DCA has several advantages, money managers prefer SCA to DCA when implementing a trend-following method. The strategy allows more capital to be allocated periodically as long as an up-trend is in place. As the trend reverses, less capital will be allocated, although trend followers generally exit completely at that point.

Value averaging (VA) is based on the following formula:

$$TV_n = IA \times n \times (1 + ER)^n$$

Where,

n = Number of time periods,

TV_n = Target value after n periods,

IA = Initial capital allocation, and

ER = Expected return (average of the expected return of investment per period and expected return of contribution per period).

The formula relies on the accuracy of the expected return (ER) supplied. If that variable is assumed as zero, the formula reduces to:

$$TV_n = IA \times n$$

This is a simplified special case of VA. It aims to increase the market value of the shares owned at a constant amount, instead of a constant rate with the original formula. Table 21.8 is an illustration of how dollar cost averaging (DCA) compares to the simplified value averaging (VA) strategy. Like its predecessor, this table also uses the month-end pricing for Bank of America (BAC) over a period of one year ending October 31, 2012.

In this table, the first four columns are the same as in Table 21.7. The figures in VA: Target Value (fifth column) shows the portfolio target value for the corresponding date: The value is targeted to increase at $1,000 per month. The figures in VA: Portfolio Value Before Transaction (sixth column) indicate the value of the portfolio for the corresponding date before any new shares are purchased or sold. It is obtained by multiplying VA: Target Value (fifth column) for the previous month by the share price at the end of the current month and dividing by the share price at the end of the previous month. The VA: Difference in Target Value (seventh column) is obtained by subtracting VA: Portfolio Value Before Transaction (sixth column) from VA: Target Value (fifth column). It indicates the value of new shares to be purchased (if it is a positive value) or sold (if it is a negative value). The last column, the number of shares to be purchased or sold, is obtained by

Table 21.8 Dollar Cost Averaging (DCA) versus Value Averaging (VA)

Purchase Date	BAC: Price per Share	DCA: Cash Outlay Each Period	DCA: Shares Purchased	VA: Target Value	VA: Portfolio Value Before Transaction	VA: Difference in Target Value	VA: Shares Purchased/Sold
11/30/2011	$5.44	$1,000.00	183.82	$1,000.00	$0.00	$1,000.00	183.82
12/30/2011	$5.56	$1,000.00	179.86	$2,000.00	$1,022.06	$977.94	175.89
1/31/2012	$7.13	$1,000.00	140.25	$3,000.00	$2,564.75	$435.25	61.05
2/29/2012	$7.97	$1,000.00	125.47	$4,000.00	$3,353.44	$646.56	81.12
3/30/2012	$9.57	$1,000.00	104.49	$5,000.00	$4,803.01	$196.99	20.58
4/30/2012	$8.11	$1,000.00	123.30	$6,000.00	$4,237.20	$1,762.80	217.36
5/31/2012	$7.35	$1,000.00	136.05	$7,000.00	$5,437.73	$1,562.27	212.55
6/29/2012	$8.18	$1,000.00	122.25	$8,000.00	$7,790.48	$209.52	25.61
7/31/2012	$7.34	$1,000.00	136.24	$9,000.00	$7,178.44	$1,821.52	248.16
8/31/2012	$7.99	$1,000.00	125.16	$10,000.00	$9,797.00	$203.00	25.41
9/28/2012	$8.83	$1,000.00	113.25	$11,000.00	$11,051.31	-$51.31	-5.81
10/31/2012	$9.32	$1,000.00	107.30	$12,000.00	$11,610.42	$389.58	41.80
Total		$12,000.00	1,597.45			$9,154.12	1,287.55
Average Share Price (ASP)	$7.73		$7.51				$7.11

dividing VA: Difference in Target Value by BAC: Share Price. The table illustrates the following:

- The average purchase price with VA was \$7.11 while that of DCA was \$7.51.
- Similar to SCA, the total cash outlay for VA over a given period is unpredictable. If the share price of the security is in an increasing trend through the period, the cash outlay required will be well below \$12,000; this was the scenario with BAC and the strategy required a cash outlay of \$9.154.12.
- VA allocates more capital when the share price drops from the previous period and vice-versa. This conforms to the value-investing philosophy of trying to purchase shares at low prices. The concept is illustrated in Table 21.8: When the month-over-month allocation size spiked the maximum (purchase date: 9/28/2012—the allocation size increased from \$10,000 to \$11,051.31 during that month—refer to the fifth and sixth columns), the strategy raised cash by selling some shares. On the other hand, when the month-over-month allocation size crashed the most (purchase date: 7/31/2012—the allocation size decreased from \$8,000 to \$7,178.44 during that month—refer to the fifth and sixth columns), the strategy allocated the most capital.

Though VA comes ahead in terms of the cost basis achieved, DCA is preferred by some investors for its more passive style. The uncertainty of the cash requirement each period is also unpalatable for some investors. As value investors generally maintain a respectable cash buffer in their portfolios, VA is well suited for them, since the variability in the cash allocation requirement each period is not much of a concern.

As noted previously, cash should be considered as an inexpensive asset class worth owning when the prices of other asset classes are high. If prices of other asset classes continue higher to bubbly levels, cash is elevated to be among the best asset classes to own—other assets should be sold to raise cash. On the other hand, should asset prices head down to rock-bottom levels, cash loses its position as an economical asset class; at least some of that cash should be used to purchase lower priced assets. VA provides a semi-mechanical way of implementing this concept thus making it a favored strategy among value investors.

Low Probability Positions

Just as it sounds, low probability positions are expected to lose money for the most part. Placing money in such ventures is akin to wild speculation; no way can this be labeled prudent money management. Then word comes that many money managers hold what appears to be positions with very low probability of success. Are these superinvestors oracles or is it their gambling instincts acting up?

Although the press devotes a lot of ink to it whenever a famous money manager reveals such a position, the fact is that it is something of a rarity. Such positions have a few common characteristics:

- The positions are such a minute percentage of the manager's overall assets that even if the position drops to zero, nary an impact is made to the portfolio.
- The low probability events that managers choose to bet on have such high reward potential that, in the event of success, despite the minute position sizing, there will be significant portfolio impact.
- The concerned money manager believes the market has mispriced the security in some way. In other words, the manager strongly believes he has an edge!

The vast majority of individual investors taking up low probability positions trip up on the final characteristic, as it is nearly impossible for an individual investor to have an edge in this area. Even for the best money managers, such opportunities seldom occur. Areas in which managers have historically found such securities include distressed bonds, businesses in bankruptcy, and certain types of options and swap contracts. A common theme of these areas is the specialized knowledge required to identify mispricing. Getting into these areas without doing this groundwork is on a par with gambling. On the other hand, if mispricing is identified with high conviction, the strategy has the characteristics of a low-risk high-reward investment:

- Low risk: Position size is so small that 100 percent loss of capital has minimal portfolio impact.
- High reward: Best case scenario is a multifold return of investment which will result in a significant portfolio impact.

- Mispricing: Probability of the high-reward scenario has been vastly underestimated by the market, resulting in a very low price compared to the potential reward.

The effort and expertise required to identify mispriced securities in the areas concerned are so huge that even the best money managers are known to tread with caution; they also rely on other money managers with specialized knowledge to successfully play the game: Even George Soros, a trader who normally relies on his own philosophy, sought the help of John Paulson upon hearing about the billions Paulson amassed by betting against subprime mortgages.[5] Soros learnt about ABX (an index that tracks subprime mortgages), the CDS insurance contract for that index, and how they are traded from Paulson, and made billions on his own trading them the following year. For individual investors, a similar strategy would be one that relies on identifying such positions from manager disclosures, then contemplating whether to clone them.

Summary

Picking stocks from manager bias spreadsheets and conducting fundamental analysis (FA) on them are the first steps in learning from the masters in the context of constructing the equity portion of an overall asset allocation plan. A very critical follow-through is determining the fit of the pick within the existing equity and overall asset allocation.

The key concepts employed by the best money managers while constructing their portfolios are based on the Nobel Prize winning ideas from modern portfolio theory (MPT) and capital asset pricing model (CAPM): diversification and hedging. The section on diversification and hedging illustrated the work in constructing a diversified portfolio while achieving the purpose of risk reduction without compromising expected return.

Money manager 13F filings can appear arbitrary in terms of both position sizes and adjustments to the position sizes from quarter to quarter. While this observation couldn't be any truer, there is a method to the madness. One of the reasons for this random show quarter to quarter is that managers tend to follow different strategies to build and size positions. The type of security and other parameters determine the strategy adopted. The section on building and sizing positions introduced techniques that money managers are known to use.

Keeping a cash hoard around is the toughest task investors face, for it fails to provide any return whatsoever. Viewing cash as a call option on every asset class with no strike price and no expiration allows the investor to visualize holding cash as similar to holding an inexpensive asset class. An illustration that demonstrated the concept using S&P 500 Index ETF (SPY) as the asset class drove home the point.

Low probability positions are expected to lose money most of the time, making such positions appear more like gambling than investing. The best money managers seem to play in this area occasionally, although, in reality, they are far from gambling: they are investing in positions that are mispriced—the market is pricing the security concerned as a low probability position when in fact the money manager's FA has determined it to be mispriced—as the security is discounted as the market has underestimated the probability of success by a wide margin. For individual investors and money managers alike, this is a difficult area to play as it involves both specialized skills and resources. Money managers are known to seek out other managers with the specialized skills in the areas concerned for help with initiating such positions. For individual investors, the best option is to follow a similar approach of spotting such positions from money manager disclosures and following them.

Notes

1. Edwin J. Elton and Martin J. Gruber, "Risk Reduction and Portfolio Size: An Analytic Solution," *Journal of Business*, October 1977.

2. Alice Schroeder, *The Snowball: Warren Buffett and the Business of Life* (New York: Bantam Dell, 2008).

3. William J. Bernstein, "Case Studies in Rebalancing," Efficient Frontier, www .efficientfrontier.com/ef/100/rebal100.htm.

4. Michael E. Edleson, *Value Averaging: The Safe and Easy Strategy for Higher Investment Returns* (London: International Publishing Corporation, 1991).

5. Gregory Zuckerman, *The Greatest Trade Ever: How John Paulson Bet Against the Markets and Made $20 Billion* (New York: Broadway Books, 2009).

Chapter 22

Conclusion

The book detailed several strategies for shadowing the best-performing money managers. The details of the holdings of a money manager are indeed a mine of information. Regulatory requirements mandate that the U.S. long portfolio holdings of all managers be disclosed through their quarterly 13F filings. While having an overview of what the managers are up to via their 13Fs is an advantage, the investor needs to be fully aware of the drawbacks.

- **Time delay**: There is an interval between when a manager trades a stock and when that information becomes public. Depending on when within the quarter the trade was made, the information can be from 45 days to three-and-a-half months old. This risk can be mitigated by avoiding managers who trade actively. For some of them, many trades would not make it to the 13Fs, as the round-trips are done within the same quarter. Employing manager bias spreadsheets to compare the price range the manager traded at with the price when the 13F became public can reduce this risk further. Bias spreadsheets sometimes make it possible to pocket the security at prices below the manager's cost basis; many value managers acknowledge that they expect their picks to dip immediately after stakes are established.

- **U.S. long only**: As the regulatory filings require only U.S. long stock holdings to be disclosed, it does not paint a full picture of the manager's activity. Positions such as shorts, derivatives, bankrupt businesses, international stocks, debt holdings, and so on, are outside the canvas of such reports. To mitigate this problem, avoid managers that are specialized in such areas of the market and those with minimal U.S. long stock exposure.

Manager styles and philosophies vary vastly, even among the best-performing managers. Before cloning managers based solely on their success, it is critical to analyze their style and evaluate whether it makes sense to follow them. Desirable traits include:

- **Value-oriented bottom-up**: Managers like Seth Klarman and David Einhorn, with a value-oriented, bottom-up stock selection philosophy, are a good fit for all cloning strategies. The positions are guaranteed to have passed the manager's stringent analysis with flying colors. As the focus is on the individual merit of a particular position, the risks associated with the macro environment and tail risk are ignored. They need to be addressed separately, in a portfolio context, for the best shot at success.
- **Shareholder activist**: Activist managers, whose focus is on shareholder activism, generally build large positions and have very high conviction about the outcome. Bill Ackman and Carl Icahn fall in this category. A temporary spike in stock prices following the disclosure of activist involvement is a common phenomenon to be aware of with these managers.
- **Concentrated positions**: Managers with heavily concentrated portfolios are worthy of following, as the few positions they hold are guaranteed to be their highest conviction opportunities. Ian Cumming and Mohnish Pabrai belong to this group.
- **Trend following**: George Soros is the epitome of this style; following him can produce good results for those who are familiar with the strategy. Timing can be critical, and so the time delay with 13Fs can prove a problem. Relying on the manager bias spreadsheet to

open positions only if they are trading below the manager's recent stake acquisition price is a reasonable approach to soften this risk. As trend followers generally build positions over a number of quarters, catching them early is often necessary to get comparable returns: analyzing the positions to identify underlying trends a manager is following before they become very large positions is another tactic.

- **Insurance float:** The bigwigs—Warren Buffett, Prem Watsa, and Ian Cumming—invest their insurance businesses' float. They are generally value oriented and tend to hold on to their stock positions for the very long term. In terms of asset allocation, given their need to stay very liquid, they are likely to keep lots of cash and invest in debt and other more defensive areas. Cloning the asset allocation is not ideal, as the objectives for investing insurance float is often way too conservative.

- **University endowments:** The investment objective of university endowments generally calls for preserving capital, generating a portion of the university's annual budget as income, and increasing the pool while staying defensive. Unlike most individual investor portfolios, they are unique in that the asset allocation is based around achieving perpetual growth, that is, the time horizon is forever. Many university endowments choose to invest a significant portion of their equity allocation with other fund managers. Although following individual equity allocations may not be feasible, their conservative stance makes it worthwhile to follow their asset allocation.

- **Family office:** Family offices are set up to invest a wealthy investor's money. The 13Fs of George Soros, Lou Simpson, and Stanley Druckenmiller, who have set up family offices recently, are good resources. As they have already accumulated a huge amount of wealth, they focus mostly on defensive strategies aimed at preserving capital, and generating periodic income for use in charitable purposes and so on.

Popular cloning strategies may be classified broadly into two groups:

- **Ad hoc cloning**: A manager's holding is selected based on some criteria and incorporated into one's existing equity portfolio. The strategies are largely passive, as the stock from a manager's 13F filing is bought/sold based on a set of rules.

- **Mechanical cloning**: Equity portfolios are constructed and maintained by applying a set of criteria to a group of money manager 13F positions. The main difference from the ad hoc model is that it allows modeling an equity portfolio instead of a single position. It is not as passive as the ad hoc model, as some trades are necessary each quarter to maintain the portfolio.

There is also a third active approach, which is to follow and learn from money managers, so as to implement their tactics successfully in one's own portfolio. Here, the 13F holdings information serves only as a filtering mechanism. A decision to buy/sell a filtered position is founded on fundamental analysis and on techniques (based on diversification, hedging, and sizing) that money managers are known to use. The strategies demand a fair amount of effort and expertise, but the potential rewards make it worthwhile.

The various approaches discussed throughout the book demonstrated what is involved when attempting to follow a particular strategy.

Ad Hoc Cloning Strategies

The tables in Part One, under each of the profiled managers, showing the effect of cloning the top positions, is the simplest application of ad hoc cloning. They help illustrate its strengths and weaknesses.

- **Suitability**: With ad hoc cloning, stocks can be selected individually, allowing investors to allocate funds into their existing equity portfolio without evoking major changes. This approach permits the investor to be price, value, and security agnostic. In short, it is suited for passive investors looking to invest in individual securities instead of index funds.
- **Rules for trading**: The rules for selecting a stock from a manager's 13F filing play a critical role with ad hoc cloning. The relative size of the position and trades (if any) done during the quarter work as tools for gauging the manager's bias which, in turn, can be used to make a buy/sell decision.
- **Portfolio fit**: The ad hoc method completely ignores the benefits of portfolio diversification.

Although ad hoc cloning methods have their limitations, the nature of the approach lends itself to passive investors. Being aware of the limitations and sidestepping them can prove valuable. Even though the approach is useful only when selecting an individual stock, it is beneficial as long as the asset classes in the overall portfolio are diversified and hedged. Also, analyzing whether an ad hoc selection is a fit in terms of a diversified equity portfolio is a small price to pay in the long run.

Mechanical Cloning Strategies

With mechanical cloning, rules mandate the positions to be cloned, the asset distribution among the positions selected, and their periodic rebalancing. In all, it allows the cloned portfolio to be constructed and maintained in a passive, mechanical fashion without having to fret over the fundamental characteristics of the securities involved or the overall market.

There are numerous strategies to pursue; the key variables are manager selection, asset allocation, and sentiment capture. The type of money manager to use is one who adheres to the following themes:

- **Individual merit**: Each position in the 13F portfolio has to have individual investment merit, rather than having merit as part of a composite position. As the mechanical cloning models cannot distinguish offsetting positions in the 13Fs, recommended positions would ignore offsetting positions in the source portfolio.
- **Long-term focused**: Mechanical cloning models rely on the positions listed in the 13Fs every quarter, and the changes made to the positions from the previous quarter. If the manager has only short-term goals for the positions held, the rules could mandate turning over most of them every quarter. High turnovers are detrimental both in terms of trading costs and tax implications.
- **Concentrated positions**: Cloning portfolios with hundreds of positions is impractical for individual investors. As the average size of an individual investor portfolio is tiny compared to the average manager's assets under management (AUM), cloning would result in very little money being allocated to each position. Implementing a model against multiple manager portfolios is unfeasible, as the number

of positions in the source portfolios increase. Trading costs and tax implications also rise with the number of positions.

Choosing among the different mechanical strategies depends on the comfort zone of the investor, regarding the calculations necessary to arrive at the choices and allocations recommended by the model concerned. In general, rudimentary spreadsheet skills are all that is required to implement the models. The math and trading requirements involved should help decide the best choice for a particular situation.

- **Largest positions versus largest new positions:** These two models differ primarily in the data point(s) considered. The data point for the largest positions models is the most recent 13F, while that of the largest new positions model is the most recent 13F and the previous quarter's 13F. The largest new positions model requires a larger set of managers in order to have enough positions for a portfolio. Besides, as the positions are based solely on the activity in the latest quarter, portfolio turnover is usually much higher than the corresponding largest positions-based model. The advantage with the largest new positions model is its ability to capture the latest manager sentiment.
- **Equal allocation:** For models based on equal allocation, assets are equally divided among recommended positions. Trading requirements can be kept very low by shadowing managers whose styles are suited for mechanical cloning. Rebalancing with a rule similar to the one used in the sample portfolios (rebalance when the largest position is 50 percent over the smallest position) ensures trades to rebalance the portfolio are done only when there is a significant shift to the recommended allocation ratio.
- **Weighted allocation versus 10-5-2 allocation versus exact match approximation:** These three models differ in the way in which the assets are distributed among the recommended positions. A fixed set of positions from each manager's 13F are used, and weightages are assigned to each one, based on the relative size of the position in the source portfolio. These models involve a little bit more calculation but, as the illustrations in Part Two showed, a spreadsheet comes in really handy. Trading requirements are higher

than the equal allocation based portfolios as a weightage change in the source portfolio can result in more trades. Also, frequent rebalancing is required as the objective is to closely mimic the source portfolio allocation.

- **Weighted allocation**: The weightages and number of positions are fixed, and correspond to the allocation ratios designed to mimic the source portfolio allocations.
- **10–5–2 allocation**: The weightages and positions are set so as to conform to the 10-5-2 philosophy. This translates to a very small number of highest conviction positions (>10 percent), an average number of large high conviction positions (>5 percent), and the rest in smaller positions (<2 percent).
- **Exact match approximation**: The weightages match the allocation ratios of the significantly large positions in the source portfolios. Choosing between them boils down to using a strategy that best conforms to the allocations in the source portfolios.

Matching the model used to the investment styles of the selected managers is another aspect to consider. For example, the simplest model (equal allocation largest positions) would be most suited for use with a set of managers who hold heavily concentrated positions over the long term. On the other hand, for managers known to target a weighted allocation or an allocation based on percentages, one of the other three allocation models would serve well.

Alternate mechanical models that clone the asset allocation and the variations that incorporate market sentiment help demonstrate how they can provide good absolute returns independent of market conditions.

Manager bias spreadsheets combined with the information on the price ranges managers realized allow for creating portfolios that guarantee better prices than the manager. A variation uses corporate insider filings (Forms 3, 4, and 5) and beneficial owner filings (13D and 13G) to construct portfolios holding high- conviction manager positions at prices comparable to that which the manager paid. The former strategy sits well with managers who trade frequently, while the latter works well with activist managers.

Implementing Manager Strategies

Selecting stocks using fundamental analysis (FA), and portfolio construction and maintenance, using techniques that allow optimization of the type of positions and their sizing are the key ingredients in the armor of the vast majority of superinvestors. Individual investors will need to tread carefully when attempting to implement these strategies. Superinvestors are fortified with knowledge, experience, and resources that consistently allow them to generate good absolute returns; as a group, individual investors are below par in all of these. A divide-and-conquer approach, whereby the bulk of the portfolio is initially allocated to passive mechanical strategies is a viable option. Adhering to selections from manager bias spreadsheets and applying the techniques to them is a good sandbox approach—picking stocks from bias spreadsheets as opposed to the entire universe of stocks helps minimize mistakes while learning the ropes. With time and effort, one gains confidence implementing the manager strategies. When this happens, more of the passive money can shift into these strategies, getting you on the road to becoming a superinvestor!

About the Author

John Konnayil Vincent received his BTech in Computer Science from Kerala, India and his master's in Information Systems from the University of Hawaii, Manoa. John worked with various software development groups in the San Francisco Bay Area for almost two decades. Highlights of that career include several inventions in the database technology field that were awarded patents, as well as performance awards. Recently, he made a career shift into wealth management. His writings related to stock market activity have appeared on Seeking Alpha and other websites.

Index